How to Set Parameters

How to Set Parameters: David Lightfoot
Arguments from Language
Change

A Bradford Book
The MIT Press
Cambridge, Massachusetts
London, England

Second printing, 1992
© 1991 Massachusetts Institute of Technology

The book was set in Times Roman by Asco Trade Typesetting Ltd. in Hong Kong and was printed and bound in the United States of America.

Library of Congress Cataloging-in-Publication Data

Lightfoot, David.
  How to set parameters: arguments from language change / David Lightfoot.
    p. cm.
  "A Bradford book."
  Includes bibliographical references (p.) and index.
  ISBN 0-262-12153-0
  1. Language acquisition. 2. Linguistic change. 3. Grammar, Comparative and general. I. Title.
P118.L46   1991
401'.93—dc20   90-13513
                                                                      CIP

Contents

Contents

Preface

For more than ten years generative grammarians have construed language acquisition as a matter of setting parameters—that is, of fixing option points defined in Universal Grammar. They have busily constructed "parametric differences" between various languages, while drum rolls and trumpet fanfares have heralded a major conceptual shift from the earlier "evaluation" of grammars. There has indeed been such a shift, which has drawn linguists closer to researchers in other fields, and this makes it all the more surprising that so little attention has been paid to what it takes to set these parameters. Sometimes this lack of attention undermines the claims being made, as when an alleged parametric difference is based entirely on data unavailable to children, on negative data, or on data about subtleties of quantifier scope. My most general goal here is to begin to correct this omission by making some claims about the child's triggering experience and about how parameters are set.

I shall argue first that the triggering experience consists only of robust elements which are structurally simple, and that parameter setting is not sensitive to embedded material. My most precise arguments are based on data from diachronic changes, and claim that grammars would not have been reanalyzed in the way that they were if complex structures influenced the form of the emerging grammars. In fact, the nature of certain changes makes it possible to define the structural limits to the triggering experience rather exactly, and to define some parameters in clearer fashion. My second major claim is that morphology plays an important role in setting parameters which have widespread syntactic effects. I shall examine some consequences of the loss of the rich Old English case system and of the breakdown of the verb classes.

Languages' histories are typically punctuated by occasional large-scale changes, corresponding to parametric shifts. French, for example, lacks some Romance characteristics and is sometimes said to have a more Germanic flavor, having set some parameters in the Germanic fashion. Examining the particular clusters of new phenomena that arose during these large-scale changes casts light on the exact nature of the parameters that were set differently and on the consequences; often one finds that a new parameter setting leads to further associated changes. Particularly illuminating, I claim, are cases of obsolescent structures: if one aims to understand language change partly in terms of the way languages are acquired by young children, obsolescence must be treated as a by-product of some new parameter setting, defined at an appropriately abstract level and set by positive primary data. Children don't stop saying things that they hear from their older models simply because they are seeking some stylistic effect or imitating new models. This observation undermines some lexicalist models of language change, which have been fashionable with historical linguists who have defined their interests too narrowly.

In general, I shall seek "ahistorical" explanations for language change, invoking no real theory of change and no "diachronic universals." In parallel fashion, I shall avoid a historicist approach to Universal Grammar, shunning principles that are motivated solely by some observed historical tendency (Lightfoot 1987). But I aim to show how the demands of language acquisition can shape the way in which languages change when certain changes occur in the triggering experience. That is not to say, of course, that all language change is to be explained in this fashion; that cannot be true if various languages change in different ways. But some very precise claims about the triggering experience will explain some old historical puzzles.

One of my claims is that the triggering experience consists not of raw data but of partially analyzed structures. Whenever one postulates non-trivial analyses, there are likely to be some theory-internal claims and a certain degree of technicality. That is true here. Moreover, in making claims about language acquisition based on evidence from language change and in using current work from syntactic theory, I am dogged by a concern for the compartmentalization of academic life and haunted by a fear that my argument will be buried in everybody's backlog of good intentions, forever piled unobtrusively in dark, unvisited corners. What can be done? Well, I have written for a heterogeneous audience, trying not to presuppose years of concern with the history of English, with the binding theory, or with acquisitional concerns, keeping my Maryland graduate students in mind. My readers must do me the favor of treating this as a specific discussion of the triggering experience, and not as a comprehensive survey of language change or language acquisition.

Several readers and audiences have reminded me many times of the wide audience I'm trying to reach, forcing me to spell out an unstated assumption, to clarify a piece of jargon, and, it must be confessed, to correct an error here and there. I am grateful to the many people who have discussed the historical material in my *Principles of Diachronic Syntax*, to the "peerage" who took some of the central ideas on language acquisition seriously enough to write commentaries on a 1989 article in *Behavioral and Brain Sciences*, and to the audiences who have endured lectures on these topics in the United States, in Europe, and in Brazil. Science is an inherently cooperative enterprise, and I have benefited enormously from all these people. I hope I have not mistaken forebearance for enthusiasm, but I now feel ready to go into print and to face another group of reviewers; no doubt they will induce me to write more.

A fellowship from the American Council of Learned Societies and an award from the Graduate Research Board at the University of Maryland gave me a reprieve from chairing a young and vigorous department, enabling me to work where the telephone didn't ring. Research grant BNS-8812408 from the National Science Foundation supported the work reported in chapter 3. Kathi Faulkingham delicately transformed messy material into scripts neat enough for others to read, and resisted the temptation to press the "delete file" command in desperation. And now some old friends have helped in the final stages: I am greatly indebted to Peter Coopmans, Norbert Hornstein, and Anthony Warner, who read the whole manuscript from quite different angles and made enough constructive suggestions to earn a dinner at Sergio's. There they will no doubt convince me that I should have followed more of their advice.

Also welcome at that dinner will be anybody who publishes an unequivocally generous review.

Chapter 1
Parameters and Triggers*

1.1 A Selective Theory of Language Acquisition

Linguists have traditionally maintained that language is not acquired by children only on the basis of experience; rather, children must themselves contribute something, if only an appropriate "disposition to learn." As careful studies were conducted, "discovery procedures" and "analogical principles" of increasing complexity were postulated as part of the child's contribution to the process of acquiring a language.

Over the last thirty years generative grammarians have been developing a selective theory of language acquisition. We have sought to ascertain what information must be available to children, independent of any experience with language, in order for the eventual mature linguistic capacities to emerge on exposure to some typical triggering experience. Cutting some corners, we have assumed that this unlearned information is genetically encoded in some fashion, and we have adopted (1) as our explanatory model.

(1) a. trigger (genotype → phenotype)
    b. primary linguistic data (Universal Grammar → grammar)

The goal is to specify relevant aspects of a child's genotype such that a particular mature state will emerge when a child is exposed to a certain triggering experience, depending on whether the child is raised in, say, a Japanese or a Navaho linguistic environment. (1b) reflects the usual terminology: "Universal Grammar" contains those aspects of the genotype that are directly relevant for language growth, and a "grammar" is taken to be a phenotypic property, a part of a person's mental makeup that characterizes his or her mature linguistic capacity. The *primary* linguistic data are those data to which children are exposed and which actually determine or "trigger" some aspect of their grammars, having some long-term effect.

The theory is "selective" in the same sense that current theories of immunology and vision are selective and not "instructive." Under an instructive theory, an outside signal imparts its character to the system that receives it, instructing what is essentially a plastic and modifiable nervous system; under a selective theory, a stimulus may change a system that is already highly structured by identifying and amplifying some component of already available circuitry. Put differently: a selective theory holds that an organism experiences the surrounding environment and selects relevant stimuli according to criteria that are already present internally. Jerne (1967) depicts antibody formation as a selective process whereby the antigen selects and amplifies specific antibodies, which already exist. Similarly, Hubel and Wiesel showed that particular neurons were preset to react only to specific visual stimuli (for example, to a horizontal line); exposure to a horizontal line entails a radical increase in the number of horizontal-line receptors, and a horizontal line can be said to elicit and select specific responses within the organism. Changeux (1980, 1983) argues along similar lines for a theory of "selective stabilization of synapses" whereby "the genetic program directs the proper interaction between main categories of neurons." "However," he continues, "during development within a given category, several contacts with the same specificity may form," and other elements, which are not selected, may atrophy (1980, p. 193). Thus, to learn is to amplify certain connections and to eliminate other possibilities (see also Mehler 1974 and Edelman 1987). Jerne (1967) argues as follows: "Looking back into the history of biology, it appears that wherever a phenomenon resembles learning, an instructive theory was first proposed to account for the underlying mechanisms. In every case, this was later replaced by a selective theory." For more discussion, see Piattelli-Palmarini 1986 and Jerne 1985.

Under current formulations of grammatical theory, the linguistic geno-type, Universal Grammar, consists of principles and parameters that are set by some linguistic environment, just as certain receptors are "set" on exposure to a horizontal line. So the environment may be said to "select" particular values for the parameters of Universal Grammar. Universal Grammar must be able to support the acquisition of any human grammar, given an appropriate triggering experience. Of course, Universal Grammar need not be seen as homogeneous; it may emerge piecemeal, parts of it being available only at certain stages of a child's development. Grammars are not only attainable under normal childhood conditions; they are also usable for such purposes as speech production and comprehension, they are vulnerable to the kinds of aphasias that are actually found, and one expects that they will provide part of the basis for understanding the developmental stages that children go through. There is no shortage of empirical constraints on hypotheses about the elements of (1).

1.2   Arguments from the Poverty of the Stimulus

The "logical problem of language acquisition" has provided much of the empirical refinement of (1). Apparent poverty-of-stimulus problems have led grammarians to postulate particular principles and parameters at the level of Universal Grammar. The stimulus or triggering experience that children have appears to be too poor to determine all aspects of the mature capacities that they typically attain. It is too poor in three distinct ways: (a) The child's experience is finite, but the capacity eventually attained ranges over an infinite domain and therefore must incorporate some recursive property not demanded by experience. (b) The experience consists partly of degenerate data which have no effect on the emerging capacity (see section 1.4). (c) Most important, it fails to provide the data needed to induce many principles and generalizations manifested by the mature capacity. Of these three, (a) and (b) have been discussed much more frequently than (c), although (c) is by far the most significant factor and provides a means for elaborating theories of Universal Grammar, as I shall now illustrate.

Any argument from the poverty of the stimulus makes crucial assumptions about the nature of the triggering experience. One simple argument, which has been used frequently, concerns the relationship between a statement (e.g., *the book on the shelf is dull*) and a corresponding question (*is the book on the shelf dull?*). There is an operation that places *is* at the front in this particular example, but how is this operation to be stated? It might be stated in structure-dependent fashion, locating *is* to the right of a subject noun phrase and moving it over that noun phrase (here, *the book on the shelf*). Alternatively, the operation might be structure-independent, making no reference to structural notions such as *noun phrase* and being sensitive only to the sequence of words; such an operation might simply identify the first *is* and move it to the front. Both proposals are adequate for the simple cases, but a slightly more complex case necessitates the first option. In (2a) the structure-independent operation would move the first *is* to the front and yield the nonoccurring (2b) (where *e* indicates an empty position); the structure-dependent operation would identify *the book which is on the shelf* as a noun phrase and would move *is* from the position immediately to its right, yielding—correctly—(2c).

(2) a. the book which is on the shelf is dull.

   b. *is the book which *e* on the shelf is dull?

   c. is ₙₚ[the book which is on the shelf] *e* dull?

The crucial evidence for the structure-dependent formulation and for the nonavailability of structure-independent operations is the nonoccurrence of (2b). However, children are not systematically informed that certain forms do not exist, or that they are "ungrammatical," and so the crucial evidence—the nonoccurrence of forms like (2b)—is not contained in normal childhood experience. Nonetheless, despite the lack of an environmental stimulus for structure dependence, and despite the simplicity of the structure-independent formulation, children invariably use the structure-dependent operation when first uttering questions of this kind; questions like (2b) simply do not occur and are not among the "errors" made by children. There seems to be no learning in this context. Moreover, whenever grammars have movement operations they are structure-dependent. If this is invariant and not deducible directly from childhood experience, it is reasonable to suppose that structure dependence is part of what the mind brings to the analysis of experience, not something hypothesized on the basis of evidence. One arrives at this conclusion by noting how the stimulus fails to determine certain aspects of mature grammars, and any such argument clearly depends on assumptions about the triggering experience—here, that the nonoccurrence of (2b) is not part of that experience. Furthermore, if the arguments to be offered in this book are correct, the relative clause in (2c) is also not part of the triggering experience.

Arguments from the poverty of the stimulus reveal not only gross properties of Universal Grammar, such as structure dependence, but also more fine-grained aspects of actual structures. To illustrate, I shall briefly rehearse an argument of Baker (1978), discussed by Hornstein and Lightfoot (1981) and then further by Lightfoot (1982). It has long been generally agreed that linguistic expressions are made up of subunits and have an internal hierarchical structure. It is also generally agreed that a grammar (in the sense defined) is not just a list of expressions but is a finite algebraic system that can "generate" an infinite range of expressions. One might imagine, in that case, that English noun phrases have the structure of either (3a) or (3b); proposals have been made along both lines. If a noun may project to a phrasal category in the manner defined by the phrase-structure rules of (3a), a phrase like *the old man from the city* will have the internal structure of (4a). If the projections are along the lines of the rules in (3b) the structure will be (4b) with quite different subunits. In (4a) *the old man* does not form a single phrasal unit, but in (4b) it does. The crucial difference is that the rules of (3a) refer to N′, an element intermediate between the head noun (N) and the maximal phrasal projection (NP) of that noun.

(3) a. NP → Specifier N′   b. NP → NP PP
      N′ → (Adj) [N or N′] PP   NP → Specifier (Adj) N

(4) a.   NP   b.   NP

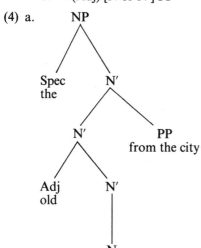
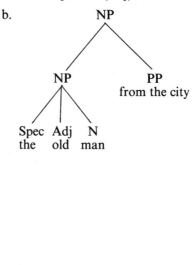

Now, it can be shown that any noun phrase that occurs in English, and thus any noun phrase that an English-speaking child is likely to hear, can be generated by both sets of projection types. However, linguists believe that something along the lines of (3a) must be correct, or at least preferred to (3b), because (3b) is consistent with certain phenomena that do *not* occur in English, unlike (3a). (3b) has no N′ node, and therefore provides no straightforward way to distinguish between (5a) and (5b) and no ready means to capture the ambiguity of (6a), which may have the meaning of (6b) or (6c). The details of the analysis need not concern us here.[1]

(5) a. *the student of physics is older than the one of chemistry
   b. the student from NY is older than the one from LA

(6) a. he wants an old suit but he already has the only one I own
   b. he wants an old suit but he already has the only suit I own
   c. he wants an old suit but he already has the only old suit I own

What *is* relevant here is the following problem: It is reasonable to suppose that children might be exposed to any noun phrase that may occur in English, but it is not the case that they are systematically informed that sentences like (5a) are not uttered by most speakers and that (6a) has two possible meanings. In fact, "negative data" (i.e., information that certain data do not exist) are generally not available to children, and perception of ambiguity is a sophisticated skill that develops late and not uniformly; most ambiguities pass unnoticed, and people take the most appropriate of the available meanings. To be sure, children come to know these things, and this knowledge is part of the output of the language-acquisition process; but it is not part of the input, not part of the "evidence" for the emerging system, and thus not part of the triggering experience. Consequently, although linguists are able to choose hypothesis (3a) over (3b) on the basis of phenomena such as (5) and (6), children have no analogous basis for such a choice if such data are not available to them. It is in this sense that the stimulus is too impoverished to fully determine the emergent analysis. In that case children must arrive at (3a) on some other, presumably nonexperiential basis. As an account of this basis, linguists have postulated genotypical information that phrasal categories have the structure of (7). By (7a) any noun phrase (NP) consists of a Specifier (e.g. an article) and a subphrase N′ in some order to be determined by the child's particular linguistic experience, the "trigger" of (1a). Similarly, a verb phrase (VP) consists of a Specifier and a V′ in some order, and likewise the other phrasal categories. By (7b) the N′ consists of a nucleus (N or N′) and perhaps some satellite material in some order. (The curly brackets indicate an unordered set, and YP covers any phrasal category or a clause.[2])

(7) a. XP → {Specifier, X′}
     b. X′ → {X or X′, (YP)}

(8) a. the house
     b. students of linguistics, belief that Susan left

Under (7), the linear order of constituents constitutes a parameter that is set on exposure to some trigger. The English-speaking child hears phrases like (8a) and, after some development, analyzes them as consisting of two words, one of a closed class (*the*) and the other of an open class (*house*); in the light of this and in the light of the parameter in (7a), the child adopts the first rule of (3a). Likewise, exposure to phrases like (8b) suffices to set the parameter in (7b), such that the second rule of (3a) emerges.[3] Because of the parameters in (7), rules like those of (3b) are never available to children and therefore do not have to be "unlearned" in any sense. Although no "evidence" for the existence of a phrasal category N′ seems to be available in a child's experience, it is provided by the genotype and therefore it occurs in mature grammars. (I shall consider an alternative account later.)

Consider, for a moment, the development that must take place before these parameters can be set. Children acquire the sounds of their languages and come to use *men* as a word and a noun with the meaning roughly of the plural of 'man'. This is a nontrivial process, and many people have examined how it happens. Having established that *men* is a noun, children later acquire the constituent structure of *men from the city*, if I am right, by setting the parameters in (7) and projecting to NP accordingly via N′, yielding

$_{NP}$[Spec $_{N'}$[$_{N'}$[$_N$[men]] $_{PP}$[from the city]]].

Lebeaux (1988) discusses this aspect of language acquisition very interestingly. In setting these particular parameters, children operate with partially formed representations that include $_N$[men], $_P$[from], $_{Spec}$[the], and $_N$[city]. They are operating not with "raw data" or mere words but with partially analyzed structures.

Men from the city and similar expressions occur in the child's environment with an appropriate frequency, and, given a partially formed grammar whereby *men* and *city* are classified as nouns, a child can assign a projection conforming to (7). Contrast this with some ill-formed expressions that a child might encounter for various reasons: *from the city men*, uttered by a guest who speaks a head-final language, is not sufficiently frequent to have any effect; a mixed form such as *men uit de stad*, uttered by a Dutch house guest, could not be analyzed by means of a partially formed grammar in which *uit* is not classified. Of course, if the Dutch guest stayed long enough and spoke often enough about city people, the child might come to classify *uit*, *de*, and *stad* as P, Spec, and N respectively, with the relevant meanings, might interpret the string correctly as a phrasal satellite of *men*, and might even use such phrases; in that case, one would witness an instance of code switching, a frequent phenomenon among children exposed to more than one language. If there is a great deal of this kind of mixture in the trigger experience, and if a pidgin is involved, the child will attain some form of creole. This extreme case reflects the quite general capacity to operate with a heterogeneous grammar.

There is much more to be said about NP structure and about its consequences. I have sketched the argument briefly here in order to demonstrate that a poverty-of-stimulus argument is based on assumptions about the triggering experience. The assumption so far has been that the non-occurrence for many people of (5a) and the ambiguity of (6a) are not part of the trigger, but that garden-variety NPs such as (8) are. It should be clear that there is a close relationship between the three entities of (1), and a claim made about any one of them usually has consequences for hypotheses about the other two.

This is by now reasonably well established for Universal Grammar and for particular grammars, but there has been a curious silence about the triggering experience. Generativists nowadays describe "parametric differences" between the grammars of, say, Japanese and Navaho, but they rarely mention how the parameters would be set for the particular grammars of these languages, or what the triggering experience would have to be for the Japanese or the Navaho child. Worse, if one tries to tease out the implicit assumptions about the trigger, they sometimes include exotic or negative data (see below). This failure to attend to the triggering experience is remarkable in that linguists have been talking for more than a decade of parameter-setting models of language acquisition, often advertising them as a major conceptual change from earlier acquisition models based on evaluation metrics that permitted the "selection" of certain grammars. As parameters are proposed to account for differences between languages, the triggering experience is rarely discussed; where there is discussion, it almost never goes beyond pointing to a class of expressions which are alleged to set the parameter in the appropriate fashion. I shall briefly discuss two examples to show that this is inadequate and that more substantive claims are needed about how certain data may set a given parameter.

Clark (1989) points to sentences like those of (9), containing an infinitival clause with a lexical subject in the accusative case.

(9) a. I believe [her to be wise]
    b. credo [eam sapientem esse]
    c. is cuimhneach leo [iad a bheith ar seachran]
       'they remember themselves being lost'
    d. *shil siad [a cheile a bheith breoite]
       'they thought each other to be ill'

(9a) is said to set an "Exceptional Case Marking parameter" whereby *believe* governs and assigns case to *her* by an exceptional procedure. The word-for-word translation (9b), however, set quite a different parameter for speakers of Latin. Here the accusative *eam* does not receive case from *credo* (which assigns dative case) and may occur where it is not governed by any lexical item: *eam sapientem esse creditur* 'her to be wise is believed'. (9c), a closely analogous sentence from Irish, involves yet another parameter in the licensing of the accusative subject of the embedded infinitive, because it is not a position in which a lexical anaphor can appear (see (9d)), unlike in Latin and English. There is no reason to believe that there is any insuperable problem here, but Clark's discussion shows that it is not* enough to point to an arbitrary sentence of the appropriate form, saying that exposure to (9a) suffices to set the "Exceptional Case Marking parameter."

Lasnik (1989), pointing to a comparable problem, notes that English allows enclitics, such as (10a), and proclitics, such as (10b).

(10) a. I want + to (wanna) win the prize
      b. Jim 's + taller than Kim is

Despite orthographic conventions, a reduced *is* is attached syntactically to the following word, which accounts for why the clause-final *is* in (10b) may not be phonologically reduced (**Jim's taller than Kim's*): there is no potential host. Also, parenthetical material may occur between *Jim* and the reduced *is*, but not on the right of *'s*: *Jim, I think, 's taller* but not **Jim's, I think, taller*.[4] The question then arises: How does a child know whether to treat any given clitic as a proclitic or as an enclitic? It is not enough to point to a phonologically reduced form and say that this triggers its analysis as a clitic; more will be needed to determine whether it is a proclitic or an enclitic, as the language allows both possibilities. Let us make the simplifying assumption that reduced elements are either proclitics or enclitics, not proclitics in some contexts and enclitics in others. A plausible account might be offered, if Universal Grammar specifies that clitics occur only where governed. (Aoun and Lightfoot (1984) make such a claim; see chapter 2 below for a definition of government.) This would entail that *to* is attached to *want* and not to *win* in (10a), if it is governed only by *want*. Similarly, sentence-initial instances of reduced *is* (*'s + Kim happy?*, reduced from *is Kim happy?*) show that it is governed by a following item, requiring the proclitic analysis shown in (10b).

We shall see in chapter 2 that an identical parameter setting with respect to the Subjacency Condition is adopted in the grammars of French and Italian, but on the basis of quite different triggering experiences. Such cases as these suggest that proponents of parametric theories of grammar need to show how data are selected as relevant to some particular parameter setting, being matched in some fashion. It is not enough to just point to relevant data, and it verges on incoherence to omit discussion of triggering experiences altogether. Despite this incomprehensible omission in much of the literature, which potentially undermines the claims being made, there is an intrinsic relationship between the items in (1). If the trigger or the "primary linguistic data" were rich and well organized, correspondingly less information would be needed in Universal Grammar, and vice versa. These are not aesthetic swings and roundabouts, and there are clear facts that limit the viable hypotheses.

I shall argue that the trigger consists of a haphazard set of utterances made in an appropriate context—utterances of a type that any child hears frequently. In other words, the trigger consists of robust data and includes no negative data—no information that certain expressions do not occur. First I will contrast this idea with some other ideas in the literature. Then, in chapter 2, I will make it more precise and argue that the trigger consists only of simple, unembedded material, and that everything can be learned from structures of "degree-0 complexity."

1.3 Negative Data

It is clear that the primary linguistic data, which trigger the growth of a child's grammar, do not include much of what linguists use to choose between hypotheses. To this extent, children are not "little linguists," constructing their grammars in the way that linguists construct their hypotheses. For example, the primary data do not include well-organized paradigms or comparable data from other languages. Nor do the primary data include rich information about what does not occur—that is, negative data.[5] It is true that some zealous parents correct certain aspects of their child's speech and so provide negative data, but this is not the general basis for language development. First, such correction is not provided to all children, and there is no reason to suppose that it is indispensable if language growth is to take place. Second, even when it is provided, it is typically resisted, as many parents will readily attest. McNeill (1966, p. 69) recorded a celebrated illustration of this resistance:

Child: Nobody don't like me
Mother: No, say "nobody likes me."
Child: Nobody don't like me
(eight repetitions of this dialogue)
Mother: No, now listen carefully; say "nobody likes me."
Child: Oh, nobody don't likes me.

Third, correction is provided only for a narrow range of errors, usually relating to morphological forms. So, the occasional *taked, goed,* or *the man what we saw* might be corrected, and on the eighth try McNeill's child perceived only a morphological correction, changing *like* to *likes.* However, not even the most conscientious parents correct deviant uses of the contracted forms of such verbs as *is* and *will*—in this case, because they do not occur in children's speech:

(11) a. *Jay's taller than Kay's (cf. . . . than Kay is)
     b. *Jay'll be happier than Kay'll (cf. . . . than Kay will)

They also do not correct errors in which anaphors such as *each other* are misused. Matthei (1981) reported that children sometimes interpret sentences like *the pigs said the chickens tickled each other* with *each other* referring to *the pigs.* This misinterpretation, discovered under experimental conditions, is unlikely to be perceived by many adults in everyday circumstances. The same is true of many other features of children's language. For a good discussion, see Baker 1979.

It is sometimes argued that although children are not supplied with negative data directly, they may have indirect access to them. Chomsky (1981, p. 9) speculates along these lines: ". . . if certain structures or rules fail to be exemplified in relatively simple expressions, *where they would be expected to be found* [my emphasis—DWL], then a (possibly marked) option is selected excluding them in the grammar, so that a kind of 'negative evidence' can be available even without corrections, adverse reactions, etc." This is illustrated by the so-called null-subject parameter, whereby finite declarative sentences like (12) occur with a phonetically null subject in Italian, Spanish, and many other languages, but the corresponding expressions do not occur in English, French, etc.

(12) a. ho trovato il libro
     b. chi credi che partirà?
     c. *found the book
     d. *who do you think that will leave?

Whatever the form of the parameter that permits this kind of variation, Chomsky, following Rizzi (1982b), suggests that if the English-speaking child picks the wrong setting, then failure to hear sentences like (12c) might be taken as indirect evidence that such sentences are ungrammatical and thus do not occur for some principled reason. Consequently the child will pick the setting that bars (12c) and (12d).

If children do have indirect access to negative data, it will have to be specified under what circumstances. That is, in Chomsky's formulation above, the phrase "in relatively simple expressions, where they would be expected to be found" will have to be fleshed out in such a way that it distinguishes cases like (12) from those like (5) and (11). While one might argue that children may have indirect access to data like (12c), it is hardly plausible to say that they have indirect access to (11). For this distinction to be made, Universal Grammar would have to be enriched to include analogical notions not yet hinted at. Consequently, there is no reason to believe that indirect access to negative data would entail less richness in Universal Grammar.

So far, the arguments for indirect access to negative data are not very strong. Certainly there are plausible alternative explanations for the null-subject phenomenon. One possibility is that the English setting for the relevant parameter is *unmarked*—i.e., the default case. Thus, Italian and Spanish children need specific evidence to adopt the other setting, and (12a) is the required evidence.[6] The fact that the Italian setting for the parameter seems to be much more common across languages than the English setting does not entail that it is less marked, since markedness values do not reflect statistical frequency. In fact, Berwick's (1985) Subset Principle predicts that the Italian setting should be marked. The Subset Principle requires children to "pick the narrowest possible language consistent with evidence seen so far" (p. 237). The Italian setting of the parameter entails a language that is broader than one with the English setting (because in Italian subjects may or may not be phonetically expressed), and therefore the English setting must be unmarked (p. 290).

A second alternative for this phenomenon is to make the variation in null subjects dependent on some other property. It has often been suggested that null subjects occur only in grammars with rich verbal inflection. However, rich inflection is not a sufficient condition for null subjects: German does not have null subjects, although its verbal inflection involves number, person, and gender (as does that of Spanish, which does allow null subjects). Consequently, the learning problem remains constant and is not affected by the richness of inflections. In another account, Hyams (1983) related the impossibility of null subjects to expletive pronouns (e.g., *it's cold, there's no more*), which occur in English, French, and German but not in Italian or Spanish, and she marshaled some interesting evidence in favor of something along these lines by considering the developmental stages that children go through. Hyams argued that early stages of children's grammars seems to have null subjects, and that the Italian value for the parameter is unmarked. This would violate Berwick's Subset Principle. Radford (1988) has offered a more radical approach, arguing that very young children lack the nonlexical projections of inflection and complementizer. If these two projections are missing, no phenomena involving such positions should occur. So Radford relates several properties which have been taken as typical of the child's grammar of this period. One of the missing positions is the structural subject; consequently, the setting of the null-subject option "cannot arise at this stage: the language has no lexical subjects but this is due to a general absence of subjects rather than to a setting of the 'null-subject parameter.'" When subjects arise (that is, when the nonlexical projections appear), the null-subject option can be adopted by Italian children on the basis of simple, positive data, as in (12a); English grammars have the unmarked option of no null subjects.

Lasnik (1989) proposed a plausible-looking scenario whereby children might acquire the appropriate distribution of contracted forms of *is* and similar words via indirect access to negative data. He noted that children must hear dozens or even hundreds of occurrences of *he's tall* for every *he is tall*; consequently, Lasnik writes, when exposed to an uncontracted form, such as *I wonder where John is*, children might conclude that the corresponding form "is not possible, since, if it were possible, it would have been used." This is not implausible but it is unnecessary: we have seen that, if clitics are subject to government, there are simple, positive data showing that the reduced form of *is* is governed by a following item and is thus a proclitic.

Indirect access to negative data may prove to be necessary for a full explanation of language acquisition, but so far no very plausible case has been made.[7] The notion raises nontrivial problems in defining the contexts in which indirect access is available. Meanwhile, if one relates the relevant phenomena to other properties and does not view them in isolation, one can suggest plausible solutions for some problems that seem to call for indirect access to negative data.

1.4   Not Every Experience Is a Trigger

Thus, putting aside the possibility of indirect access to certain negative data, one can plausibly argue that the triggering experience is less than what a "little linguist" might encounter and does not include information about ungrammatical sentences, comparative data from other languages, exotic and subtle judgments about quantifier scope, and much more that occurs in a typical issue of *Linguistic Inquiry*. Such information is simply not part of any child's linguistic experience. Consequently, we may persist with the idea that the trigger consists of nothing more than a haphazard set of utterances in an appropriate context. In fact, we can restrict things further: the trigger is something less than the total linguistic experience. Neither the occasional degenerate data that a child hears nor idiosyncratic forms necessarily trigger some device in the emergent grammar that has the effect of generating those forms. For example, (13a) might occur in a child's experience without triggering the formation of a rule that generates an unusual kind of subject-verb agreement. Similarly, children growing up in New York might hear (13b) without adopting *y'all* as a word in their grammars.

(13) a. the person who runs the stores never treat people well
     b. y'all have a good time in South Carolina

A child might even be exposed to significant quantities of linguistic material that does not act as a trigger. So, if a house-guest speaks an unusual form of English, perhaps with different regional forms or with the forms of somebody who has learned English imperfectly as a second language, this normally has no noticeable effect on a child's linguistic development. Even children of heavily accented immigrant parents perpetuate few non-standard aspects of their parents' speech.

I take it that this is fairly obvious intuitively, and that it shows that there is little to be learned about the trigger experience from simply tape-recording everything uttered within a child's hearing. The triggering experience cannot be the sum of what a child hears or understands. We know that young children can understand quite complex structures, such as the multiply embedded relative clauses in the nursery rhyme *this is the cow that kicked the dog that bit the rat that ate the cheese that lay in the house that Jack built*. Comprehensive studies such as those reported by Wells (1981) are very useful and inform us about what children can understand at what ages, but they are not studies of the triggering experience, which is a subset of the total experience. More can be learned from the historical changes that languages undergo. It is well known that certain kinds of syntactic patterns become obsolete in certain speech communities at certain times. This means that sometimes children hear a form that does not trigger any grammatical device permitting it to be generated by the grammar and thus to occur in their mature speech. The conditions under which this happens cast some light on the nature of the trigger, as will be shown in later chapters.

So then, we may now claim that the trigger experience is some subset of a child's total linguistic experience. But where exactly are the limits? This is often a crucial question in grammatical analyses, but it is rare to see alternatives discussed. Consider again the example of the structure of noun phrases. I argued above that any noun phrase that an English-speaking child could hear would be consistent with the rules of both (3a) and (3b). I also claimed that the data that lead grammarians to prefer (3a) to (3b) are generally not available to children, and that therefore the information that eliminates (3b) must come from some other, presumably genetic source. One could, however, look at things somewhat differently. The real difference between (3a) and (3b) is the existence of an N′ node in the rules of (3a). The existence of this node is required by the Universal Grammar rule schema in (7) and, on that account, does not have to be derived from relevant experience. In that case, we might ask if there is anything in a child's experience that would require postulating an N′ node; and one can indeed imagine evidence that would force the child to establish such a node.

English speakers use the indefinite pronoun *one* to refer back to an N′ (see note 1). The fact that it refers to an N′—something intermediate between the head N and its maximal projection (NP)—might in fact be learnable. (14a) would not be a sufficient basis for learning this; regardless of whether Heidi actually has a big or a small cup, the sentence could always be interpreted as specifying only that Heidi has some cup, regardless of its size (with *one* referring only to the N *cup*). (14b), however, would suffice if uttered in a situation where Heidi has a cup that is some color other than blue; only the interpretation with *one* representing *blue cup* would be consistent with the facts. In that case a child might learn, correctly, that *one* stands for a phrasal projection of N—namely, an N′.[8]

(14) a. Kirsten has a big cup, and Heidi has one too
      b. Kirsten has a blue cup, but Heidi doesn't have one

There are now two alternative accounts: the existence of N′ might be derived from a property of Universal Grammar, or it might be triggered by the scenario just sketched. My hunch was and remains that this scenario is too exotic and too contrived to be part of every child's experience, and therefore that postulating (7) at the level of Universal Grammar is more plausible. But this hunch may be wrong. It is certainly falsifiable. If a rule schema like (7) exists in Universal Grammar, then strong claims are made about the possible degree of variability in the structure of NPs that will be found in the languages of the world: in languages where this kind of structural configuration is relevant (which may or may not be all languages), there will be essentially four NP types. Type (15a) is represented by English and French, and type (15b) seems to be manifested in Basque,

Burmese, Burushaski, Chibcha, Japanese, Kannada, and Turkish (see Greenberg 1966, note 20). Types (15c) and (15d) are more problematic; I know of no carefully studied grammar that manifests them. Greenberg (1966) and Hawkins (1979) discuss several languages in which demonstratives follow the head noun and which therefore might be of type (15c) or (15d), but they do not distinguish between demonstratives that have the syntax of adjectives (as in Latin) and closed-class items that manifest Spec (as in English). If it should turn out that types (15c) and (15d) do not occur, then the rule schema of (7a) will be tightened to allow only the Spec-N′ order.

(15) a. $_{NP}[\text{Spec } _{N'}[\text{head complement}]]$

b. $_{NP}[\text{Spec } _{N'}[\text{complement head}]]$

c. $_{NP}[_{N'}[\text{head complement}] \text{ Spec}]$

d. $_{NP}[_{N'}[\text{complement head}] \text{ Spec}]$

Also, the rule schema (7) suggests that one will find developmental stages corresponding to the fixing of the two parameters by a child. Building on work by Klima and Bellugi (1966) and Roeper (1979), I argue on page 179ff. of Lightfoot 1982 that this is indeed the case. Children seem to acquire noun-phrase structures in four identifiable stages. Examples (16a) and (16b) list some noun phrases that occur in stages 1 and 2, respectively.

(16) a. car   b. a coat   that Adam
        baby   a celery   more coffee
        wa-wa (water)   a Becky   two socks
        mama   a hands   big foot
        hands   my mommy

Every child goes through the four stages, although the ages at which individuals go through particular stages may vary. Most children utter the stage 2 forms between the ages of 1 and 2 years. At stage 3 there is more sophistication, as the examples in (17) show.

(17) mama   my doll   a blue flower
     cracker your cracker a nice cap
     doll   a your horse
     spoon   that a horse
                            that a blue horse
                            your blue cap

At stage 4 the mature system emerges, and it normally remains more or less constant for the rest of the individual's life. But consider (18), which lists some forms that never occur in children's speech.

(18) *blue a flower   *a that blue flower   *flower a
      *nice a cup   *blue a that   *house that a
      *my a pencil   *that a
      *a that house   *a my
                           *my a

Recall the parameters for noun phrases developed in section 1.2. These were hypotheses about how NP structure could vary from grammar to grammar. Stage 1 arises after some development has taken place, as was noted above: children have identified some of the sounds and words. At this stage our parameters are irrelevant, because the child has only one-word structures. Other cognitive capacities are relevant, such as the conceptual system that involves properties and conditions of reference, knowledge and belief about the world, conditions of appropriate use, and so on. These play a role in explaining why *mama* and *cup* are more likely than *photosynthesis*, *quark*, or *grammar* to be among the earliest words in a child's speech.

At stage 2 the child seems to have fixed the linear-order parameter of rule schema (7a) and determined that the order is Spec N': all specifiers appear at the front of the noun phrase. The occurrence of phrases like *a Becky* and *a hands* suggests that at this stage children cannot distinguish definite and indefinite articles, and that they do not know that *a* is singular. There is no evidence that the child can distinguish subtypes of specifiers (articles, possessives, numerals, demonstratives), which all occur one at a time in front of a noun.

By stage 3, the child discriminates some kinds of specifiers and establishes more of the relative orders. In fact, the child knows that all specifiers precede adjectives, which in turn precede nouns, and that specifiers are optional whereas the noun is obligatory. The stage 3 grammar differs from the mature system in that the child does not yet know that an article may not co-occur with a demonstrative or with a possessive such as *your*. This suggests that the child now has the rules NP → Spec N' and N' → (Adj) N, but that it will be a little longer before the child will be able to determine the status of a demonstrative and whether a form like *your* is a specifier or an adjective. After all, in other languages demonstratives and possessives are often adjectives instead of specifiers.

Consequently, there is reason to believe that postulating the rule schema in (7) at the level of Universal Grammar is more plausible than claiming that the existence of N' is *learned* on the basis of exposure to sentences like (14b) uttered in relevant contexts. But, more important, alternatives such as this must be sketched and evaluated, and grammarians must explicate their assumptions about the triggering experience required to set the parameters of Universal Grammar that they hypothesize.

So I persist with the idea that the trigger is a subset of a child's experience, and that it probably does not include exotic events like the one sketched in the context of (14b). The trigger consists only of robust data that can be analyzed in a manner consistent with genotypical principles and with those parameters of the child's grammar that have already been fixed. There remains the question of how small the subset is.

There is a theory, advanced by Snow (1977) and earlier by Jespersen[9] (1922, p. 142), that the crucial input for language growth is very small, and that it consists of a specially structured form of speech transmitted through mothers and caretakers. This "motherese" is supposed to provide a set of patterns which are generalized by children on an inductive basis. This view was held fairly widely for a while.

There are at least four reasons why this kind of pattern generalization is not the means by which children acquire speech.

First, although children no doubt register only part of their linguistic environment, there is no way of knowing exactly what any individual child registers. Hence, a factual basis is lacking for the claim that children register only what is filtered for them through their parents' deliberately simplified speech. Children have access to more than this, including defective utterances.

Second, even if children registered only perfectly well-formed expressions, that would not be enough to show that they have a sufficient inductive base for language acquisition. As was noted in section 1.1, the child's stimulus is "deficient" in three distinct ways. The motherese hypothesis would circumvent only the degeneracy problem; it leaves untouched the infinity problem and the far more important absence of evidence in primary linguistic data for certain partial generalizations. The poverty-of-stimulus problems still hold, and the child would need to know that the contractability of the first *is* in (11) could not be extended to the second *is*. One wants to know why quite ordinary inductive generalizations like this are in fact not made; the so-called motherese does not show where inductive generalizations must stop.

Third, if the child registered only the simplified and well-formed sentences of motherese, the problem of language learning would be *more* difficult because the child's information would be more limited. That is, if children who are exposed to unrestricted data must circumvent problems of an impoverished stimulus (in the sense that the stimulus does not alone provide evidence for all the generalizations manifested by the mature capacity), then this will be all the more true of children who are exposed to more restricted data. So if children with access to unrestricted data need principles of Universal Grammar in order to attain the systems that they acquire, because of the absence of certain kinds of evidence, this will be true *a fortiori* of children with access to less extensive data.

Fourth, careful studies of parents' speech to children (e.g., Newport, Gleitman, and Gleitman 1977) show that an unusually high proportion consists of questions and imperatives; simple declarative sentences are much rarer than in ordinary speech. This suggests that there is very little correlation between the way the child's language emerges and what parents say in their speech directed at children. Thus, the existence of motherese in no way eliminates the need for postulating a genetic basis to explain language acquisition. The child is primarily responsible for the acquisition process, not parents or older playmates. (For a good discussion of this topic see Wexler and Culicover 1980, pp. 66–78.)

Furthermore, while it is by no means clear exactly what this motherese consists of, the general phenomenon is not uniform and does not occur in all households or cultures. Even where motherese is not practiced, children nonetheless attain a normal linguistic capacity. This suggests that the child's trigger experience need not be limited artificially along the lines of motherese.

1.5 Conclusion

The computational system supporting the human language capacity has some distinctive properties. One is its plasticity—the fact that it is compatible with many different mature states, depending on the environmental factors a child is exposed to. This kind of "phenotypic plasticity" has not been studied extensively by biologists. The variation found in human languages promises to extend our understanding of this concept.

We shall need to characterize the robustness of the data which may act as a trigger. Robustness is presumably a function of saliency and frequency. One can be sure that parameters are not always set by single events; that would make the child too "trigger happy" and inclined to draw long-term conclusions (a metaphor) from insufficient data. However, some parameters may require more triggering experience than others. Indeed, some parameters may be set by single events: for example, some child might "learn" (another metaphor) the meaning of the words *add* and *giraffe* from one exposure, particularly if that single exposure focused much attention on the word and provided a simple definition. Even some structural parameters might require little by way of triggering experience; no more than a few instances of *men from the city*, *student of physics*, and the like may be necessary to fix a prepositional satellite as following its nominal head. As has been noted, raw data do not act as triggers, so it is not enough to count how many such phrases are heard by the child under investigation. This parameter can be set only when the child has a partial analysis whereby *men* is classified as a noun and *from the city* as a PP; one will want to know what experience is needed at that stage before the relevant parameter is set. So any counting has to involve significant analysis and has to presuppose a good account of the primitives involved in the preceding analyses. For example, is it enough to know that *men* is a noun and *from the city* a PP, or does the child also need to know *in advance* that the PP is in a modifying relation?

The required robustness might also vary from one word to another. Consider the problem of why children, having first generalized a double object from the core verb *give* to *donate* (*I donated them $1000*), then back off from that generalization, ceasing to use such forms. It is possible that expressions like *I gave $1000* are less robust in children's experience than *give him a book* and therefore unlikely to override the learned stipulation that *give* incorporates a thematic role of goal which it may assign directly to a NP, thus permitting a double object. However, *I donated $1000* is robust enough, in comparison with the occasional *donate them $1000* that a child might come across, to block the incorporation of an extra thematic role, and thus to cause the child to stop using *donate* with two objects. If something along these lines is correct, it suggests that what is at issue is the robustness of one expression *relative to* some corresponding form. This, of course, leaves open the question of how such lexical discrepancies might have arisen in the language, and thus in children's experience.[10]

There are substantive matters here which so far have received little attention, reflecting a pathological lack of interest among generativists in the triggering experience. It is clear that not everything a child hears has a noticeable or long-term effect on the emergent mature capacity; some sifting is involved. Some of the sifting must surely be statistical, some is effected through the nature of the genetically endowed properties, and some results from the cumulative nature of language acquisition and from the fact that children may not make any sense of certain expressions at some stage of development. All these points raise substantive questions. However, I shall now turn my attention to the complexity of the triggering experience, arguing that it consists only of very simple structures. If a plausible case can be made, then there will be one more tool for evaluating analyses, and linguists will question proposals that entail more complex triggering experiences.

Chapter 2
Simple Triggers

2.1 Degree-0 Learnability

Wexler and Culicover (1980) argued for limits to a child's trigger with their notion of degree-2 learnability. They offered the first "learnability proof," showing that, given certain constraints on grammatical processes, if children were confronted with (b, s) pairs (where b is a base structure, in which transformational and phonological rules have not applied, and s is a surface string), they would identify the relevant grammar in finite time when exposed only to sentences with at most two levels of embedding, such as *Jay said [that Kay asked [if Ray was home]]*; this is "degree-2 learnability." The first learnability proof was bound to be important, and many interesting assumptions were made about language learners, not all of them very plausible (Baker 1982; Morgan 1986). In particular, the notion that children must have access to very complex sentences seems worth examining.

Wexler and Culicover used a particular kind of error-detection procedure which effectively added an extra level of sentence embedding to whatever triggering experience is needed. They argued that the relevant information is contained in structures with one level of embedding, but their error-detection procedure then required another level of embedding to reveal possible errors. Morgan (1986) adopted a different error-detection procedure and offered a degree-1 learnability proof based on the assumption that children receive as input not only Wexler and Culicover's (b, s) pairs but also a surface string with constituent structure assigned.

However, the error-detection procedure reflects a more fundamental difference in orientation. Wexler and Culicover were not much concerned with variation in grammars, and they used a selection model of acquisition wherein the child tests various hypotheses and selects one in accordance with a specific evaluation metric. I am adopting the recent parameter-setting model, however, in which Universal Grammar contains rich information about, say, possible projection types and specifies certain option points which are set on exposure to particular data sets. The issues I raise in the following case studies would also be important for a selection model of acquisition not making rich assumptions about parameters in Universal Grammar. I shall not compare the two models here, however; this would be an extremely complex matter, since selection models have not addressed the kind of language variation that I shall deal with.

Since Wexler and Culicover 1980 there have been real advances in grammatical theory—notably the development of the parameter-setting model of Universal Grammar, which replaced the selectional model of Chomsky (1965). Also, since the 1960s grammarians have been seeking to develop locality restrictions, such that grammatical processes affect only elements that are not too far apart. This work suggests that grammatical processes affect only items that are clause mates (members of the same clause), or that they operate only where an item in a lower clause is, loosely, at the front of that clause. Locality restrictions have been formulated somewhat differently at different stages of the development of Universal Grammar and by different authors. The details of various locality restrictions need not concern us immediately, but they do raise the following question: If grammatical processes are generally limited to clause mates, or at most to items of which one is at the front of an embedded clause, why should children need to hear more than a single clause (plus the front of a lower clause) in order to hear the effects of all possible grammatical processes in their language? In other words, can everything be learned from main clauses (degree-0 learnability) plus a little bit?

This work has suggested a tight restriction on the trigger experience (Culicover and Wilkins 1984; Joshi 1989), but there is no demonstration effect (Lightfoot 1986, 1989). Locality conditions are necessary to ensure degree-0 learnability, but not sufficient. The simplicity of the trigger is quite a separate, empirical matter. This will be illustrated as we consider some cases which are consistent with the usual locality conditions but which seem to require degree-2 learnability, being apparent counterexamples to degree-0 and even to degree-1 learnability. It is important to distinguish the existence of locality conditions from the need for simple triggers, but I shall argue that these cases are in fact compatible with a degree-0-learnability account.

2.2 Bounding Nodes

Chomsky (1973) proposed a Subjacency Condition that required syntactic movement to be local, crossing no more than one "bounding" node. *Wh* phrases move to a complementizer position ("Comp") at the front of a clause; hence, a clause, S', consists of Comp and S, and S in turn consists of a subject NP; an inflection element INFL (including tense and an agreement marker), which acts as the head of the clause; and a VP.[1] Consequently, a *wh* phrase must move stepwise from within an embedded clause to the front of a main clause, leaving a "trace" at each stage; so *who did Jay say Kay met?* would be derived as in (1), and each movement crosses only one bounding node, S.

(1)

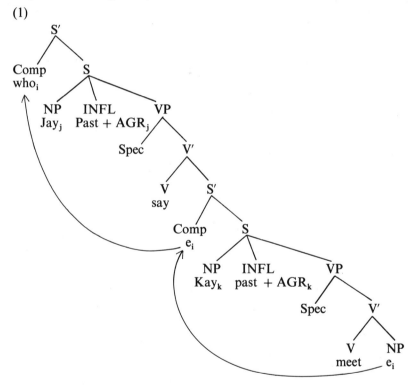

Rizzi (1982a, p. 73, n. 25) and Sportiche (1981) argued for a parametric difference between English on the one hand and French and Italian on the other, such that English speakers have S as a bounding node while French and Italian speakers have S'. Rizzi pointed to (2a) and Sportiche to (2b) and (2c), which have a long-distance movement as in (3) (which is Sportiche's analysis for (2c)).

(2) a. tuo fratello, a cui mi domando che storie abbiano raccontato, era
        molto preoccupato
        'your brother, to whom I wonder which stories they told, was very
        troubled'
     b. c'est à mon cousin que je sais lequel offrir
        'it's to my cousin that I know which one to offer'
     c. voilà une liste des gens à qui on n'a pas encore trouvé quoi
        envoyer
        'here's a list of the people to whom we've not yet found what to
        send'

(3) [à qui$_i$] $_S$[on n'a pas encore trouvé $_{S'}$[[quoi$_j$] $_S$[envoyer e$_j$ e$_i$]]]

In (3) à qui moves over two S nodes but only one S' node. Consequently,
if the Subjacency Condition proscribes movement over more than one
bounding node, (2) suggests that in French and Italian S' and not S must
be the bounding node. If the English equivalents of (2) are ungrammatical
(see Rizzi and Sportiche), then English grammars have S as a bounding
node and a movement like that of (3) would violate Subjacency. In one of
the rare instances of a grammarian's discussing the needed trigger experience, Rizzi (1982a) argues that if the Subjacency Condition is parameterized such that either S or S' or both may be a bounding node, then S
must be a less marked value than S'. The reason is that if S' is unmarked,
then it is hard to see how the English-speaking child could learn the S value
without having access to negative data, namely that the English analogues
to (2) do not occur. On the other hand, Italian and French children could
learn the S' value by hearing sentences like (2). Hence a trigger is provided,
but the trigger is a complex structure with two levels of embedding, which
is consistent with degree-2 but not with degree-0 learnability.[2]

Rizzi assumed a fairly strict notion of locality: in the least marked case,
wh movement operates only within a clause (see note 2); in the next most
marked case (English) it crosses a clause boundary but affects only the
frontmost position of the embedded clause; only in the most marked case
(Italian and French) is the movement nonlocal. Even in the most marked
case, where movement may cross two S nodes, the actual triggering experience, if Rizzi is right, involves not just one level of embedding, as might
suffice, but two levels of embedding. There is nothing inconceivable or
strange about this analysis, and it suggests that the issue of locality is
partially independent of questions about the richness of the triggering
experience. Whether or not there is a degree-0 or degree-1 trigger for the
bounding-node parameter is quite unrelated to the existence of locality

conditions; the existence of locality conditions does not, *ipso facto*, require degree-0 learnability. Also, I shall point in a moment to degree-0 triggers for the nonlocal, marked operations.

Continuing to assume Rizzi and Sportiche's analysis and its factual basis, one may ask whether there is an alternative way to learn what is needed: that S′ and not S is a bounding node in French and Italian. A simple sentence like (4a) might appear to provide the relevant trigger if it is analyzed along the lines of (4b). In (4b) there is movement over NP and S, suggesting that both cannot be bounding nodes. However, there is an alternative analysis in which movement takes place from outside the NP, as in (4c), as Hornstein and Weinberg (1981) showed was needed for English; this is illustrated by (4d). If (4c) is a possible analysis for children, then (4a) would not provide crucial evidence for S′, i.e., trigger the choice of S′ as a bounding node as opposed to S.

(4) a. de qui as-tu vu un photo?
    b. de qui$_i$ $_S$[as-tu vu $_{NP}$[un photo e$_i$]]
    c. de qui$_i$ $_S$[as-tu vu $_{NP}$[un photo] e$_i$]
    d. who$_i$ $_S$[did you see $_{NP}$[a photo] of e$_i$]

However, there are simple main-clause data that require that S not be a bounding node. (5a) must be analyzed as (5b), as is argued by Kayne (1981a) and others. This movement of *combien* from within an object NP, across both NP and S, requires that S cannot be a bounding node in addition to NP.[3]

(5) a. combien as-tu vu de personnes?
        'how many people have you seen?'
    b. combien$_i$ $_S$[as-tu vu $_{NP}$[e$_i$ $_{N'}$[de personnes]]]

I have argued here that, at least for French (I shall return to Italian in section 2.5), the relevant parametric value can be triggered by unembedded data such as (5), and therefore that Rizzi and Sportiche's analysis of (2) does not motivate degree-2 or degree-1 learnability.

I shall consider two further examples of analyses which seem to require a more complex trigger than would be permitted under degree-0 learnability, but I shall argue that the relevant parameters may be set on the basis of unembedded material. These examples require discussion of some theoretical machinery.

For both cases I shall adopt the usual model of grammar, diagrammed in (6), and the specific Universal Grammar proposals of Aoun, Hornstein, Lightfoot, and Weinberg (1987). Under (6), a D-structure (which represents the underlying grammatical relationships) is mapped into an S-structure through successive movement operations. The S-structure, in turn, is mapped into both a phonological form (PF), which is the basis for a phonetic representation, and a logical form (LF), which represents a significant part of the meaning of an expression, indicating the scope relations of quantifiers, anaphoric relations among NPs, and so forth.

(6)

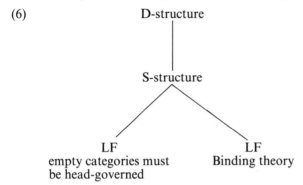

D-structure

S-structure

LF
empty categories must
be head-governed

LF
Binding theory

Aoun et al. propose two locality conditions. They argue that an anaphor must be *bound* (i.e., coindexed with some higher element) within its Domain at Logical Form (see (7a)), and this is part of a more general Binding Theory (see (7)).

(7) Binding Theory
   a. an anaphor is bound in its Domain
   b. a pronoun is not bound in its Domain
   c. a referential expression is not bound by an argument (for our purposes, a D-structure NP position).

Aoun et al. also require an empty element in PF to occur only where it is *governed* by a coindexed X^0 element other than INFL—that is, head-governed. A government relation holds if two elements share all maximal projections; more technically, (8).

(8) a (X^0, or head in our earlier terminology) governs b, if
   i. all maximal projections dominating a also dominate b,
   and
   ii. a is dominated either by (a) all maximal projections dominating b or by (b) all maximal projections dominating the maximal projection of b.

Consider how (8) applies to a more detailed version of the structure of *an old man from the city*, given as (9).

(9)

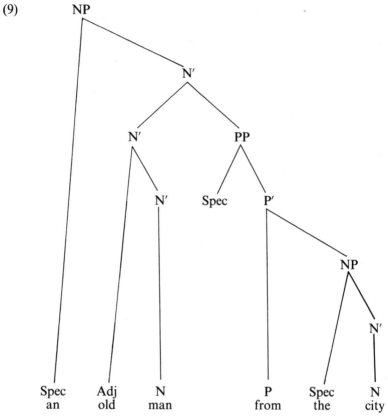

NP and PP are maximal phrasal projections of the heads N and P, respectively. In (9), the relationship between the N *man* and Spec *an*, Adj, and PP satisfies conditions (8i) and (8iia). Thus, the N *man* governs these elements. It also governs the P *from* via (8i) and (8iib), since *from*'s maximal phrasal projection PP is dominated by all the maximal phrasal projections dominating the N *man*. However, the N *man* does not govern the N *city*, because *city*'s maximal phrasal projection NP is dominated by another maximal phrasal projection PP which does not dominate the N *man*, in violation of (8iib); consequently, *man* and *city* do not share all maximal projections in the relevant sense.

2.3 Dutch Government

This formulation of Universal Grammar permits a degree-0 account of some phenomena that have been widely discussed for the last several years. As is often noted, English speakers do not move subjects from a position immediately to the right of an overt complementizer. Structures like (10b) violate the Universal Grammar condition that empty elements at PF must be governed by a coindexed element. Hence, corresponding sentences like *who did Jay say that saw Kay? do not occur in English. (By contrast, sentences corresponding to (10a) and (10c) do occur: who did Jay say that Kay saw? and who did Jay say saw Kay?).

(10) a. $_{S'}$[who$_i$ did + AGR$_j$ Jay$_j$ say $_{S'}$[[e$_i$ that] Kay$_k$ AGR$_k$ saw e$_i$]]

　　b. *$_{S'}$[who$_i$ did + AGR$_j$ Jay$_j$ say $_{S'}$[[e$_i$ that] e$_i$ AGR$_i$ saw Kay]]

　　c. $_{S'}$[who$_i$ did + AGR$_j$ Jay$_j$ say $_{S'}$[e$_i$ e$_i$ AGR$_i$ saw Kay]]

Dutch speakers, however, use sentences equivalent to (10b): wie denk je dat het boek gelezen had? 'who do you think that had read the book?'. Such sentences have a structure like (11a): the Subjacency condition forces wie to move first to its local Comp, leaving a trace there which makes the empty subject governed via a Comp indexing procedure, by which Comp assumes the index of an element that it contains.[4] Similarly, in structures like (11b) the indexed Comp head-governs an empty subject despite the presence of the complementizer.

(11) a. wie$_i$ denk je $_{S'}$[[e$_i$ dat]$_i$ $_S$[e$_i$ het boek gelezen had]]
　　　who think you　that　　the book read　　had
　　b. ik vraag me af $_{S'}$[[wie$_i$ of dat]$_i$ $_S$[e$_i$ het boek gelezen had]]
　　　I wonder　　who whether　the book read had
　　　'I wonder who read the book'

Hilda Koopman (1983) discussed these phenomena, raised the question of what the relevant parameter was that distinguished Dutch and English grammars, and argued that this parameter could be set on the basis of main-clause data. The essential idea is that a Dutch speaker has to learn that an item in Comp may percolate its index to Comp and make an empty subject head-governed despite intervening material, as in (11b). In English, however, percolation is blocked by the presence of other material in Comp; so in (10b) the trace in Comp may not percolate its index, and thus the subject trace is not head-governed. Koopman argued that this distinction can be learned from main-clause data such as (12). Dutch has an underlying object-verb order, and heeft must therefore move toward the front of the sentence, as indicated. The empty subject must be governed by the Comp despite the presence of heeft, just as the empty subjects in (11) are governed by the coindexed Comp despite dat and of dat.

(12) $_{Comp}$[wie$_i$ heeft$_j$]$_i$ $_S$[e$_i$ het boek gelezen e$_j$]
　　　who has　　　the book read
　　'who has read the book?'

English, however, does not have structures like (12), and thus there is no main-clause evidence that an item in Comp may effectively govern across intervening material (via the Comp indexing procedure). So sentences like *who has read the book?* have a structure like (13a), where *has* does not move from its S-internal position. Since English does not have underlying object-verb order, there is no reason to require *has* to move. In fact, the non-occurrence of **who did read the book?* (where *did* is not stressed) suggests that an auxiliary verb may not move toward the front in such structures; the structure would have to be (13b), because the unstressed *do* occurs only nonadjacent to the main verb. The nonoccurrence of (13b) can be attributed to the fact that the empty subject fails to be governed by a coindexed Comp because of the presence of *did*. (13c) does occur, but here the trace of *what* is governed by the verb *read* and is coindexed with it (see note 4).[5]

(13) a. $_{Comp}[who_i]_i \ _S[e_i$ has read the book]

b. $_{Comp}[who_i \ did_j]_i \ _S[e_i \ e_j$ read the book]

c. $_{Comp}[what_i \ did_j] \ _S[Jay \ e_j$ read $e_i]$

So, on hearing simple sentences like *wie heeft het boek gelezen?* and analyzing them as (12), the Dutch child relaxes the restriction on government, such that the empty subject is head-governed. This entails the well-formedness of complex sentences like (11). The English-speaking child hears no equivalent main clauses that motivate such a relaxation and therefore does not use structures like (10b). Consequently, if there is a Universal Grammar condition that empty items at PF must be head-governed, a degree-0-learnability account can be provided for the striking differences between Dutch and English embedded clauses.

This last case demonstrates that some properties of Comp that crucially affect the well-formedness of embedded clauses can be derived from main-clause properties, under certain formulations of Universal Grammar. However, this is not to say that all properties of Comp can be so derived. For example, English, unlike Dutch, French, German, Italian, Spanish, and many other languages, allows an element in Comp to be deleted, subject to certain conditions (primarily the Universal Grammar condition, already mentioned, that empty elements at PF, including empty items and deletion sites in Comp, must be head-governed):

(14) a. Jay said (that) Kay left

b. Jan zei *(dat) Marie vertrokken was

c. Jean a dit *(que) Marie est partie

Similarly, French has a process whereby the complementizer *que* takes on the form *qui* if it governs an empty subject in an embedded clause:

(15) a. qui$_i$ crois-tu $_{S'}$[[qui/*que] [e$_i$ est parti]]
       who do you think that   has left

    b. qui$_i$ crois-tu $_{S'}$[[que/*qui] [Marie a vu e$_i$]]
       who do you think that   Marie saw

Also, many (perhaps all) languages have words like *if* and *whether*, which occur only in embedded Comp positions. I cannot see how main-clause data could motivate these properties, or how they could motivate the marked device in English whereby the embedded subject of a nonfinite verb may be governed and assigned case by the higher verb: *I expect [her to win]*. A higher verb does not govern a lower subject unless the maximal projection (S′) dominating the lower clause is removed in some way, on the assumption that *a* governs *b* only if they share all maximal projections (see Chomsky 1981 and (8) above). The removal of this projection (often referred to as S′ Deletion) is a marked process found in certain grammars and triggered by sentences like *I expect Jay to be happy* and *Jay was expected to be happy*. I shall discuss this process in chapter 4, offering a different account.

Such phenomena require that children have access to at least the front of an embedded clause in order to set some parameters. This would suggest that the notion of degree 0 needs to be amended to "degree 0 plus a little," as was noted earlier. However, this messiness can be avoided if we think not in terms of clauses, which are merely convenient pretheoretical entities in generative formulations of Universal Grammar, but rather in terms of binding Domains (see (7)). This involves some technicalities, which I shall spell out briefly, but the results are straightforward: a child with access only to material from unembedded binding Domains has access to certain well-defined elements of an embedded clause. These are elements that children must have access to, and I shall argue in later chapters that they suffice and that children set their parameters on the basis only of data from unembedded binding Domains.

A binding Domain is defined in terms of a SUBJECT. The Domain for an element *x* is the first S′ or NP that contains an accessible SUBJECT. A SUBJECT is a higher ("c-commanding") NP or AGR, and a SUBJECT is accessible to *x* if assigning the SUBJECT's index to *x* violates neither the "i within i" condition (not relevant here) nor condition (7c). This will be illustrated in section 2.4. The fixing of some grammatical parameters depends on access to a lower Comp and the subject of an infinitival, as has been noted. For each of these elements, the Domain in which there is a higher SUBJECT can only be the next higher S' and not the local one, if we assume as usual that an infinitive occurs where there is no agreement marker. So in a structure like (16), if the lower S' lacks AGR, the only higher SUBJECT for the embedded subject is an element in the matrix S'. Similarly for Comp, regardless of whether there is AGR in the lower S', because a lower AGR would not be higher than the Comp.

(16) $_{S'}[\ldots$ NP AGR $\ldots _{S'}[$Comp [NP $\ldots]]]$

If this is correct, it seems plausible that some current formulations of Universal Grammar allow us to maintain a strict version of degree-0 learnability. The child's triggering experience seems to consist only of robust positive data which may be analyzed within the framework of Universal Grammar, given already established parameters of the particular grammar. Furthermore, it is restricted to data occurring in an unembedded binding Domain, and we may claim that there is nothing new to be learned from embedded Domains. This is the hypothesis that will be examined in later chapters. First, however, we shall see that it permits a degree-0 account of a parametric difference between English and Chinese and a solution for the Italian material discussed in section 2.2.

2.4 Chinese AGR

Aoun (1986), reanalyzing work by Huang (1982), argued that Chinese (whose verbs do not vary morphologically depending on the choice of subject) lacks AGR in INFL. His evidence consisted of sentences like (17).

(17) zhangsan$_i$ shuo $_{S'}$[ziji$_i$ hui lai]
      Zhangsan say   self can come
      'Zhangsan said that himself will come'

Such sentences indicate that the binding Domain for the anaphor *ziji* is the matrix S', because it is only in the matrix S' that *ziji* has a binder. This entails that there is no accessible SUBJECT (i.e., no AGR) in the embedded S' containing *ziji*. In the English analogue to (17) (see the gloss) AGR would occur in the embedded clause and would act as an accessible SUBJECT for *himself*; consequently the embedded clause would be the binding Domain for *himself*, which would fail to be bound in that Domain, hence violating (7a).

(17) does not seem to be a particularly exotic datum. It is also consistent with degree-0 learnability, if we define degree 0 in terms of binding Domains: the Domain for *ziji* is not an embedded Domain, and therefore

ziji is available to a language learner who has access only to unembedded material and (17) may set the relevant parameter such that there is no AGR in this language.

Defining the parametric difference between Chinese and English such that Chinese lacks AGR accounts for several superficial differences, notably differences in subject-object asymmetries and in the interpretability of the adjunct "why". We have already seen that the parameter may be set by data from unembedded binding Domains; now we will examine this parameter with some care in order to get a clear idea of how a single parameter setting may account for many superficial differences between languages if it is defined at an abstract level. In addition, this case illustrates the notion of a binding Domain, and it will enable readers who want to follow the technicalities to see them at work in some detail. Other readers may skip this section and proceed directly to section 2.5, if they are willing to grant in general that analyses must involve an appropriate level of abstractness and some theory-internal claims. To begin, I will devote a technical paragraph to reexamining the English sentences of (10) as an exercise in calculating binding Domains.

We need a simple assumption: All subject NPs are coindexed with their AGR, under the usual subject-verb agreement. Consequently, in (10a) the lowest e_i has no accessible SUBJECT. The local candidates are *Kay* and AGR, but in each case assigning the index k to the e_i would entail that e_i would be coindexed with an argument position, that of *Kay*; this would violate (7c). The same holds for the higher AGR and *Jay*. Therefore, in (10a) the lowest e_i has no accessible SUBJECT, hence no Domain, and so the binding theory does not hold for this element and it has no locality restriction. Consequently, direct objects may move long distance generally. But now compare an empty element in subject position, as in (10b). Here the lowest e_i does have an accessible SUBJECT; assigning it the index of the local AGR does not entail a coindexing with some other argument position, and therefore AGR is "accessible." As a result, e_i must be coindexed with a higher element in its local S′ in order to satisfy (7a). Since it has no local antecedent, the structure violates the binding theory (in addition to the PF condition of head government—see section 2.3). Compare now (10c), which lacks an overt complementizer at the front of the embedded clause. Again the empty subject in the embedded clause has an accessible SUBJECT for the same reason as in (10b), but here there is a local antecedent if the Comp indexing operation has taken place, namely the indexed Comp, and condition (7a) is satisfied.[6] This analysis provides a way of accounting for certain subject-object asymmetries, whereby extraction of a *wh* word from object position (whether taking place in the syntax or in logical form) is quite free, but extraction from subject position is sensitive to the presence of a complementizer, as the sentences in (10) show. Although such asymmetries are widespread in the languages of the world, they do not occur in Chinese (Huang 1982). Saying that Chinese lacks AGR provides an explanation. In general, Chinese has its interrogative words occurring not at the front of the sentence but in the position in which they must be understood ("in situ"). Most languages allow this possibility (consider English *I wonder who bought what*, where *what* remains in situ), but Chinese has no general alternative of syntactic movement. For such constructions the relevant scope relations are usually expressed through a process of "movement" in logical form (LF), the level of representation at which quantifier-variable binding is expressed. (18) is ambiguous between the readings (18a) and (18b); it has the two possible LF representations (19a) and (19b), corresponding to (18a) and (18b) respectively.

(18) ni xiang-zhidao [shei mai-le sheme]
      you wonder   who buy-ASP what
      a. 'what is the x such that you wonder who bought x?'
      b. 'who is the x such that you wonder what x bought?'

(19) a. $_{S'}$[sheme$_j$ $_S$[ni xiang-zhidao $_{S'}$[shei$_i$ $_S$[e$_i$ mai-le e$_j$]]]]
          what   you wonder   who   buy-ASP
      b. $_{S'}$[shei$_i$ $_S$[ni xiang-zhidao $_{S'}$[sheme$_j$ $_S$[e$_i$ mai-le e$_j$]]]]
          who   you wonder   what   buy-ASP

Because Chinese lacks AGR, neither *shei* nor *sheme* in (18) has a binding Domain, and therefore both may move long distance in LF. In (19a) and (19b), e_i, corresponding to *shei*, has no accessible SUBJECT; there is no AGR, and *ni* is not accessible. Also, the object e_j, corresponding to *sheme*, has no accessible SUBJECT for the same reason as the empty object in the English example (10a): assigning the index of the NP e_i to e_j would make e_j argument-bound, violating (7c). So, lack of AGR in Chinese entails that neither a subject nor an object has a binding Domain and therefore there are no subject-object asymmetries analogous to those of (10).

However, the binding theory is relevant in Chinese, and (20) is not ambiguous in the same way as (18). "What" may have wide scope over the matrix clause, with "why" having narrow scope over the embedded clause under "wonder", but not vice versa. (20) has only the meaning indicated by the gloss, i.e. (21a) but not (21b).

(20) ni xiang-zhidao [Lisi weisheme mai-le sheme]
     you wonder   Lisi why   buy-ASP what
     'what is the x such that you wonder why Lisi bought x?'

(21) a. sheme$_j$ $_S$[ni xiang-zhidao $_{S'}$[weisheme$_i$ $_S$[Lisi e$_i$ mai-le e$_j$]]]
     b. weisheme$_i$ $_S$[ni xiang-zhidao $_{S'}$[sheme$_j$ $_S$[Lisi e$_i$ mai-le e$_j$]]]

Here *sheme* has no accessible SUBJECT and thus no binding Domain, for the same reason that *who* had no Domain in (10a): the candidate SUBJECTs for e_j in (21) are *Lisi* and *ni*, but coindexing with these elements would lead to a violation of condition (7c) (which requires that a referential expression be argument-free). Hence the binding theory is irrelevant for *sheme* and there is no locality restriction. *Weisheme*, however, is not a referential expression and therefore is not subject to condition (7c); hence *Lisi* is accessible to the trace of "why", e_i in (21), and the embedded S' is its binding Domain. Hence (21a) is a possible LF for (20), but (21b) is not.

It is a general property of "why" and "how" that they are not referential expressions, and thus they are not subject to principle C of the binding theory (7c). Hence the contrast in English between (22a) and (22b); similarly in main clauses ((23a), (23b)).

(22) a. Jay wondered who lives where
     b. *Jay wondered who left why

(23) a. who lives where?
     b. *who is leaving why?

(24) a. $_{S'}$[who$_i$]$_i$ $_S$[e$_i$ AGR$_i$ is leaving why]
     b. $_{S'}$[who$_i$ why$_j$]$_i$ $_S$[e$_i$ AGR$_i$ is leaving e$_j$]

The structure of (23b) is (24a), and the LF is (24b). When *why* moves to Comp at LF, its trace e_j has an accessible SUBJECT and thus a binding Domain but fails to have an antecedent high enough in that Domain. The Comp must bear the index of the subject e_i because otherwise the empty subject, for which AGR is an accessible SUBJECT, would fail to be bound in its Domain. The identical structure with *where* instead of *why* is well formed because *where* is a referential expression and therefore has no Domain and is not subject to the demands of the binding theory (7). Consequently, saying that Chinese lacks AGR also accounts for some puzzling similarities between English and Chinese.

Furthermore, although (23b) does not occur in English, the corresponding sentence is well formed in Chinese. (25a) has the LF (25b). e_j has an accessible SUBJECT, namely e_i, and therefore must be bound in its

Domain, as it is. On the other hand, e_i has no Domain, there being no AGR in Chinese, and therefore needs no local binder.

(25) a. shei weisheme mai-le shu
         who why   buy-ASP books
         'who buys books why?'

   b. $_{S'}$[[shei$_i$ weisheme$_j$]$_j$ $_S$[e$_i$ e$_j$ mai-le shu]]

Hence, the distinction between (23b), which is ungrammatical in English, and (25a), which has the well-formed LF (25b) in Chinese, lies in the fact that Chinese lacks AGR.

This case has involved some theory-internal claims, as one should expect by now. In this example, the locality conditions formulated by Aoun, Hornstein, Lightfoot, and Weinberg enable us to establish a single parameter—the presence or absence of AGR—which accounts for many superficial and subtle differences between English and Chinese and which can be set on the basis of unembedded data, if we define "unembedded" in terms of binding Domains and not of clauses. The absence of AGR may follow from the fact that Chinese has an impoverished verb morphology, if Universal Grammar prescribes a tight relation between morphological properties and abstract syntactic elements. However, if a syntactic trigger is needed for lack of AGR, then a simple trigger is available. (25a), involving only material in an unembedded binding Domain, may (like (17)) act as a trigger for the correct parametric value: that Chinese lacks AGR.

Again, there is no logical relationship between the existence of locality restrictions and degree-0 learnability; the Chinese operations just discussed were quite local, but it remained an empirical question whether there were parameters to be fixed which required access to complex sentences. The same point can be made with an *ad hominem* observation: Some of the most insightful commentators on Lightfoot 1989 took grammatical operations to be local while holding that children need access to complex structures to set their grammatical parameters. This is a perfectly coherent position, although not empirically justified in my view. It illustrates the partial independence of notions of locality and the data needed to set parameters: to be a localist does not necessarily entail being a minimalist with respect to the triggering experience.

2.5 Italian Again

If one thinks of unembedded binding Domains rather than unembedded clauses as the basis for language acquisition, then a solution to the Italian problem (section 2.2) becomes available, as Guglielmo Cinque pointed out in a personal communication. Recall that Rizzi and Sportiche argued that S′ but not S is a bounding node in Italian and French. It was shown above how the French child could derive this conclusion from simple data such as (5). However, it is not clear that comparable structures are available to the Italian child. Analyses vary, and children seem to be free to treat (26a) as (26b), or (26c), or (26d); it is not obvious that children must analyze *quante* as extracted from within a NP and moved across S to Comp in one operation.

(26) a. quante ne hai viste?
      'how many have (you) seen of them?'
    b. $_{NP}[$quante $e_i]_k$ $_S[$ne$_i$ hai viste $_{NP}[e_k]]$
    c. $_{QP}[$quante$]_k$ $_S[$ne$_i$ hai viste $_{NP}[e_k$ $e_i]]$
    d. $_{QP}[$quante$]_k$ $_S[$ne$_i$ hai viste $[e_k]$ $[e_i]]$

However, if (27a) and (27b) are well-formed structures for the corresponding sentences, then movement has taken place across NP and S, showing that S cannot be a bounding node. For arguments that such "small clauses" are not dominated by a maximal projection (S′), see Hornstein and Lightfoot 1987. In such a structure, the NP indicated, being a subject, cannot be reanalyzed. Furthermore, its binding Domain is the matrix clause, since the lower S contains no SUBJECT (AGR); it is not, however, a member of the matrix clause.

(27) a. ne$_i$ ho visti $_S[_{NP}[$molti $e_i]$ corrergli incontro]
      'of them (I) saw many run toward him'
    b. ne$_i$ ho visto $_S[_{NP}[$il volto $e_i]$ sbiancarsi]
      'of him (I) saw the face become white'
      ne$_i$ ho visti $_S[_{NP}[$molti $e_i]$ affaticati]
      'of them (I) saw many tired'

Hence, simple, degree-0 data are available to make S into a nonbounding node in the grammars of Italian speakers, if one defines "simple" in terms of unembedded binding Domains. Although simple, the data are slightly exotic and probably do not occur frequently in any child's experience. Consequently, it is not surprising that there is variability among Italian speakers in the setting of this parameter—conspicuously more variability than there is among speakers of French, for whom the relevant trigger is quite robust.

2.6 Conclusion

The viability of this hypothesis, that the primary linguistic data are restricted to data occurring in an unembedded binding Domain, will depend on further case studies, and I shall present some in later chapters. Here I have examined some crucial cases which would seem to have motivated richer and more extensive triggers, and I have shown that, given certain formulations of Universal Grammar, one can fix the relevant parameters on the basis of data in nonembedded Domains. Further cases, of course, may be less tractable, and this deliberately strong hypothesis may have to be revised and relaxed.

The hypothesis depends on particular analyses, as is clear from the cases discussed in this chapter. Similarly, any potential refutations will be as persuasive as the analyses on which they depend. It will not be enough to cite unanalyzed phenomena that appear to be limited to embedded Domains. For example, Higgins (1973) pointed out that the complement to the verb *serve* is always transitive, as (28) illustrates.

(28) a. *the ice served to melt
     b. the ice served to chill the beer

On the face of it, such an observation might be construed as a counterexample to degree-0 learnability. However, as Higgins showed, the correct generalization is that the subject of the embedded infinitive must be interpretable as an instrument. What is wrong with (28a) is that the understood subject of *melt* is not an instrument. Similarly, in (29) the complement verb is transitive but there is no instrumental subject.

(29) *Edison served [PRO to invent the light bulb]

The correlation that complements to *serve* are always transitive follows from the fact that "any verb in English whose subject can be understood as an instrument of necessity has an object" (Higgins 1973, p. 174). Consequently, the observed phenomenon does not pose a problem for degree-0 learnability. Our degree-0 learner has access to the subject of an infinitival complement (because its binding Domain is the matrix S'), and nothing more is needed: the selectional property of *serve* makes no reference to an embedded object, contrary to initial appearances.

The fact that certain morphological forms occur only in embedded clauses might also be a *prima facie* problem for degree-0 learnability. For example, certain predicates are followed by verbs in the subjunctive mood in the Romance languages. This is presumably a form of complementation, marked in the embedded Comp or in the head of the clause (INFL) or in both. Each of these positions is accessible to our degree-0 learner. As was noted in section 2.3, parameter setting is often sensitive to properties of an embedded Comp. This permits a child to learn whether an element in Comp may be deleted, to learn whether a relative pronoun may only be nominative (as in Malagasy), and, indeed, to learn the existence of words like "if", "whether", and "because", which occur only in an embedded Comp. It will be shown in section 4.2 that parameter setting is also sensitive to an embedded INFL, as is expected if INFL is the head of a clause; in that case, the binding Domain of INFL could not be its own projection and thus would have to be the next S'. So the existence of subjunctive forms in embedded clauses poses no problem for our degree-0 learner, who has access to an embedded Comp and to INFL.[7] Similarly, there is no difficulty in learning that in English the subjunctive *were* occurs only in counterfactual conditional clauses, such as *if I were the boss, I would.* ... Such forms are probably archaisms, more taught than acquired through the usual process of parameter setting and thus by no means uniform in the speech of English speakers. But in any case, *were* occupies INFL and therefore is accessible to parameter setting.

Other cases may raise more serious difficulties. In chapter 3 I shall discuss the acquisition of underlying object-verb order, which in Dutch and German seems to be manifested only in embedded clauses. I shall show that the relevant parameters may in fact be set by unembedded data, and that such an account solves some old mysteries about the acquisitional data.

Some languages have morphemes bound to a higher NP which may be in a higher clause. These morphemes, known as "long-distance anaphors," have different properties in the various languages in which they occur. Consider the following cases, which are from English, Chinese, and Icelandic:

(30) a. the children$_i$ thought that $_{S'}$[$_{NP}$[each other's$_i$ pictures] were on sale]

   b. John$_i$ xiangxin Bill$_j$ dui Sam$_k$ shuo ziji$_{i,j,*k}$ taoyan Mary
         believe   to   say self   hate
       'John believes that Bill said to Sam that self hated Mary'

   c. John$_i$ segir að Mary$_j$ elski sig$_{i,j}$
       'John says that Mary loves self'

The exact parameterization manifested by these phenomena has been discussed extensively in recent years; the topic deserves a book of its own. Pica (1987) keys the syntactic properties of these morphemes to their morphological form. Hyams and Sigurjónsdóttir (1990) treat Icelandic *sig* as a pronominal anaphor, a lexical variant of the familiar "PRO," and not as a pure anaphor. If it were an anaphor, then the Subset Principle would predict that early grammars would allow only local binding (because that defines a smaller language than a grammar allowing also long-distance binding). However, Hyams and Sigurjónsdóttir show that children control the complex constraints on long-distance binding at a relatively early age and that both children and adults show a strong preference for long-distance readings where the anaphors are ambiguous, as in (30c). Pronominal elements, on the other hand, typically have long-distance dependencies (*everybody hopes that his mother is happy*). The development data for Chinese and Korean are different, and therefore they require a different analysis. Wilcoxon (1988) argues that apparent embedded reflexives in Chinese are better treated as instances of an "intensive adverb." If the analysis of Hyams and Sigurjónsdóttir and that of Wilcoxon are along the right lines, there may be no such thing as a long-distance anaphor and children may not learn sets of exceptions to the binding theory. This is reinforced by the arguments of Sigurdsson (1986), who showed that long-distance reflexives in Icelandic are not subject to a syntactic analysis under any version of the binding theory. The idea that the binding theory should not be parameterized to allow long-distance anaphors derives more plausibility from the work of Cole, Hermon, and Sung (1990), who reduce some apparent long-distance dependencies in Chinese and Korean to sequences of local dependencies, thus changing the acquisitional questions substantially.[8]

Rather than try to resolve these matters here, I shall pursue a different line of argumentation in later chapters, arguing that the nature of some historical changes suggests that children are degree-0 learners. Under certain conditions they are insensitive to complex data that should have inhibited the new parameter settings actually adopted.

The claim that children are degree-0 learners stands alongside the Subset Principle and reflects a property of their "learning" capacity and not of Universal Grammar. Universal Grammar constitutes the initial state of a person's linguistic capacity and incorporates the principles and option points of the eventual mature capacity. It cannot say anything about the conditions under which its parameters are set. If children set their parameters on the basis of simple, unembedded data, this must follow from the learning strategies available to them: children may "learn" only from simple structures. In that case, one must leave open the possibility that the definition of "simple structures" may eventually be stated in quite different terms, perhaps in more general terms which subsume the syntactic learning discussed here as one special case. I have invoked the notion of an unembedded binding Domain as the basis for parameter setting, because it seems to provide the most accurate characterization for the instances discussed. This may have to be restated in other terms, perhaps in terms of phonetic units. In that case, the relevant phonetic units will coincide with the limits of binding Domains, if our central hypothesis is along the right lines. Consequently, it is premature to address questions about the appropriateness of using an LF notion to define the limits to triggering experiences. Nor are we ready to ask whether binding Domains are themselves subject to parameterization (note the skepticism just expressed) and, if so, whether triggering experiences may vary in complexity from language to language according to that parameterization. Nor shall I ask about the status of embedded direct objects, which have no binding Domain (except by default) by the definitions of Aoun (1986); as will be shown, they cannot be accessible to parameter setters. These are intriguing questions, but first we need some more motivation for degree-0 learnability.

Recall the most fundamental point: An intrinsic relationship exists among claims made about the three entities in our explanatory model, and any claim made about Universal Grammar entails certain assumptions about particular grammars and about triggers. Those assumptions should be spelled out, because they may vary in their plausibility, with consequences for the claim about Universal Grammar and for the particular grammars under investigation. In view of the richness of current theories and the productivity of comparative work on parametric variation, claims about the triggering experience can be used as one basis for evaluating hypotheses. In fact, if one ignores the trigger at this stage one runs the risk that one's hypothesis may be off the mark.

The hypothesis of degree-0 learnability, as we have it so far, directs attention toward discrepancies between phenomena occurring in embedded and unembedded Domains, but such discrepancies raise no particular learnability questions if embedded Domains may be part of the trigger experience. I shall state my central claims with enough precision and detail to make them readily testable, but it will be important to distinguish technicalities from fundamentals. A fundamental concern cannot be eliminated on a technicality. Let us see whether a bifurcation between embedded and unembedded Domains is plausible from the perspective of learnability. I shall argue that it is. The notion of an unembedded binding Domain provides the relevant distinction for the cases discussed here, but there may be other ways of making the division.

Chapter 3
Loss of Object-Verb Order

3.1 An Empirical Argument for Degree-0 Learnability?

So, some well-studied parameters which appeared to depend on complex experiences can in fact be set by simple triggers. This makes one wonder whether children acquiring the usual mature linguistic capacities ever need access to complex triggering experiences. Indeed, once one treats the trigger with proper respect as a legitimate entity in one's theorizing, there are good methodological reasons to assume that children respond only to simple triggering experiences and to impose the burden of proof on linguists who invoke richer triggering structures. However, Occam's razor can be dulled by empirical arguments that more is needed, and it can be made into an irrelevant tool. If linguists offer necessity arguments and argue that richer fodder is needed, it would be useful to have a strong empirical argument to counter them, since empirical arguments are more effective in many ways, and certainly more refined, than methodological razors.

It will be hard to construct such an argument from the usual kind of grammatical analysis. For one phenomenon after another, one might argue that a simple trigger will suffice, as in chapter 2, but then the general conclusion that simple triggers always suffice will be reached only by induction. This is a notoriously fallible form of reasoning, even when the inductive base seems to be wide and firm. One might try to supplement such arguments by showing that the wrong grammars would emerge if children were sensitive to embedded Domains, i.e., that phenomena from embedded Domains could be misleading; but that would involve showing that some property or operation manifested in embedded Domains was not manifested in any matrix Domain, and that could not occur under the hypothesis of degree-0 learnability (or, indeed, under the familiar assumption that processes affecting embedded or nonroot domains must be structure-preserving). Consequently a different form of argument is needed.

One possibility would be to expose a child to a language artificially modified to include some robust phenomenon manifested only in embedded clauses, and to examine whether it had any effect on the child's development. A skillful and very lucky observer might even exploit a natural experiment along those lines: if a pidgin language manifested a special property in embedded Domains, one might examine the fate of that property in the ensuing creolization process. I shall discuss an example along those lines, from Berbice Dutch, in section 7.3. Here, however, I shall offer a diachronic argument.

It is well known that Old English had similar gross word-order properties to what one finds today in Dutch and German: object-verb order appears quite consistently in embedded clauses, but in main clauses one finds a strong tendency toward verb-object order. It is also well known that this embedded-clause word-order property was lost early in the history of English. The first question is how Dutch, German, and Old English children have acquired grammars yielding these effects in embedded clauses. I shall show in section 3.2 that data from matrix Domains suffice to trigger the relevant properties of Dutch and German, and that there is no reason to invoke the "subordinate clause strategy" of Roeper (1973), whereby children must pay particular attention to embedded clauses. In section 3.3 I will show that matrix Domain data, albeit different, also suffice to set the relevant parameters for Old English. Then in section 3.4 I will show how changes affecting those matrix Domains yielded different primary linguistic data, which triggered a different grammar for English speakers, which generated embedded clauses with verb-object order. My general argument is that changes affecting embedded clauses were an automatic by-product of certain changes in unembedded Domains, but only if one assumes that children are degree-0 learners. If they are not degree-0 learners, the fact that the changes coincided remains a remarkable accident of history that should exhaust the tolerance of all but the most whimsical. The form of the argument is that if parameter setting were sensitive to embedded material, there would have been plenty of robust data to warrant object-verb order. However, since word order did change, there will be good reason to believe that children must be degree-0 learners; that is, they ignored potentially decisive data that lay outside unembedded structures. This, in turn, requires that we seek alternatives to analyses that require children to have access to embedded Domains in order to set grammatical parameters. The argument is based on diachronic data, and claims that

English could not have changed in the way that it did unless children are degree-0 learners.

3.2   Acquiring Object-Verb Order

A striking feature of Dutch, German, and Old English, particularly from the viewpoint of degree-0 learnability, is the discrepancy in predominant word order between clause types: embedded clauses have a fairly consistent subject-object-verb order, whereas main declarative clauses have the verb in second position, preceded by a subject or any other constituent. To this extent the three languages are parallel, although Old English shows some different patterns—for example, the subject-object-verb order characteristic of embedded clauses occurs also in conjunct clauses (that is, clauses introduced by a coordinating conjunction, such as 'and' or 'but'). The two phenomena do not necessarily go hand in hand; the Scandinavian languages (Danish, Norwegian, Swedish, and Icelandic) all typically have the main-clause verb in second position (with some minor differences) but have subject-verb-object order in embedded clauses. An extensive literature has been devoted to these phenomena, and a central problem is usually taken to be the position of the verb in main clauses: what is that position, why must the verb occur there in main clauses, and by what is the verb preceded? This is the so-called verb-second problem. For good surveys, see the collection of essays in Haider and Prinzhorn 1986, the introduction to Hellan and Koch Christensen 1986, Platzack 1985, and chapter 2 of Weerman 1989; Koopman (1984) analyzes some partly analogous phenomena in some West African languages.

This literature shows agreement on some central aspects of the analysis of these phenomena, and great diversity in other respects. Following den Besten 1983 (first circulated in 1977), generative analyses of the Germanic and Scandinavian languages agree in postulating two operations, one whereby the finite verb is moved into a complementizer position and one whereby some other phrasal category is moved into a preceding position— perhaps a topic position, or the Specifier of a Complementizer Phrase (CP) in the framework of Chomsky 1986. So the Dutch sentences *Jan woont in Utrecht* 'Jan lives in Utrecht' and *in Utrecht woonden drie haringen* 'in Utrecht lived three herrings' are derived as in (1a) and (1b).

(1) a. $_{NP}[Jan_i]$ $_{Comp}[woont_j]$ $_S[e_i$ in Utrecht $e_j]$

     b. $_{PP}[in$ Utrecht $_i]$ $_{Comp}[woonden_j]$ $_S[drie$ haringen e_i $e_j]$

Norwegian *Jon kjøper aldri bøker* 'Jon never buys books' and *bøker kjøper*

Jon aldri 'books buys Jon never' are analyzed in similar fashion, but the verb precedes its complement at D-structure, as in (2a) and (2b).

(2) a. $_{NP}$[Jon$_i$] $_{Comp}$[kjøper$_j$] $_S$[e$_i$ aldri e$_j$ bøker]

  b. $_{NP}$[bøker$_i$] $_{Comp}$[kjøper$_j$] $_S$[Jon aldri e$_j$ e$_i$]

Consequently, verbs do not move into Comp in embedded clauses, because the position is already occupied by a lexical complementizer ('that', 'if', etc.).[1]

It has been useful to distinguish two movements that verbs may undergo: from V to INFL and from INFL to Comp. So a more articulated structure for (1a) would be (3), where AGR indicates the features of tense and person contained in INFL and the verb *won-* adjoins first to INFL, from where it head-governs the trace e_w, and then INFL (now containing *won-*) moves to Comp.

(3) $_{NP}$[Jan$_i$] $_{Comp}$[won$_w$ + AGR]$_j$ $_S$[e$_i$ $_{VP}$[in Utrecht e$_w$] $_{INFL}$[e$_j$]]

Given such a distinction, one notes that V-to-INFL applies quite generally in all clause types, and that INFL-to-Comp usually applies in main clauses.

On this much there is general agreement. There is consensus not only on the position to which a verb moves in main clauses, but also on its underlying position in these languages. Bach (1962) and Bierwisch (1963) analyzed German as object-verb at D-structure; similarly, Koster (1975) gave many reasons to analyze Dutch as underlyingly object-verb and having the movement rules that I have indicated. Koster's general argument is that it is far simpler to base-generate verbs to the right of their complements and allow a "root" transformation to move them to second position in main clauses than it is to base-generate them in second position (whether defined as in Comp or otherwise) or elsewhere and postulate a rightward movement operation applying in embedded clauses. Koster's discussion was couched in terms of the distinction between "root" and "structure-preserving": his favored analysis involved a root transformation moving a verb leftward in main clauses, whereas the rejected analyses would involve a unique operation, applying only in embedded clauses and not conforming to his rule typology. Den Besten's approach, keying the movability of the verb to an available Comp position, makes the root vs. structure-preserving distinction irrelevant here: rather, the verb moves to a governing INFL position, and thence to a governing Comp position. This is an instance of head-to-head movement, the verb moving from one head position to another and leaving a bound trace in each position. The reverse process, moving downward from Comp to INFL and then to an empty V in embedded clauses would leave an unbound trace in Comp.

From our point of view, such a process, applying only in embedded Domains, would clearly be inaccessible to a degree-0 learner. I will return below to the question of how a child might attain Koster's analysis. Koster's form of argument, purged of the root vs. structure-preserving distinction, carries over to the Scandinavian languages with a different conclusion: verbs are base-generated to the left of their complements, hence sentence-medially, and moved to INFL and then in main clauses to Comp, as in (4), which is a more articulated structure for (2a).

(4) $_{NP}[Jon_i]$ $_{Comp}[[kjøp_k + AGR]_j]$ $_S[e_i$ aldri $_{INFL}[e_j]$ $_{VP}e_k$ bøker]]

A problem has been noted for Icelandic (Hellan and Koch Christensen 1986, p. 3): although Icelandic shows verb-second effects similar to those illustrated by (1) and (2), embedded clauses show the same adverb order as main clauses—see (5).

(5) a. hvort Jon kaupir aldrei bökur
        'if Jon buys never books'
    b. Jon kaupir aldrei bökur
        'Jon buys never books'
    c. $_S[Jon$ $_{INFL}[kaup_k + AGR]$ $_{VP}[aldrei$ e_k bökur]]

If the verb *kaupir* moves across the adverb *aldrei* to Comp in (5b), then the structure of (5a) is unclear, where Comp is filled by the complementizer *hvort* but the verb nonetheless occurs to the left of the adverb. This suggests that Icelandic grammars treat adverbs like *aldrei* as VP adverbs or as Specifiers of VP and that a verb moving to INFL moves across the adverb (Ottósson 1989), yielding a structure like (5c). Meanwhile, comparable adverbs in mainland Scandinavian are sentential and are not affected by the movement of a verb to INFL; see (4) for Norwegian.

There is widespread consensus on what I have sketched so far, although it is implemented in quite different ways (for discussion see Haider and Prinzhorn 1986, p. 4). The details need not concern us now; my goal here is not to give a properly worked out analysis of verb-second phenomena, but to provide enough structure to allow discussion of the acquisition of the relevant parameter settings. There is great diversity, however, in the explanations offered for why verbs should move to Comp in these languages, why there should be a general "topicalization" process fronting some other constituent in all declarative main clauses, and, most important, why these processes should be obligatory in declarative main clauses. The processes themselves are not unusual; operations that topicalize a constituent by moving it to the front of a main clause appear in many of the grammars that have been studied carefully. The movement of INFL to Comp would be an instance of one head moving to an immediately c-commanding head position in the framework of Chomsky 1986, where INFL is the head of an INFL phrase (IP) and Comp the head of a Comp phrase (CP), and is a widely attested option occurring in the grammars of English, French, and Italian. What requires explanation in the so-called verb-second languages, whether underlyingly verb-object or object-verb, is the apparent obligatoriness of INFL-to-Comp movement in all main clauses and the apparent obligatoriness of "topicalization" in declarative main clauses.

Some element of Universal Grammar will be needed to explain the obligatoriness of the processes in the verb-second languages. Since children generally do not have access to negative data (see chapter 1), the Dutch child cannot "learn" that, say, INFL-to-Comp movement is obligatory directly on the basis of the ungrammaticality of *in Utrecht drie haringen wonen 'in Utrecht three herrings live'. If that datum is not available to the child, there can be no consequence or inference or learning based on it. One must leave open the possibility that this learning might take place if children have indirect access to such data; that is, failure to hear such a simple expression might lead the child to deduce its ungrammaticality and thus to acquire some specific device that will block its derivation. This cannot be ruled out in principle, but we saw in chapter 1 that there are reasons to be skeptical of appeals to indirect negative data. If one is eventually forced to admit indirect access to negative data, one would expect to find that deductive learning based on it would emerge in children somewhat differently than the usual parameter setting, perhaps later or after a stage of misgeneralization. Certainly an argument will be required that children do have indirect access to negative data under certain narrowly prescribed circumstances.

Nonetheless, one finds several proposals in the extensive verb-second literature postulating language-specific devices, and in such a way that they implicitly (but never explicitly, as far as I know) presuppose indirect access to negative data. For example, the proposals of den Besten (1983), de Haan and Weerman (1986), Haider (1986), Koopman (1984), and others each postulate some element in Comp which must, given some principle of Universal Grammar, "attract" INFL (or the finite verb) to that position, but the evidence for this element (and thus of the principle of Universal Grammar that forces movement to it) is the obligatoriness of the movement, i.e., the ungrammaticality of structures where movement has not taken place. In the absence of an appropriate learning theory whereby children have access to the relevant negative data, the proposal simply restates the problem. Platzack's (1986) proposal suffers from the same defect when he postulates different projections in verb-second and non-verb-second languages. His idea is that S is a projection of INFL in English and in other languages that do not have verb-second properties, and a projection of Comp in verb-second languages. He also allows grammars to differ in terms of whether the subject NP is base-generated as part of the projection of INFL or part of the projection of Comp. Then a principle of Universal Grammar, Platzack's "Case assignment rule," forces a verb to move to Comp in grammars where the projection of INFL does not include the subject NP. This postulates major differences in projection types. The evidence for the particular projection scheme for a verb-second language is the obligatoriness of INFL-to-Comp movement and the ungrammaticality of structures where INFL fails to move to Comp, and again there is no discussion of how the child would have access to such data. It is unclear how one might treat grammars (like those of earlier forms of English) allowing verbs to move to Comp as an option, and the proposal also fails to account for the necessity of topicalization in declarative main clauses, a point to be taken up below.

The same sort of attainability problem arises with the quite different proposals of Safir (1981) and Evers (1982). Safir has Universal Grammar require that verbs (and other heads) be uniquely governed, and he makes the structure of German such that verbs must move to Comp in main clauses in order for this requirement to be satisfied. Evers keys movement of the finite verb to the assumption that the tense element has a scope-bearing property and must c-command the clause; in embedded clauses the verb does not need to move because the matrix verb determines the scope of tense. In each case the child has to learn something specific about verb-second languages: Safir's child must learn the structural properties that entail that a verb in a base-generated INFL position (it is assumed that verbs move to INFL in all clause types) fails to be uniquely governed in the appropriate sense (unlike, say, equivalent verbs in French). Evers' child must learn that Comp is the only position that c-commands the clause, in contrast with English, French, and Italian. In each case the evidence is not explicitly discussed but it would appear to be the ungrammaticality of structures where movement to Comp has not taken place. Also, neither Safir nor Evers discusses the relationship between movement to Comp and topicalization.

One solution to the problem of an appropriate triggering experience for the proposed analysis would be to make the verb-second phenomenon unmarked. If, for example, one postulates that INFL moves to Comp by attraction to some element there, one might argue that generating that element in Comp reflects the unmarked situation; English and French children, on the other hand, are exposed to positive data which show that the attractive element is absent, namely the occurrence of the finite verb in some other position. This might lead one to expect English and French children to go through an early verb-second stage, just as Hyams' (1983) English children go through an early pro-drop stage reflecting the alleged unmarked status of the null-subject option in her analysis. I know no evidence along these lines.

A striking feature of the basic properties of verb-second languages is the correlation between the "topicalization" operation and the obligatory movement of INFL to Comp.[2] Since the INFL-to-Comp movement is a common option in many languages which are not verb-second, it is unlikely that the obligatoriness of the movement would entail obligatory "topicalization" or fronting of some phrasal category. Indeed, some verb-subject-object languages seem to have obligatory verb fronting without any obligatory "topicalization"; for example, Welsh seems to have underlying INFL-subject-verb-object order and surface verb-subject-object order in all clause types by virtue of the verb's moving obligatorily to INFL (Harlow 1981; Sproat 1985), but there is no requirement that another phrasal category be moved forward. It is possible, of course, that the verb must be not just at the front of the clause but actually in Comp to entail "topicalization," but it is hard to see why the obligatoriness of the movement should require "topicalization"—that is, why "topicalization" should not be required in English or French when a verb happens to be in Comp.

However, the reverse relationship might be more plausible: "topicalization" or a fronted XP might entail verb movement. Taraldsen (1986), developing work by Cinque and Kayne, argues interestingly that a topicalized argument phrase must be locally licensed, and that a verb in Comp effectively turns the position filled by the topic into an argument position by yielding a predicate structure; so verb movement has the effect of providing a local licensing environment for a displaced argument phrase, which in turn permits its trace to be construed as a variable. He offers some intriguing evidence based on the absence of verb-second effects with bare *wh* words introducing root interrogatives in certain northern dialects of Norwegian. It is a theory of the right type in that Universal Grammar forces movement to Comp in order to license initial argument phrases; in that case the child has to learn that Dutch and German sentences begin with some argument phrase of arbitrary function, which is not implausible. Hellan and Koch Christensen (1986, introduction) note that the verb-second phenomenon occurs in those languages that allow long-distance anaphors, which are sometimes argued to be sensitive to predication (e.g., some of the contributions which they introduce); they go on to speculate that the common denominator of these languages may be some sort of predication sensitivity. However, there are two fundamental problems. First, it does not seem natural to construe expletives like Dutch *er* and German *es* as elements requiring predication. Second, topicalization does not entail verb movement in languages that are not verb-second (English, French, etc.). If one keys this to a *structural* difference in the position of the topicalized item, then the requirement of a certain kind of predication relationship becomes unclear.

A comparable approach, which does not involve notions of predicate formation, can be stated in terms of constraints on phrase structure, if those constraints hold of S-structures. Suppose that Dutch children learn that sentences generally begin with an arbitrary phrasal category (NP, PP, etc.), which has no fixed functional or thematic role (and therefore is not necessarily a subject NP licensed by a governing INFL). Since the category is utterance-initial, it cannot be a complement of some head and must therefore be a specifier, since these are the only two positions in which a phrasal category may occur, if one adopts the convention of chapter 1 (repeated in (6) below). Lexical specifiers must be dominated by another phrasal category which must have a head; call it YP. Since the initial phrasal category has no fixed thematic or functional role, the corresponding head cannot be INFL or any other element associated with a particular thematic, functional, or case-assigning role, and therefore will be an empty position at D-structure, which is subsequently filled as another head moves to that position. The only element that is local enough to move to the empty head position and head-govern its trace is INFL (with its associated verb).

Under this approach, children acquiring a verb-second language such as Dutch learn that initial phrasal categories are locally licensed in a fashion that, in turn, requires obligatory movement of a finite verb to Y^0 (Lightfoot 1990). If $_{INFL'}$[NP INFL VP] represents the internal structure of a clause (where INFL' projects from INFL and is equivalent to S in other notations), then INFL' may be maximalized with an initial Comp or (in the marked case) via the extra projection superimposed by Dutch children. In that event the extra YP would not be distinct from INFL-P (or IP). If the extra projection represents the marked case, then it is data-driven and emerges in response to some triggering experience. This means, first, that it would not generalize to embedded clauses unless specifically triggered.

So, Dutch has only the unmarked $_{IP}$[Comp $_{I'}$[NP INFL VP]] in embedded clauses, and no embedded verb-second properties. Second, grammars vary in the class of phrases which occur as the Specifier of an extra YP: in Dutch all phrasal categories require the extra YP, and therefore all matrix clauses have the structure $_{YP}$[XP Y^0 $_{INFL'}$ [NP INFL VP]], even if the XP is an expletive like *er*; but in English only interrogative elements have this effect and so require fronting of the finite verb. Initial topics (*Kim, Tim likes*) and noninterrogative *wh* words (*what a team that was*) are not associated with moved verbs. (Weinberg (1990) argues that sentences with "subject-verb inversion" are dominated by an extra projection CP, whereas other types are dominated by IP. Similarly, Ottósson (1989) distinguishes Icelandic main clauses dominated by IP from those dominated by CP.)

These ideas raise many questions and may be implemented in various ways, but this will not be the focus of my attention here. It is worth noting parenthetically Universal 11 of Greenberg (1966, p. 83), drawn to my attention by Amy Weinberg: "Inversion of statement order so that verb precedes subject occurs only in languages where the question word or phrase is normally initial. This same inversion occurs in yes-no questions only if it also occurs in interrogative word questions." If languages generally do not have a verb-fronting operation unless they also front interrogative phrases, then it is plausible to interpret a moved verb as licensing the initial phrase, along the lines suggested above. I am not concerned here with an exact formulation, just with the essential contribution of Universal Grammar for children acquiring a verb-second language. If such children can learn that an inflected verb must occur in second position (specifically, let us assume, in Y^0) in order to license the initial phrasal category, the further question then arises of how they learn that the verb moves there and from where it moves.

With this brief sketch of some elements of grammars yielding verb-second phenomena, let us now ask how children attain these grammars. One can see that there is a ready answer to this question for a linguist who assumes a rich triggering experience: robust data from embedded clauses show that verbs occur not only in second position in matrix clauses but also at the end of a clause. Such data, however, are not accessible to a degree-0 child, for whom the primary linguistic data are confined to matrix binding Domains. Nonetheless, I shall argue that simple data from matrix Domains suffice to trigger underlying object-verb order in V'.

In chapter 1 we saw good reasons to postulate general conditions for projections: they are subject to a template given by Universal Grammar, repeated here as (6).

(6) a. XP → {Specifier, X′}

    b. X′ → {X or X′, (YP)}

(6b) requires that a complement occur adjacent to its head at D-structure, although they are unordered at the level of Universal Grammar. This forces a movement analysis. A Dutch child endowed with (6) and hearing expressions like (7) will realize that either the verb or its object must have moved, because they are not adjacent phonetically.

(7) a. in Utrecht vonden de mensen het idee gek
       in Utrecht found   people   the idea crazy
       'in Utrecht people found the idea crazy'

    b. gisteren vonden de bestuursleden de oplossing (niet)
       yesterday found the committee members the solution (not)
       'yesterday the committee members found (not) the solution'

A child relying on distributional data of the type that one finds in textbook exercises could exploit the invariant position of the verb to postulate a simple rule moving it there. This would conform to the general requirement that a head moves only to another c-commanding head position, if the verb moved from a position adjacent to the object to INFL and then to the "extra" Y^0 position. It would be more difficult to formulate an accurate rule moving the object from a position adjacent to the surface verb, given the further data of (8), where both the verb and its complement have been displaced.

(8) a. het idee vonden de mensen gek

    b. de mensen vonden het idee gek
       'people found the idea crazy'

If the verb were base-generated in an initial position, it would be impossible to generate the data in (7) and (8) through a movement operation moving the object from alongside the verb to positions that consistently c-commanded the source. So it would seem more straightforward to postulate a verb-movement process, which in fact is the only option for a child constrained to identify movement sites that are c-commanded by the moved element.

So, children equipped with (6) as part of their Universal Grammar and exposed to data like (7) and (8) would postulate a movement operation affecting finite verbs. Furthermore, given (6), they would know that the verb moves from a D-structure position immediately adjacent to the direct-object NP. But from which of the two possible positions? Verb-second languages typically have unembedded "signposts" indicating the movement site of the verb. For example, many Dutch and German verbs have separable particles, which occur *uniformly* at the end of main clauses, as in (9), indicating the position from which the verb has moved.

(9) a. Jan belt de hoogleraar op
        Jan calls the professor up
    b. Franz steht sehr früh auf
        Franz gets very early up

The fact that these verbs form a semantic unit suggests that they are base-generated together. And the uniform clause-final position of the particles would receive the simplest possible analysis if the particle-verb clusters were generated there. This is supported where the verb is nonfinite and occurs alongside the particle: *Jan moet de hoogleraar opbellen* 'Jan must call up the professor', *Franz muss sehr früh aufstehen* 'Franz must get up very early'.

Such expressions with a modal verb or perfective *hebben*, with or without a separable prefix, constitute a second unembedded indicator of the D-structure position of verbs. They might be derived from biclausal D-structures along the lines of $_{S'}$[Jan $_{S'}$[PRO de hoogleraar opbellen] moet], because *moeten* and *mussen* are independent verbs in Dutch and German and not modal auxiliaries. If so, a verb-raising process entails eliminating the S' clause boundary (and more, but that is irrelevant here), as argued by Evers (1975), and at S-structure there is only one S' (see (10)) and thus only one possible binding Domain at LF. Under the theory of Universal Grammar adopted in section 2.2 above, the lower S' (being a maximal projection) would need to delete in order to permit the trace e_k to be head-governed by the raised verb *opbellen*.

(10) $_{S'}$[Jan$_j$ moet$_i$ $_S$[e$_j$ $_S$[PRO de hoogleraar e$_k$] e$_i$ opbellen$_k$]]

If this is correct, then such "clause-union" data would be accessible to our degree-0 learner. In fact, Klein (1974) examined mothers' speech addressed to two Dutch two-year-olds and found a surprisingly high percentage of such structures (42% and 32%, respectively, of the total number of recorded utterances). The samples were small, and Klein chose to exclude several types of data, which may have skewed his statistics somewhat. However, he gives good reasons to believe that Dutch children pay much attention to such structures from an early age. Questions then arise about the nature of the structures assigned to such expressions by young children; for example, Klein suggests that an unstressed "auxiliary" is in some sense not perceived and thus plays no role in the analysis of sentences like (10). In this case, a simple monoclausal structure would be assigned and the binding Domain for *de hoogleraar* would be the only one, the matrix Domain. So in either case, on the verb-raising analysis or on a monoclausal analysis by young children, the NP-V sequence *de hoogleraar opbellen* would be accessible to our degree-0 child.

A third unembedded indicator of the movement site in these languages is the position of verbal specifiers such as negatives and certain closed-class adverbials, necessarily generated immediately to the left of the verb at D-structure (Emonds 1986).[3] In Dutch and German, verbal specifiers do not move with the verb but occur separately at the end of a main clause, thus indicating the position from which the finite verb has moved (see (11)). (Again, embedded infinitivals manifest the D-structure order directly: *Jan wil niet lopen, Jan moet de hoogleraar niet opbellen, Jan kan de hoogleraar soms/morgen/vaak opbellen.*)

(11) a. Jan loopt niet
        Jan walks not
     b. Jan belt de hoogleraar niet op
        Jan calls the professor not up
     c. Jan belt de hoogleraar soms/morgen/vaak op
        Jan calls the professor sometimes/tomorrow/often up

These elements also provide clues to the underlying position of the verb in the Scandinavian languages. The position of the verb in embedded clauses (see (12a)) is not available to our degree-0 learner, but if *ikke* and *aldri* are verbal specifiers, then their occurrence in main clauses (see (12b)) indicates to the Norwegian child the position from which the verb has moved—viz., the position preceding the direct-object NP. Consequently the child will not be surprised to find the verb occurring unmoved after the specifiers in embedded clauses.

(12) a. vi vet at Jon ikke/aldri kjøper bøker
        'we know that Jon not/never buys books'
     b. Jon kjøper ikke/aldri bøker   (cf. (2a))
        'Jon buys not/never books'

In addition to the three unembedded indicators of underlying verb position discussed so far, there is a class of uninflected, infinitival constructions in colloquial Dutch, which manifest object-verb order directly in unembedded contexts (Peter Coopmans, personal communication):

(13) a. en ik maar fietsen repareren
        I bicycles repair
        'I ended up repairing bicycles'

b. kop houden   hand uitsteken
   head hold   hand outstretch
   'shut up'   'signal'
c. Jantje koekje hebben?
   Jantje cookie have
   'Jantje has a cookie?'
d. ik de vuilnisbak buiten zetten? Nooit
   I the garbage-can outside set? Never
   'me put the garbage out? Never'

(13a) is a productive kind of historical infinitive, occurring with the particles *en . . . maar*. (13b) represents a colloquial alternative to the usual form of the imperative with the verb fronted: *hou je kop*. This may be a kind of elliptical form, with *je moet* 'you must' missing. (13c) is the kind of thing sometimes used in "motherese" and in speech addressed to young children, representing a kind of baby-talk in which the functional categories are absent (cf. Radford 1988). (13d) is an exclamatory question.

There are some ambiguities in the analyses sketched here, and I have not provided details of some of the technical issues that arise, but one sees that there are four kinds of primary linguistic data, all drawn from unembedded binding Domains, which might indicate the D-structure position of verbs. If this is correct, then children do not need access to embedded Domains to determine that Dutch verbs follow their complements underlyingly. Not only is this a possible and theoretically pleasing account, but acquisitional data strongly suggest that something along these lines is correct—that there are unembedded indicators which enable the child to adopt an object-verb setting. Clahsen and Smolka (1986) identify four stages in the acquisition of German verb-movement properties:

stage 1 (25–29 months): no fixed order between sentence constituents; all verbal elements (including verbal complexes) occur in first/second and final position with a preference for final position
stage 2 (31–33 months): verbal elements with particles occur regularly in final position; other finite verbs occur in both first/second and final position
stage 3 (36–39 months): all and only finite verbs occur in first/second position; verbal complexes with finite and nonfinite parts appear in discontinuous positions
stage 4 (41–42 months): as soon as embedded sentences are produced, their finite verbs are in final position.

Strikingly, from the earliest relevant stage children identify sentence-final position as one of the possible positions for verbs—including finite verbs, despite the fact that they are almost never heard in this position in main clauses. At stage 3 there is a dramatic increase in the frequency of verb-second structures: in stages 1 and 2 they are used in only 20–40% of the utterances, but at stage 3 they are used in 90%; Clahsen and Smolka (p. 149) report that this increase takes place explosively, within a month for all the children studied. Children seem at this stage to have the object-verb D-structure order and an operation moving a finite verb obligatorily to some fronted position; to this extent the adult system is in place. Importantly, when they begin to use embedded structures (stage 4), the finite verbs are invariably in final position and there seems to be no "experimentation" or learning based on embedded-clause data. This is exactly what one would expect if children are degree-0 learners, and not at all what one would expect if children depend on embedded Domains to set grammatical parameters.[4]

In short, it seems reasonable to suppose that in so-called verb-second languages, where verbs move to INFL and then to the extra Y^0 position, the underlying position of the verb is degree-0 learnable whether it precedes its complement, as in the Scandinavian languages and in Yiddish (den Besten and Moed – van Walraven 1986), or follows them, as in Dutch and German. If there are unembedded indicators in these languages for the D-structure position of the verb, one can go on to ask whether there are analogous unembedded indicators in Old English, which also seems to have had underlying object-verb order. We shall see that there were such in-dicators and, indeed, that they must have provided the basis for setting the relevant parameters, whereas data from embedded Domains had no effect on parameter setting.

3.3   Old English

Like Dutch and German, Old English was fairly strongly verb-second in main clauses and verb-final in embedded clauses. However, the evidence suggests that these properties were neither stable nor long-lasting, and we shall see that Old English was unlike modern Dutch and German in significant ways. This should caution one against too much of a procrus-tean approach, adopting Dutch or German analyses where Old English data are inadequate to support particular hypotheses (cf. van Kemenade 1987).

There are many statistical studies of the word-order properties of Old and Middle English, all conducted from somewhat different points of view and adopting different criteria for what is to be counted. Bean (1983) offers good commentary on the caution needed in interpreting the results of these surveys. Barrett (1953), Bean (1983), Canale (1978), Dahlstedt (1901), Denison (1981), Fourquet (1938), Gardner (1971), Gorrell (1895), Hiltunen (1983), Jacobsson (1951), Macleish (1969), Reszkiewicz (1962), von Schon (1977), Shannon (1964), Smith (1893), Swieczkowski (1962), and others have dealt with the position of verbs in relation to their subjects and to their complements. From these surveys one can extrapolate significant differences in the prevailing word order of main and embedded clauses along the general lines of what is found in Dutch and German.

For example, Smith (1893) reported that Alfred's *Orosius*, dating from ca. 900 A.D., has simple verbs occurring at the end of subordinate clauses 82% of the time (259 out of 314 cases, and this excluded short clauses where the verb had no complement and was necessarily final), whereas main clauses typically show either "normal order" (subject-verb-complements-adverbs) or "inverted order" (verb-subject...). If one ignores his distinction between auxiliary and regular verbs, which imposes a modern English distinction on Old English (Lightfoot 1979, chapter 2), Gorrell (1895) reports 90% of indirect declaratives ending in a verb (whether simple or part of a compound) in the *Orosius* (372 out of 414) and 90% in *Bede* (704 out of 782), which is also attributed to Alfred. Such figures could easily be expanded, and, although statistics alone cannot motivate an analysis, they suggest that an analysis along the lines of Dutch and German is appropriate: many Old English grammars had an underlying object-verb order, and the finite verb was fronted. As in Dutch and German, main clauses typically began with phrases of arbitrary thematic and functional roles (often called "topics," misleadingly; see note 2), and this in turn entailed movement of the finite verb to the extra Y^0 position, putting it into second position, for the reasons discussed earlier. An analysis of this general type is outlined by Canale (1978), van Kemenade (1987), and Pintzuk and Kroch (1985), and these authors show how it interacts with other processes to account for much of the data found in the texts.[5]

However, Old English does differ in some ways from Dutch and German. First, in coordinate sentences the second conjunct often shows the object-verb order typical of subordinate clauses, and sometimes it shows inverted order. (14) and (15) are examples of each from the Parker manuscript of the Anglo-Saxon Chronicle.

(14) a. & his eagan astungon   (797)
        'and his eyes they put out'
     b. & þone æþeling ofslogon & þa men   (755)
        'and the prince they slew and the men'
(15) a. & þy ilcan geare w̃s gc̃oren Æþelheard abbud to bisc̃   (790)
        'and that same year was chosen Abbot Ethelheard as bishop'
     b. & þa cuædon hie   (755)
        'and then said they'

In general, conjunction may involve any level of projection, so that heads, X′s, and phrasal categories may be conjoined. Consequently, if verbs may move to an empty Y^0 as in Dutch and German, this suggests that the second conjunct may or may not have the extra position, being either YP or IP (alternatively either CP or IP, in the system of Chomsky 1986). There seems to be nothing more systematic involved in this alternation; authors vary in whether they use verb-second or object-verb order in second conjuncts, and analysts sometimes treat them as main clauses (Hiltunen 1983) or as embedded clauses (Andrew 1940; Canale 1978). If it is correct to say that the second conjunct is either YP or IP, then in this regard Old English reflects what one would expect, and an explanation is needed for why Dutch and German never allow object-verb order in the second conjunct of a matrix clause—that is, why only YP and not IP is conjoined in these grammars.

Second, Gorrell (1895, p. 472) reported that the complementizer þæt may occasionally be absent in Old English (unlike the equivalent complementizers in Dutch and German). This is supported by Mitchell (1985, section 1981ff.). However, Gorrell also claimed that in the 13 cases he noted he found 12 instances of subject-verb-object order and only one of subject-object-verb. This can be understood if Old English had an operation moving a verb to an initial position, applying also in the rare instances of complementizerless embedded clauses (which occur never in Dutch and only rarely in German; see Haider 1986). But the correlation between subject-verb-object order and absence of þæt is problematic. Gorrell cited examples which are not true complements (e.g., (16a), where *ic secge* is clearly parenthetical, as indicated by my gloss), and he mysteriously miscited (16b) with the verb *wolde* misplaced: *cuæð he wolde on mergenne meces ecgum getan*. On the other hand, his single example of object-verb order has a pronominal object, which might be analyzed as cliticized onto the verb.[6]

(16) a. ða getreowan freond þonne ic secge *seo* þæt deorweorþeste
þing (Boethius, ed. Fox 82, 27)
'the true friends, I say, would be the most valued thing'

b. cwæð he on mergenne meces ecgum getan *wolde*   (*Beowulf* 2940)
'said he would in the morning cut-them-to-pieces with the
sword's edge'

c. sægde he he hit *gehyde* from þæm seolfon Uttan mæssepreoste
(*Bede* 200, 25)
'said he he would hide it from the seven priests of Utta'

Third, literary Dutch and German almost never show object-verb order
in main clauses, but this order occurs in Old English. For example,
Smith (1893, p. 232) noted verb-final main clauses in Alfred's *Orosius*—
particularly with preposed dative and accusative pronouns, "which often
draw other words with them." This might reflect the fact that the text was
translated from Latin, but Andrew (1940) observed that the order was
frequent in verse. Bean (1983) examined 593 main clauses in the first four
sections of the Anglo-Saxon Chronicle (up until 891) and found 65 cases
(i.e., 11% of all main clauses) where the verb could not plausibly be
analyzed as fronted; these are sentences of the form object-subject-verb or
subject-X-verb. In addition, there were 141 main clauses where the verb
was in third position, following an arbitrary phrase (usually indicating time
or place) and a subject NP. If these are also taken as cases where the verb
is not in the initial Y^0 position, then 34.7% of the main clauses in this
portion of the Chronicle show a verb in some other position, and perhaps
in its base-generated position.

Fourth, Old English shows more variation than Dutch or German texts
in the position of its verbs. To some extent this may reflect the fact that
our information is based on somewhat fragmentary texts of different
genres, which have been filtered through a complex editorial and scribal
tradition and which predate the standardization of the literary language,
which was one of the consequences of the Norman Conquest. It may also
reflect the fact that changes were taking place affecting the position of the
verb, as will be discussed in the next section. Nonetheless, one finds a
significant number of verb-final main clauses, as noted, and a significant
number of embedded clauses with the so-called normal order of subject-
verb-object, sometimes reflecting a direct object that has been "extraposed" from the V'.

Although I have identified four differences between Old English, on the
one hand, and Dutch and German, on the other, they strongly suggest that
many Old English grammars had underlying object-verb order with the

option of moving a finite verb to an initial Y^0 position; as in Dutch and German, this option was forced if some arbitrary phrase occurred initially (as was almost uniform in main clauses), presumably because of the phrase-structure template and the requirement, discussed above, that lexical specifiers have a corresponding lexical head at S-structure. Assuming this to be correct and bearing in mind the variation manifested by the texts, one can proceed to ask how the relevant parameters were set by Old English children.

When we posed the analogous question for the modern European verb-second languages, we found unembedded signposts indicating the underlying position of the verb, which would be accessible to our degree-0 learner. These signposts explained how Dutch and German children could acquire object-verb order so easily and how they could use object-verb order in the very first occurrences of embedded clauses, having already set the relevant parameter. We have no acquisitional studies corresponding to those of Clahsen and Smolka for German, but we can only assume that Old English grammars with some of the above-described central properties were attainable by children under usual conditions, and that they were attained fairly readily.

Recall that robust sentences in which verbs were on the left of their complements and nonadjacent to them showed Dutch, German, and Scandinavian children that the verbs had moved to their fronted position. Precisely analogous data presumably would have driven Old English children to a similar analysis, showing verb-second as one option:

(17) a. þa gegaderode Ælfred cyning his fierd   (*ASChr* A.894.6)
       then gathered Alfred king his army
    b. þær hæfdon Romane sige   (*Orosius* 232.11)
       there had Romans victory
    c. ... & feng Ælfric Wiltunscire bisceop to þam arcebisceoprice
       (*ASChr* A.994.1)
       and succeeded Ælfric, Wiltshire's bishop, to the archbishopric

So far so good, but what are the unembedded indicators for the position from which the verb has moved? Here there are differences with Dutch and German which will assume some importance when we discuss the diachronic changes in the next section. There were potentially four types of indicator found in main clauses.

First, Old English verbs had prefixes which could occur in a separate position. There were three possible orders. The most usual order in main clauses was ... verb ... particle (see (18)). The particle sometimes moved with the verb to its fronted position (see (19)), and occasionally one finds the particle between the subject and object, which might reflect a rightward movement of the object or an intermediate position of the verb in INFL (see (20) and note 7). Visser (1963, section 668) gives a handy collection of examples of the three types.

(18) a. þa *sticode* him mon þa eagon *ut*   (*Orosius* 168.4)
        'then stuck him someone the eyes out'

     b. þa *geat* mon þæt attor *ut* on þære sæ   (*Orosius* 258.16)
        'then poured somebody the poison out into the sea'

     c. ond þa *ahof* Drihten hie *up*   (*Blickling Homilies* 157.22)
        'and then God raised them up'

     d. þa *astah* se Hælend *up* on ane dune   (*Homilies of the Anglo-Saxon Church* I, 182)
        'then rose the Lord up on a mountain'

(19) a. he þa *ut awearp* þa sceomolas þara cypemanna   (*Blickling Homilies* 71.17)
        'then (he) threw out the benches of the dealers'

     b. Stephanus *up-astah* þurh his blod gewuldorbeagod   (*Homilies of the Anglo-Saxon Church* I, 56)
        Steven up-rose through his blood glory-crowned

(20) a. þa *ahof* Paulus *up* his heafod   (*Blickling Homilies* 187.35)
        'then lifted Paul up his head'

     b. *nime* he *upp* his mæg   (*Ancient Laws* (Thorpe) i, 296,10)
        'he should take up his kinsmen'

     c. þær *bær* Godwine eorl *up* his mal   (*ASChr* an.1052)
        'then set forth Earl Godwin his case'

In subordinate clauses these particles generally appear prefixed to the verb in final position (see (21)), as one would expect if prefixes are base-generated alongside their verbs and if Old English had an operation moving the verb from VP-final position to an initial Y^0 in main clauses.[7]

(21) a. ... þæt he ðone cwelmbæran hlaf *aweg bære*   (*Homilies of the Anglo-Saxon Church* II, 162.23)
        that he the deadly loaf away bear

     b. ... þæt hie mid þæm þæt folc *ut aloccoden*   (*Orosius* 222.3)
        that with that they entice the people out

The prevalence of the order in (18) may have helped to trigger an underlying object-verb order, with the separated particle marking the D-structure position of the verb, as in Dutch and German. However, the availability of alternative orders would have made this a somewhat less reliable trigger than in Dutch and German.

Second, VP specifiers, as in Dutch and German, typically occur separate from the verb in main clauses, in their base-generated VP position (see (22)). However, simple negatives in Old English are always attached to the verb: *ne* at the left with the option in later stages of the language of *noht* to the right. Consequently, since these negatives move with the verb, they provide no clue about the underlying position of the verb, in contrast with Dutch and German.

(22) ne geseah$_i$ $_S$[ic $_{VP}$[næfre ða burh e$_i$]]   (Ælfric, *Homilies* I.572.3)
     'never saw I the city'

Third, sentences corresponding to the clause-union structures of Dutch and German also occur in Old English, with a more limited class of verbs, and they may manifest a grammar with the verb-raising analysis of Evers (1975):

(23) Swa sceal geong guma gode gewyrecean   (*Beowulf* 20)
     'thus shall young men good things perform'

Dutch and German are each consistent in adjoining the lower verb (respectively) to the left and to the right of the higher verb. Old English, on the contrary, shows much variation in this regard, and individual authors use both orders. Mitchell (1985, section 3941) observes that the relative percentages of left and right adjunction in different clause types is sometimes useful in determining authorship. However, for reasons to be discussed in section 4.1, it is not obvious that verbs such as *cunnan*, *sculan*, and *motan* permit raising of a lower verb, or that they occur in clause-union structures. (See Pintzuk 1988 for good criticisms of this analysis in the context of the variation in particle position in (18)–(20).) Consequently, it is not clear whether their complements lack their S'. If the S' is not deleted in structures like (23), then the binding Domain for the lower VP is the embedded S', which would not be accessible to a degree-0 learner. However, even if adult grammars in the Old English period did not have a monoclausal analysis of sentences like (23), it is likely that children's grammars did, and that two-year-olds did not perceive or analyze the modal verb, as Klein (1974) suggested for modern Dutch (see above). So, although there is some question about the analysis of sentences like (23) in Old English, I shall assume that the position of the lower verb was accessible to our degree-0 learners.

As was noted earlier, there is a fourth indicator: verb-final main clauses, usually occurring as the right-hand element of a conjoined structure, as in

(24a) (these have no equivalent in Dutch and German), and sometimes occurring in nonconjoined structures, as in (24b).

(24) a. & Cuþan mon ofslog   (*ASChr* A.584.2)
        and Cutha-acc somebody slew
        'and somebody killed Cutha'
   b. þa him Hroþgar gewat   (*Beowulf* 662)
        'then Hrothgar recognized him'
   c. he Gode þancode   (*Beowulf* 625)
        'he thanked God'
   d. he hine an bigspell ahsode   (OE Gospels, Mark 7, 17)
        'he asked him about the parable'

Another possible indicator of the underlying verb position is sentences with object pronouns, which occur overwhelmingly in object-verb order even in unembedded Domains: *he hine seah* 'he saw him'. However, it is not obvious how children would have analyzed these forms. It may well be that the pronominal form was treated as a type of clitic, attached to the verb. But cliticized forms do not necessarily reflect D-structure order; in, French, VPs are clearly verb-initial but object pronouns are cliticized in a preverbal position. So one must remain agnostic on this point: object pronouns may or may not have been critical. Similarly, nothing is known about colloquial data equivalent to the Dutch example in (13), providing unembedded indicators of object-verb order in the spoken language.

3.4   Reanalysis in English and Its Consequences

Dutch and German have three clear unembedded triggers for underlying object-verb order, in addition to the colloquial data illustrated in (13): the separated particles, the verbal specifiers (including negative markers), and object-verb order in verb-raising structures. We have seen that the separated prefixes and verbal specifiers consistently occur in the D-structure position of the verb. The Old English situation, however, is not as clear-cut. First, at no point in Old English did separated particles occur consistently in the D-structure position of the verb, and therefore they were not a reliable indicator of the underlying position of the verb. Second, the negative marker, being always attached to the verb and moving with it, never indicated the underlying position of the verb; the VP specifiers, which did not move with the verb (e.g., *næfre* in (22)), were significantly less robust and, in any case, show nothing of the position of the verb inside the VP. The third potential trigger, structures corresponding to sentences like (23), would have been as available to Old English children as they are to Dutch and German children today, if the monoclausal childhood structures are relevant. If the adult structures provide the relevant concept for determining accessibility, then structures like those of (23) would not have revealed anything about the underlying position of the embedded verb if Old English grammars lacked a Dutch-style verb-raising operation. There was a fourth possible trigger: object-verb order in main clauses should have been a good indicator of underlying verb order, but it was not a predominant order in the texts, and it diminished over the course of the Old English period.

The net result is that we have four potential triggers for underlying object-verb order, but none of them is as reliable or robust an indicator as any of the triggers in modern Dutch and German. One thing, however, is clear: throughout the Old English period embedded clauses were predominantly object-verb, and they were overwhelmingly so for most of the period. This is the heart of the argument. Readers: If your attention has flagged, this is the time to take a deep breath, prepare to catch your second wind, gird your loins, or at least decide on an appropriate metaphor. If children were sensitive to embedded material as they set their parameters, there would have been abundant experience pointing to object-verb order at D-structure. Nonetheless, we shall see that embedded instances of object-verb order could not have been part of the trigger experience. If we examine some changes affecting two of the four potential unembedded triggers, we shall gain a better sense of what actually set the verb-order parameter.

There was a steady decline of object-verb order in matrix clauses through the Old English period. This is tracked nicely by Bean (1983), who examined nine sections of the *Anglo-Saxon Chronicle*, taking them as representative of different stages of Old English. Her results must be treated with some caution: it is generally supposed that the original compilation of the Chronicle was initiated by King Alfred and completed in the year 891, but it is not obvious that Bean's four sections covering the period up to 891 were also *linguistically* pre-891. This is an important caveat, but nonetheless she shows some clear patterns which will be useful for our purposes. She counted various word-order patterns in different clause types, and these included matrix clauses where the verb could not be analyzed as in its usual fronted position. Four types are relevant here:

a. subject-X-verb (where X indicates any specifier or phrase)
b. object-subject-verb

c. subject-X-verb-X

d. adverbial phrase-subject-verb

Types a and b seem to be manifested mostly in conjunct clauses introduced by *ond* or *ac*, which may or may not have an initial Y^0 position, as we have noted. These forms were available to our degree-0 learner, because such conjunct clauses, whether projecting to YP or not, represent unembedded binding Domains. Type c involves movement of an element to the right of the verb, and type d is usually introduced by expressions like 'in this year' (recall that this is a chronicle). In contrast with modern Dutch and German, the fronting of the verb was never obligatory in Old English, as can be seen from the fact that types a–c, which are quite impossible in Dutch and German, make up a significant proportion of main clauses, ranging from 10% to 23% in the nine sections that Bean examined. Therefore, there is no reason to treat type d as involving "topicalization," verb fronting, and an otherwise unmotivated extrasentential position for the initial adverbial; instead the verb occurs either in its base-generated position or in INFL.

Taking these four types together, we observe a steady decline in matrix clauses where the verb needs to be analyzed in some position other than the initial Y^0 and often in its base-generated position. The total number of such sentences reported by Bean and the percentages of the main clauses are as follows: section I (until 755): 122 (50%); section II (755–860): 64 (37%); section III (865–884): 29 (25%); section IV (885–891): 14 (23%); section V (892–900): 13 (13%); section VI (958–1001): 5 (12%); section VII (1048–1066): 36 (18%); section VIII (1122–1124): 19 (17%); section IX (1132–1140): 23 (22%). The steady decline in these patterns, plotted in figure 3.1, corresponds to an increase in structures where the verb can be analyzed as in the initial Y^0 position: verb-subject-X, adverbial phrase-verb-subject, subject-verb-X, and object-verb-subject. If one aggregates Bean's figures for such patterns, one finds a steady increase, leveling off at around 80%: I 48%, II 60%, III 73%, IV 77%, V 85%, VI 84%, VII 81%, VIII 76%, IX 78%. One need not rely entirely on the *Anglo-Saxon Chronicle*; these figures are matched by a comparison of four prose texts: King Alfred's *Letter on Learning*, *Ohthere*, *Wulfstan*, and Ælfric's preface to Genesis. Verb-final main clauses decline, occurring in 32%, 8%, 10%, and 14% of the respective texts; correspondingly, sentences manifesting the verb in initial Y^0 increase and level off at the 80% level: 47%, 80%, 82%, 85%.

Another change in the primary linguistic data, taking place during the course of Old English, concerns the rise of separable particles or "phrasal

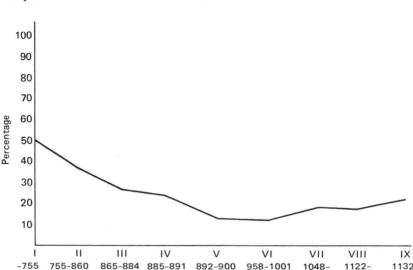

Figure 3.1

adverbs," described by Denison (1981), Hiltunen (1983), and von Schon (1977). In the earliest records one finds bound morphemes prefixed to verbs and, in matrix clauses, moving with them (see (19)). This pattern became less uniform over the next several centuries, and the bound morphemes gradually became less productive and came to occur as particles, separated from their verb in matrix clauses (see (18) and (20)). This gave rise to a situation raising questions of classification for grammarians; Mitchell (1985) discussed this in a section entitled "Prepositions, adverbs, prepositional adverbs, postpositions, separable prefixes or inseparable prefixes?" Hiltunen (1983) distinguished phrasal verbs (*call up*) from prepositional verbs (*call on*). During the Old English period these particles consistently occurred prefixed to their verb in embedded clauses, as in (21) (see Koopman 1985), so, whatever the later problems of classification, it seems clear that at this time they were generated as $_V$[particle V]. In that case, the gradual rise of patterns in which the particle was separated from its verb in main clauses manifests the movement of the verb to INFL and to initial Y^0; such stranded particles, as they developed, could be taken as indicating to a child the underlying position of the verb. The increasing frequency of patterns in which the main clause ended with a particle was plausibly an indicator of underlying order. Hiltunen examined a set of early Old English prose texts and counted 235 (unconjoined) main clauses with phrasal verbs of the *call up* type, and 57% of them had the verb preceding the particle.

The corresponding figure for late Old English was 71%, and for early Middle English it was 97%. These figures are plotted in figure 3.2. As noted earlier, however, particles showed variable positions (to the extent that Koopman was led to argue that VPs showed free word order except insofar as they were verb-final—see note 7) and were never as consistent an indicator of verb position as in Dutch and German.

There were no changes, as far as I am aware, in the robustness of the clause-union structures of (23) during the course of Old English.

The two changes in the primary linguistic data just discussed work against each other for the purposes of a child setting the verb-order parameter. As main-clause object-verb order decreased and reduced the clues for underlying object-verb order, so separated particles became more frequent and provided a new indicator of underlying verb order. The actual trigger for setting the verb-order parameter was largely a function of the interaction of these two phenomena: in the early stages, presumably, main-clause instances of object-verb were robust enough to set the parameter appropriately; as they became less robust, the increasingly frequent separated particles provided some more evidence of object-verb order. However, variability in the position of the particles entailed that they never became as reliable an indicator of underlying verb position as in Dutch and German, and as a result they were not able to offset totally the effects of the diminishing instances of main-clause object-verb order. Consequently, as matrix instances of object-verb diminished to a certain point, underlying object-verb order became unlearnable and the verb-order parameter came to be set differently. Canale (1978) showed that this change in parameter setting had taken place by the twelfth century, basing his argument largely on the fact that the new verb-object order was standard in embedded clauses by that time.

When one examines how the new word-order patterns emerged in embedded clauses, one finds some striking and well-known facts. These facts have so far not been understood, but they now suggest strongly that children are degree-0 learners. The changes discussed so far, affecting main clauses, were slow and gradual and probably involved no change in grammars. That is, Old English grammars permitted options of moving the verb to an initial Y^0 and of leaving a separable particle in its D-structure position. The texts suggest that these options tended to be exercised more and more over a period of several hundred years. This no more reflects a difference in grammars than if some speaker were shown to use a greater number of passive or imperative sentences. Rather, it reflects the kind of accidental variation that is familiar from studies in population genetics.

Nonetheless, changes in the primary linguistic data, if they show a slight cumulative effect, might have the consequence of setting a grammatical parameter differently. That is what seems to have happened with English verb order.

There are two striking facts. First, while main clauses were showing a slowly diminishing number of object-verb orders, embedded clauses remained consistently object-verb. Gorrell's (1895) massive study of embedded clauses in Old English showed verbs occurring in final position between 80% and 90% of the time in all prose texts examined. He presented statistics on *Orosius*, *Bede*, the *Cura Pastoralis*, *Boethius*, the *Blickling Homilies*, the *Anglo-Saxon Chronicle*, the Gospels, the *Lives of Saints*, *Wulfstan*, and Ælfric's *Homilies*, which I have listed in (25) in their rough chronological order.

(25)

	Or	Bede	CP	Boe	BH	Chr	Gosp	LS	AH	W
%	90	90	85	81	87	82	84	82	80	81
N	414	782	561	466	456	164	451	519	1348	591

Second, when the new verb order began to affect embedded clauses, it did so rapidly and catastrophically, showing a very different pattern from that observed in main clauses. Figures 3.2 and 3.3 illustrate the difference

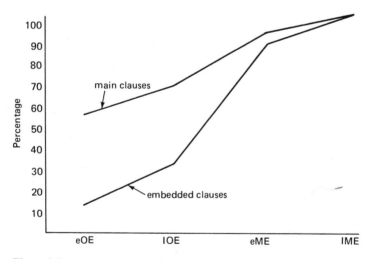

Figure 3.2
The rise of V(...) particle order. (Based on Hiltunen 1983.)[8]

graphically. Figure 3.2 plots the increasing frequency from early Old English onward of verbs of the *call up* type preceding their associated particles; the graph is based on Hiltunen's (1983) study of prose texts from four periods. The gradual change in main-clause patterns does not reflect a change in grammars but merely illustrates the fact that writers increasingly exercised the option of moving the V to initial Y^0 and leaving the particle in place. However, since embedded verbs could generally not move to a filled Comp and since they were base-generated to the right of their particle, an embedded verb could not precede its particle until the grammar was reanalyzed in such a way that verbs preceded their complements and thus their particles at D-structure or until INFL came to precede VP (whichever came first—see note 7). Consequently, a verb preceding its particle in an embedded clause reflects a change in grammars, or at least a change in specific lexical entries such that certain particle-verb strings became verb-particle. The graph shows that this change took place relatively rapidly. Hiltunen (1983, p. 92) comments that the loss of the prefixes and the development of analytical expressions became fully manifest in early Middle English: "Right from the first pages of [*The Ancrene Riwle*], for instance, one cannot avoid the impression of the prefixes having been swept away almost overnight. The suddenness of the change is remarkable in view of the longish and stable OE period."

Figure 3.3 is based on the statistics offered by Bean's (1983) study of nine sections of the *Anglo-Saxon Chronicle*. As was shown in figure 3.1, main

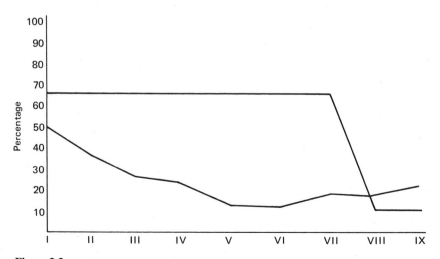

Figure 3.3

Table 3.1
Decline of object-verb order in the *Anglo-Saxon Chronicle* (based on Bean 1983).

	I	II	III	IV	V	VI	VII	VIII	IX
Relative clauses									
Total number	24	7	10	18	37	6	46	26	22
% object-verb	21	71	90	33	84	83	65	27	14
Subordinate clauses									
Total number	11	8	10	15	49	9	84	41	48
% object-verb	64	63	100	27	55	13	49	7	19
Conjunct clauses									
Total number	49	32	60	17	34	16	91	40	70
% object-verb	52	84	86	77	59	50	53	2	6

clauses show steadily declining object-verb order, leveling off below 20%; I reproduce this line in figure 3.3. However, a very different pattern emerged in embedded and conjunct clauses. First, note that conjunct clauses are relevant here in that while in the earliest stages they may show either verb-second or verb-final order when unembedded (depending on whether the conjoined clause projects to YP or IP), they could show the verb preceding the object only after grammars were reanalyzed and had underlying verb-object order. As a result one would expect to see a significant drop in verb-final order as the D-structure parameter is set differently. Bean counts as conjunct clauses only those that are conjoined and lack an overt subject, so I have computed as verb-final her instances of types a, c, and d without overt subjects, i.e., X-verb, X-verb-X, and adverb-verb. Second, the sharp dips in section IV for relative clauses and in sections IV and VI for other subordinate clauses should presumably be attributed to the exceptionally small samples (see table 3.1). The remaining picture is one of robust object-verb order in embedded and conjunct clauses, declining sharply in section VIII and uniformly in all three clause types. If one aggregates relative, subordinate, and conjunct clauses, one finds that object-verb order occurs in 66% of clauses (380 of 572) in sections I–VII and 11% (27 of 247) in sections VIII and IX. Furthermore, the sharp drop between sections VII and VIII is uniform for each clause type: relative clauses drop from 65% object-verb in section VII to 27% in section VIII, subordinate clauses from 49% to 7%, and conjunct clauses from 53% to 2%.

The historical record, then, shows that matrix clauses underwent some gradual statistical shifts through the Old English period: particles were increasingly separated from their associated verbs and appeared to their right, often but not always in their base-generated position, and instances of object-verb order diminished as the verb-second option was exercised more and more. If the prose texts are reliable indicators, in the eighth century matrix clauses showed verb-final and verb-fronted order about equally, but by the eleventh century children heard verb-final matrix clauses only 20% of the time, while 80% were analyzable with the verb in an initial Y^0. This in turn entailed an increasing number of subject-verb... sentences, as one instantiation of verb-in-Y^0 (associated with an arbitrary phrasal category in initial position), but this increase was relatively modest. Bean's statistics show the following percentages of matrix-clause subject-verb... order for the various sections of the *Chronicle* (numbers in parentheses): I 29% (70), II 34% (59), III 19% (22), IV 38% (23), V 34% (34), VI 26% (11), VII 45% (89), VIII 39% (43), IX 36% (38); cumulatively, the first three sections have 28% and the last three sections 41%, a significant but not enormous increase. The net result was that by the eleventh century there were fewer unembedded indicators of object-verb order and more data pointing to verb-object order.

The historical record also shows that by the twelfth century most grammars had been reanalyzed such that they had underlying verb-object order. The new parameter setting manifested itself primarily in new patterns in embedded clauses, which emerged comparatively suddenly, as has been noted by almost every traditional grammarian who has examined aspects of the transition, from Kellner (1892) and Gorrell (1895) to Kohonen (1978) and Mitchell (1985). Kellner (p. 290) noted a "sudden stop" in embedded object-verb order, and Kohonen (pp. 101, 125) a "dramatic" change in embedded clauses; Stockwell and Minkova (1989) write of "an abrupt halt" in embedded "verb-lateness." Certain properties of the Old and Middle English grammars remain obscure or ambiguous, and some things may have to be formulated somewhat differently from what I have offered here, but the contrast in the way the word-order changes were manifested in matrix and embedded clauses is a big and robust fact. It would be extremely difficult to explain if parameter setting were sensitive to embedded data, and this is the core of my argument. Until the twelfth century, embedded clauses were robustly object-verb, providing plenty of potential evidence of underlying object-verb order for a degree-1 learner, who would be sensitive to data from an embedded Domain. In view of the abundance of such evidence, it is hard to imagine how a degree-1 learner could have attained underlying verb-object order when exposed to what the texts suggest was available in early Middle English. On the other hand, in view of the changes in matrix clauses over the preceding three centuries, it is easy to see how degree-0 children attained verb-object order, setting parameters only on the basis of unembedded material and ignoring (for these purposes) data from embedded binding Domains which might have suggested a different parameter setting. Indeed, if children are degree-0 learners, the central changes are largely what one might expect.

3.5   Comparisons

This account of verb-order change differs fundamentally from most others. One common approach (Aitchison 1979; Canale 1978; van Kemenade 1987; Lightfoot 1979; Stockwell 1977) has made the change in D-structure order a function of steadily increasing patterns of verb-object order due to a putative rightward movement of complement elements. In Lightfoot 1979, the fact that the innovative orders occur first in matrix clauses was attributed to the structure-preservation hypothesis: since the rightward movement of complement elements was not structure-preserving, it could only occur in root clauses. These analyses addressed the attainability of the new grammar insofar as they postulated steadily changing primary linguistic data which eventually had the effect that children had verbs preceding objects at D-structure. However, such accounts make sense only if children are degree-0 learners, with no access (for the purposes of establishing their grammar) to the position of the verb in embedded clauses, where such rightward movements would have been much less common. Furthermore, it is not at all clear that processes of rightward NP movement played a significant role or that they increased during the Old English period. They typically have limited scope, affecting "heavy" elements, and they tend to be uncommon in object-verb languages. Rather, verb-object sequences emerged by virtue of the operation moving INFL and its associated verb leftward to the Y^0 position, yielding the familiar "verb-second" phenomena. That operation was used increasingly during the Old English period, as we have seen, giving an increasing number of verb-object sequences and changing the primary linguistic data to which children had access.

The verb-second phenomena, therefore, were crucial to the emergence of the new verb-object order at D-structure. However, several things preclude linking the new verb order more directly to the operations moving verbs to INFL and to Y^0. First, Dutch grammars, which have had such operations for several hundred years, still show underlying object-verb order—presumably because, on the analysis offered here, matrix-clause indicators of the D-structure verb order remain robust. Gerritsen (1984) reports that spoken German and Dutch show about 60% of all main clauses with subject-verb... order (significantly higher than the percentage in even late Old English texts; see above), so a large proportion of objects follow their verbs; but this shows no signs of making D-structure object-verb order less attainable. Second, the Scandinavian languages are as strongly verb-second as Dutch and German, but have underlying verb-object order, like English. And Gerritsen reports the same percentage of subject-verb... order for main clauses in spoken Norwegian. So there would seem to be little chance of relating the order of elements in VP to processes moving verbs to Y^0. Third, the development of underlying verb-object order in English, which was complete by the twelfth century, does not correlate with the emergence or loss of operations moving verbs to Y^0. Those operations had emerged as options in the earliest texts and remained productive through the seventeenth century and the entrenchment of periphrastic *do*. Indeed, some verb-second forms increase in productivity as late as the seventeenth century. Jacobsson (1951) reported that verbs preceding their subjects in *not only... but also...* constructions were "strikingly rare" in the late Middle and early Modern English periods, emerging only in the seventeenth century. Similarly, such inverted forms with *nor* and *neither* (*neither has Kim seen this*) underwent a significant increase in the sixteenth and seventeeth centuries.

These factors also militate against Vennemann's (1974, 1975) idea that subject-object-verb order changes to subject-verb-object via an intermediate stage of topic-verb.... It is possible (but undemonstrated) that such an intermediate stage is a necessary condition for such a shift in verb order, but it cannot be a sufficient condition. Dutch and German are, in Vennemann's terms, consistently topic-verb in main clauses, and have been stable for a long period, showing no signs of developing verb-object order. In our terms, as long as the main-clause indicators of underlying verb position remain robust, there is no reason to expect a change of order in VP. However, it is worth noting that Vennemann's claim would have to be complemented by a notion of degree-0 learnability: if topic-verb order represents a necessary intermediate stage of development, then we can observe that it occurred in English only in matrix Domains and not at all consistently in embedded clauses. Since English underwent a shift in its verb order, the lack of topic-verb structures in embedded clauses was clearly not an inhibiting factor. This would make sense only if the relevant conditioning factors are what one can observe in matrix Domains, where

Vennemann's precondition is met. That is, Vennemann's child would have to be a degree-0 learner.

Weerman (1989) takes D-structure to express only hierarchical relations, while linear relations are determined at S-structure through case assignment or "S-identification." His theory allows case to be assigned to the left or to the right, thereby accounting for the fact that object-verb and verb-object co-occur in the texts as grammars change. He claims that this permits him to account for the gradualness of the change, but it seems not to be compatible with the chronology observed here: gradual reduction of main-clause instances of object-verb order, leading to a catastrophic loss of the order in embedded clauses.

Battistella and Lobeck (1988) key the change in verb order to the development of a new structural case system. Their idea is that Old English verbs assigned only inherent case, which did not depend on directionality. Then, as the morphological case system began to erode, from late Old English onward, case came to be assigned structurally. Furthermore, there is a default setting for structural case assignment in that it takes place to the right. Consequently, "when inherent case was replaced by structural case assignment, VP would have been restructured so that the verb preceded its arguments, shifting from head-final to head-initial" (p. 27). There are some flaws in this account. First, while it is plausible to assume that Old English grammars assigned inherent case (see Lightfoot 1981a and chapter 5 below), Battistella and Lobeck do not do so exclusively. For example, simple passive sentences can arise only if verbs may assign case structurally. If verbs assigned only inherent case, an object would have received case even when the verb was in its participle form (because inherent case does not depend on government by the case assigner) and thus could not have subsequently acquired nominative. Furthermore, nominative case may be assigned to NPs which move to subject position in the course of a derivation and thus must be structural. Second, even if structural case assignment did emerge only in late Old English, this would not have entailed a change in VP order at D-structure; since structural case is assigned at S-structure, NPs could presumably have moved derivationally to positions where they would receive case. However, Battistella and Lobeck's account allows no link between the gradual changes that we have observed in main clauses and the catastrophic changes affecting verb order in embedded clauses. Nor could it be profitably amended by incorporating a form of degree-0 learnability, because there is no reason to suppose that structural case assignment should appear first in matrix clauses; languages do not have different case systems for different clause types.

In the light of all this, Stockwell and Minkova (1989) offer an interesting twist. They argue that certain historical changes may progress in exactly the opposite direction from what I have argued here, being first established in embedded clauses and only later affecting main clauses. It is unclear what assumptions would be needed about children's acquisition of language in order for such a development to take place, but the argument of Stockwell and Minkova is flawed because it is based on an epiphenomenon. They claim, quite plausibly, that subject-verb order was firmly established in embedded clauses before becoming the norm in matrix clauses, taking over from verb-second order. The factual basis for this claim is sound, but the facts require a different interpretation. There is no subject-verb/verb-second parameter analogous to the object-verb/verb-object parameter, i.e., one instance of the more general (6b). We have seen how this verb-order parameter came to have the verb-object setting, being quite general by the twelfth century. We have also seen that for the next few hundred years the language continued to have productive "verb-second" properties in matrix clauses: main clauses began with an arbitrary phrasal category, with the inflected verb having to move into an initial Y^0 position. These properties generally did not occur in embedded clauses during this period (the twelfth to seventeenth centuries), partly because there was no empty initial position for the embedded verb to move to. During this period, embedded clauses were uniformly subject-verb, as Stockwell and Minkova note, because verbs were base-generated to the left of any complement and did not move to the left of the subject. Consequently there were two relevant changes: the replacement of object-verb order by verb-object (which resulted from changes in unembedded primary data, as has been shown in this chapter) and the loss of "verb-second" (which took place much later and affected main clauses). There is no reason to believe that the loss of "verb-second" took place "by analogy" to the consistent subject-verb order in embedded clauses, and the loss was certainly a distinct diachronic development, not just a delayed instantiation of a change that had already affected embedded clauses.

3.6   Conclusion

In this chapter I have offered a new account of the emergence of the modern verb order in English, which must constitute one of the most extensively studied changes in the literature on diachronic syntax. There are many aspects of the change that I have not discussed and some aspects of the grammars on which I have deliberately sought not to take a position, focusing instead on certain big facts which have not received sufficient attention and which point emphatically to a requirement of degree-0 learning. Only if children are degree-0 learners, setting parameters on the basis of simple, unembedded triggering experiences, can one understand the contrast in the ways in which the new order permeated matrix and embedded clauses. The mere fact that the change took place strongly suggests degree-0 learning, for otherwise one is at a loss to see why the change was not inhibited by robust evidence of underlying object-verb order in embedded clauses; the nature of the change is quite incompatible with anything along the lines of Roeper's (1973) "subordinate clause strategy," by which children were thought to pay disproportionate attention to embedded clauses (presumably Stockwell and Minkova (1989) assumed something of this nature for language acquisition).

With this perpective on the changes affecting English, it will be interesting to examine comparable changes in other languages. For example, grammars of the Scandinavian languages have also come to have verb-object order (like English), while still having a very productive verb-second operation moving the verb to initial Y^0 (unlike English). One would like to know whether there is an enlightening account to be had in terms of gradual loss of main-clause indicators of underlying object-verb order, followed by rapid and dramatic changes in embedded clauses as the parameter came to be set differently. Similarly, it has been argued that Old French had underlying object-verb order, and Adams (1987) has shown that French grammars used to move verbs to an initial position in the Germanic fashion; both properties were lost, at different times. Dutch and German are particularly intriguing cases, if Gerritsen (1980) is right. She argues that subject-verb-object patterns became increasingly frequent through the fourteenth century, declining thereafter as the languages reverted to a more consistent object-verb order. She analyzed a short thirteenth-century text and showed, for example, that infinitival complements to such verbs as "must", "can", and "try" showed verb-object order in 46% of the cases and object-verb in 54%. She also found a significant percentage of verb-object order in relative clauses (46%) and other subordinate clauses (67%). The samples were not large, but it is possible that some grammars were reanalyzed and had D-structure verb-object order, or at least that the simple triggering experiences became more heavily verb-object without necessarily provoking a new parameter setting. In either case, the results will have interesting implications for our notions about what it takes to set a parameter one way or another. On the analysis offered here, it will be particularly interesting to know whether there were changes affecting the simple, unembedded triggers for object-verb order—separated particles, negative markers and other VP specifiers, verb-raising constructions, and so forth. If so, one will want to compare them with analogous changes in English, asking how the Dutch data fell short of triggering a new parameter setting.

By undertaking this kind of comparative study, one may expect to learn something about the nature of triggering experiences and about how parameters are set. For example, it is sometimes said that parameters are set by the properties of lexical items, and that children may have access to any lexical items during the parameter-setting process (see, e.g., Rizzi 1989). Such an approach would permit access to an embedded object-verb sequence, and one can now see that this is too permissive: the diachronic data discussed here suggest that if parameters are set by the properties of lexical items, then it is by lexical items as manifested in unembedded Domains. In the next chapter we shall examine the structural cutoff point in more detail, seeing that the notion of a binding Domain seems to make the cutoff at the right point and that parameter setting is sensitive to certain elements of embedded clauses but not to the position of a complement with respect to its head verb.

Chapter 4
Infinitives

4.1 New Accusative Subjects and Passives

If children set parameters only on the basis of data from matrix binding Domains, then only certain parts of an embedded clause will influence the form of the emerging grammar. In chapter 2 we saw that embedded Comps and subjects of nonfinite clauses are accessible to our degree-0 learner, because they have no local c-commanding NP or AGR (see definition of binding Domain in section 2.2) and therefore have the next higher clause as their binding Domain; this may be a matrix clause. Similarly, if INFL is the head of S', it is plausible to take its binding Domain as the next clause up (where it might be "bound" by the higher INFL); this would make an embedded INFL accessible to a degree-0 learner. In that case, one may wonder how children determine the syntactic properties of infinitives: infinitives themselves occur characteristically in embedded clauses, generally in their D-structure position and not in INFL. An infinitive in that position is therefore not accessible to a degree-0 learner. Presumably children can learn that infinitives exist as an uninflected morphological category from "citation forms" and unembedded instances, such as those that were pointed to in chapter 3 from Old English and Dutch. But how do children learn the distribution of infinitives (i.e., how to use them in embedded Domains) if embedded infinitives are not accessible to influence the shape of the emerging grammar?

I shall again take a diachronic perspective on this puzzle. The distribution of infinitives may change over time, and one will want to know how those changes could have been effected: how did people come to use infinitives differently? In this section I shall investigate two long-standing puzzles in the history of English: the rise of infinitives with lexical (often accusative) subjects and the rise of passive infinitives. I shall argue that they arise as a by-product of the new parameter setting discussed in chapter 3, the new verb-object order.[1] The correlations follow naturally if children are degree-0 learners; otherwise they are mysterious or accidental. Along the way, I shall offer a new analysis of an old problem in English concerning the occurrence of the *to* infinitival marker in the complements of causative and perceptual verbs. Let us begin with accusative and infinitive constructions.

Traditional grammars offer extensive discussion of infinitive constructions with lexical subjects and run into various classificational problems. They note, for example, that a lexical NP intervening between the matrix and the embedded verbs may be dative or accusative in Old English, as is illustrated in (1), and this observation has shaped some of the classifications.

(1) a. ða het he *heora æghwylcum*[dat] gesomnian his byrþene wyrta
       (Gregory's Dialogues, Pref 3(C)14.202.13)
       'then commanded he of them each to gather his bundle of herbs'
    b. se cing het *hi*[acc] feohtan agien Pihtas   (*Chron.* 12, 449A)
       'the king ordered them to fight against the Picts'

So, Callaway (1913) distinguished "objective" from "predicative" infinitives, where in the latter case both the NP and the embedded verb depended directly on the matrix verb. If the NP was dative, the construction was objective; if the NP was accusative, the construction might be either objective or predicative. Other grammarians discussed whether the NP was most naturally construed as the direct object of the higher verb or as the subject of the lower verb. The criteria were usually semantic, based on notions that, in something like *I'd hate my dear friend to go to London, my dear friend* is not hated (or, in current jargon, receives no thematic role from *hate*). Sometimes the classifications were fairly subjective, like Callaway's distinction between infinitives that were substantival (acting as a subject or an object), verbal (occurring with pre-modals, with copulas, or as a predicate to an accusative subject), adverbial (indicating purpose or result, or modifying an adjective), or adjectival (modifying a noun). Callaway often invoked modern intuitions in classifying particular infinitives, and paid little attention to the matrix verb or to whether the infinitive is "plain" (with the *-an* ending) or "inflected" (preceded by the preposition *to* and with the dative ending *-anne* or *-enne*).[2] Bock (1931) offered the following classification:

(2) a. verb and accusative are more strongly linked than verb and
       infinitive: verbs of forcing, hindering, persuading, etc.

b. verb is linked equally to accusative and to infinitive: verbs of causation, perception, calling

c. accusative and infinitive together make up the complement of the verb: verbs of saying, thinking.

Visser (1973, section 2055) tried to avoid the confusion by ignoring the status of the intervening NP and setting up a construction type of "verb object/subject infinitive," but then was forced to introduce many subclasses of verbs and new confusions.

One can cut through this imbroglio and build on Bock's classification, distinguishing verbs (such as *expect*) which are followed by clausal structures and those (such as *persuade*) which assign a thematic role to the following NP, which in turn is not part of the lower clause. The usual structures postulated are those of (3), where the bracketed unit indicates a clausal structure and PRO indicates an empty subject which is coindexed through some control property with a NP in the higher clause.

(3) a. expect [NP infinitive...]
     b. persuade NP [PRO infinitive...]

Since *persuade* assigns a thematic role to the following NP, it follows that it imposes selectional restrictions on the NP, which is characteristically animate or at least "persuadable." *Expect* imposes no comparable restrictions on the following NP, which is selected entirely by the lower infinitive; the clearest illustration of this is that the NP may be an expletive, with no intrinsic meaning of its own:

(4) a. I expected there to be somebody raising these issues
     b. *I persuaded there to be somebody raising these issues

The structures of (3) also lead to assignment of the same thematic roles to active and passive complements to *expect*, but not to *persuade*. Hence, the complement to *expect* is "voice transparent," and (5a) and (5b) are roughly synonymous in a way that (5c) and (5d) are not.

(5) a. I expected the doctor to examine Kim
     b. I expected Kim to be examined by the doctor
     c. I persuaded the doctor to examine Kim
     d. I persuaded Kim to be examined by the doctor

Furthermore, since complements generally may be finite or nonfinite (subject to selectional restrictions), postulating the structures of (3) leads one to expect that *persuade* would be a three-place predicate when occurring with a finite complement, as in (6a), whereas *expect* would be a two-place predicate, as in (6b).

(6) a. I persuaded Jim that Kim/he was sick

    b. *I expected Jim that Kim/he would be sick

Mitchell (1985) pointed to a few examples of sentences of the form of (6b) in Old English, but Fischer (1988a) shows that the finite clauses are purpose or result clauses rather than complements. This alone suggests that it is at least plausible to attribute the structural distinction in (3) to *expect*-type and *persuade*-type verbs in Old English.

Perhaps a more persuasive reason to invoke a structural distinction between the two types of verbs in Old English is that *expect*-type verbs were ungrammatical with the accusative and infinitive construction, whereas *persuade*-type verbs occurred freely with an accusative NP and an infinitival. This historical discrepancy is missed necessarily by Visser and by others who see no structural distinction in the two types. Furthermore, the distinction is actually denied by Zeitlin (1908), who sought to show that the "genuine" accusative and infinitive construction (i.e., with *expect* and such verbs) was native. However, Bock (1931, p. 153) pointed out that all Zeitlin's relevant examples were drawn from texts heavily influenced by Latin originals (for example from Bede's *History*, Wærferth (*Gregory's Dialogues*), translations of the gospels, and from glosses). Gorrell (1895) had shown that when *gefrignan* 'find', *ongietan* 'perceive', *witan* 'know', and *findan* 'find' occurred with infinitives with accusative subjects, they were actually instances of perception verbs (which have a different analysis —see below) and they always occurred with a plain infinitive; they were not instances of *expect*-type structures, although they were sometimes treated as such. Fischer (1988a) claims that the accusative and infinitive constructions in Callaway 1913, Visser 1973, and the Toronto Concordance never occur after native (Germanic) verbs (*think, read, know, learn, hold*, etc.) except in glosses. In fact, this construction is limited overwhelmingly to *hatan* 'order', *lætan* 'let', *seon* 'see', *hieran* 'hear', and their compounds.

Consequently, we emerge from the thicket saying that "exceptional case marking" structures (ECM, Chomsky 1981) such as (3a) represent innovations in the history of English. Although this is not immediately obvious, they were in fact ungrammatical in Old English, occurring only in literal translations.

This means that the only accusative and infinitive constructions that were grammatical in Old English were those of (7), with *persuade*-type verbs, which appear to take double objects ((7a)), causatives ((7b)), and perceptual verbs ((7c)).

(7) a. se cing het hi feohtan agien Pihtas   (*Chron.* 12,449A)
'the king ordered them to fight against the Picts'

 b. he ... let itt eornenn forþwiþþ   (Orm 1336)
'he forthwith set it running'
swa ðu dydest minne broðer his god forlætan   (*Ælfric Homilies* i,468,21)
'as you made my brother forsake his god'

 c. þa þa he geseah his fostormoder wepan   (*Gregory's Dialogues* (C) 97.14)
'then he saw his fostermother weep'
ic gehyrde hine ðine dæd & word lofian   (*Gen.* 508)
'I heard him your deeds and words praise'

Constructions like (8), on the other hand, emerge only in Middle English. Warner (1982) offers good discussion of these and related forms in his examination of Wyclif (late Middle English), who was the first writer to use accusative-and-infinitive constructions extensively. (8a) is an example of Zeitlin's "genuine" accusative and infinitive form, in which *Kim* receives its case from an epistemic verb by some exceptional process. (8b) is the comparable interrogative form, which also does not occur in the texts before Middle English. The nonoccurrence of (8b) illustrates the dangers of arguing *ex tacito*: it might be a function of the kinds of texts that have survived from the early period, in that such interrogative forms are unlikely to be attested in poetry, chronicles, and the other literary genres which make up the extant body of Old English material. It is possible, after all, that Old English was like modern French in this regard and that (8b) was in fact grammatical. I shall continue to assume that it was ungrammatical, but this is not central to any of the claims to be made.[3]

(8) a. you expect [Kim to win]
 b. who$_i$ do you expect [e$_i$ to win]?
 c. you$_i$ were expected [e$_i$ to win]
 d. Kim$_i$ seems [e$_i$ to be happy]
 e. Kim$_i$ is certain [e$_i$ to win]
 f. Kim$_i$ was seen [e$_i$ to leave]

The corresponding (8c), where the matrix verb is passive, also seems to represent a Middle English innovation, as I shall discuss below. The fact that comparable passives with desiderative verbs (such as *he was wanted to take the cake) did not emerge at this time indicates that forms like *I want Kim to win* must be analyzed differently: *Kim* receives its case from the complementizer *for*, always present underlyingly with desiderative verbs, which in turn may be deleted by a late, post-S-structure process. Consequently, an empty subject of the infinitive either has case and is a variable (*who$_i$ do you want [e$_i$[e$_i$ to take the cake]]?*, where the lower e$_i$ receives case from the deleted *for* and is head-governed by the local Comp) or is not head-governed (*you want* $_{S'}$[*PRO to take the cake]*); it can never be a head-governed trace without case, as would be required for the passive sentence.

(8d) and (8e) are examples of subject-to-subject raising, which has long been known not to be productive in Old English (Traugott 1972, p. 102; Kageyama 1975; Lightfoot 1979, p. 301ff.). Passive causative or perceptual verbs with a *to* infinitive, as in (8f), also seem not to have existed in Old English and to have been Middle English innovations.

Alongside the innovations of (8), it is useful to recall some other contexts in which infinitives with lexical subjects did not begin to be attested until well after the corresponding forms with no lexical subject. In (9), drawing mostly on Visser 1966, I list the first instances of various types of *for to* infinitives, all of which occur with no lexical subject. In (10) I list the first instances of the corresponding forms with lexical subjects, which consistently occur about 200 years later.

(9) a. for to go is necessary   (1205)
  b. it is good for to go   (1300)
  c. ...that stood in aunter for to die   (1205)
  d. the king did it for to have sibbe   (1100)
  e. this is a fouler theft than for to breke a chirche   (1205)
  f. he taketh of nought else kepe, but for to fill his bagges   (1385)
  g. for to say the sothe, ye have done marvellously   (1300)

(10) a. for us to go is necessary   (1567)
  b. this would make it imprudent for him...   (1534)
  c. I'm afraid for them to see it   (1391)
  d. he brought it with him for us to see   (1422)
  e. what would be better than for you to go?   (1534)
  f. there is nothing to do but for him to marry Amanda   (1568)
  g. for this low son of a shoemaker to talk of families...   (1673)

These constructions were discussed in Lightfoot 1979 (p. 186ff.), where it was argued that the early *for to* sequences in (9) manifested a complex infinitival marker and that *for* was neither a preposition nor a complementizer. The structures in (10) reflected a reanalysis whereby *for* came to be construed as a preposition in Comp governing the lexical subject. Something along these lines still seems to be correct, and the emergence of the *for* NP *to* VP forms in (10) cannot be related directly to the innovations in (8), contrary to what was suggested in an erroneous comment in Lightfoot 1981a. There may be an indirect relation, but I shall not treat these forms here; in this section I shall make a limited point about the triggering experience rather than give a comprehensive account of infinitival subjects.

These, then, are some of the manifestations of the Middle English development that greatly expanded the contexts in which infinitives could occur with lexical and NP trace subjects. The development has long been noted, and various explanations have been offered for the new accusative and infinitive forms. Probably the most frequently offered explanation has been that the development represents Latin influence. There is some evidence for this view, insofar as the first instances with *expect*-type verbs were in translations and glosses, as noted. But a number of questions arise. Since Latin had at least as widespread a social role among French, Dutch, and German speakers, one must wonder why its influence did not promote the rise of accusative and infinitives analogously in these languages. Moreover, one asks why Latin influence was so selective: lexical subjects came to occur in English under conditions of government by the higher verb, but infinitival subjects in Latin were not bound by this limitation. So, for example, if Latin influence was the source of the innovation, why does one not find new subjects in contexts like *I expected last week Kim to win* (cf. *last week I expected Kim to win* and *I expected last week that Kim would win*), or *Kim to win would be a pity*, which would have been grammatical in Latin? (There are some instances of lexical subjects occurring in ungoverned positions, appearing for the first time in Chaucer and Wyclif: *the thridde grevance is a man to have harm in his body*. It is not clear how these forms should be analyzed, but they do not survive into modern English and therefore should not, I assume, be analyzed in the same way as the other innovations discussed here.)

Another explanation sometimes offered for the new accusative and infinitive forms is that they represent an analogical extension to epistemic and other verbs of patterns already found with causative and perceptual verbs, and even, some writers suggest, with small clauses (*I consider him a fool*). However, such small clauses were rare almost to the point of nonexistence before the thirteenth century. They represent a Middle English innovation, according to Callaway (1913, p. 212) and Einenkel (1916, p. 25), being rare before the thirteenth century and quite popular from then on. In that case, they could not have provided an analogical base. Furthermore, they and the complements to causative and perceptual verbs actually attested in Old English have quite different properties from all the innovative forms in (8), as we shall see.

A third account, offered in chapter 4 of Lightfoot 1979, is that the infinitive was originally an NP, with more or less the distribution of gerunds, which are also verbal nouns. In Middle English it underwent a category change and came to be treated as a verb projecting to a VP and therefore could co-occur with a subject NP. This unified some of the novel properties that entered the language at roughly the same time, but it was mysterious why such a category change should have taken place, and why language learners should have treated infinitives differently from the way they had been treated by earlier generations.

Since the existing explanations all leave something to be desired, a wise and sober reader will seek alternatives. Let us begin by distinguishing the causative, perceptual, and *persuade*-type verbs, which already manifested accusative and infinitive forms in Old English. *Persuade*-type verbs are relatively straightforward and show an accusative NP that is not part of the complement clause. Here I shall assume the usual structure, as in (3b).[4] Complements to causative and perceptual verbs, however, have provided more puzzles. In (12) I list some analyses that have been offered; none of these will suffice for Old English.

(12) a. see NP to VP

b. see $_{NP}[_{Spec}[NP]\ N]$

c. see $_S[\quad]$

d. you $_{S'}[$Jim [Kim kiss]$]$ saw —V-R→ you Jim [Kim e_i]
saw + kiss$_i$
you $_{S'}[$PRO [Kim kiss]$]$ must —V-R→ you [Kim e_i] must + kiss$_i$

e. $_{V'}[$see $_{VP}[\ldots\ldots$ subject]$]$

f. you saw $_{S'}[$Jim$_j$ kiss$_k$ $_S[e_j$ Kim $e_k]]$

(12a) is due to Akmajian (1977) and involves an idiosyncratic subcategorization frame for *see*. It also entails distinct subcategorization frames for the passive and active *see* (with and without *to*: *Kim was seen to leave* and *I saw Kim leave*). (12b) is the analysis advocated in Lightfoot 1979. In current terms one might say that the lower NP receives case by Spec-head agreement (along the lines of Chomsky 1986): because *see* always assigns accusative case to its direct-object NP and its head, the Specifier also receives accusative uniformly, which explains the absence of dative cases in these contexts (although it is common to find dative cases on NPs following *persuade* and such verbs). However, as noted, we are left with no explanation for why structure (12b) became unattainable for children in the Middle English period. (12c) leaves no account for the extractability of embedded objects (*who did* s[*you see* s[*Jim kiss*]]), if S was a bounding node for Subjacency in Old English as it is in the modern language: if there is no intermediate Comp, the movement of *who*, which was presumably well formed in Old English, would cross two bounding nodes.

(12d) illustrates the verb-raising process motivated by Evers (1975) for Dutch and German, and advocated for early English by van Kemenade (1987, p. 55ff.) and carried over by Fischer (1988a). Van Kemenade claims that the rule applied to causative, perceptual, and pre-modal verbs like *must*, but all of her examples involve pre-modals. It is quite unclear how the analysis would apply to causative and perceptual verbs. For example, special mechanisms are required to ensure that the lower subject, here *Jim*, would receive case or would receive the arbitrary interpretation when empty (see below); these might be the same mechanisms needed for equivalent structures in Dutch and German, but this is not examined. Van Kemenade asserts that the embedded infinitive is adjoined to the matrix verb, but gives no evidence for the adjunction and considers no alternatives.[5]

(12e) would treat the complements to causative and perceptual verbs as VP complements, analogously to Burzio's (1986) analysis of comparable verbs in Italian. The VP-final subject is not a D-structure position, but results from movement and allows long passives, clitic climbing, and anti-causative constructions. However, such subjects do not occur in Old English; nor does one find even agentive *by* phrases in this position, as pointed out by Fischer (1988b, p. 88). It is also unclear how one would treat empty subjects with arbitrary interpretations, which I shall discuss later in the context of (19).

(12f) might be a possible structure at a stage where the language was verb-second and permitted a verb and one other phrasal category to occur in an initial projection. This option will be discussed at the end of this section and shown to be inadequate for English.

Since the existing analyses of causative and perceptual complements do not suffice, we need an alternative. Ideally it should solve a long-standing puzzle in modern English. An active complement to causative and perceptual verbs generally has a bare infinitive with no *to* marker, while the corresponding passives require the *to* (see (13a)–(13d)). Moreover, impersonal forms such as (13e) do not exist, with or without the *to*.

(13) a. Jill saw [Bill leave]

    b. *Bill$_i$ was seen [e$_i$ leave]

    c. *Jill saw [Bill to leave]

    d. Bill$_i$ was seen [e$_i$ to leave]

    e. *it was seen [Bill (to) leave]

This paradigm can be accounted for if *saw* can assign case into the embedded constituent in (13a), but not where it is headed by *to* in (13c), and if *seen* head-governs a trace in the embedded constituent if and only if it is headed by *to* (compare (13b) and (13d)). Norbert Hornstein points out that these results can be derived on the basis of some commonplace assumptions allied with a suggestion in Hornstein and Franks 1988 and a reanalysis operation. Let us assume that clauses generally may have the minimal structure of (14a), where INFL acts as the head of the S'; this includes the complements of causative and perceptual verbs. Also, constituents without lexical heads do not count as maximal projections, as argued by Hornstein and Lightfoot (1987) (see (14b)). Following Aoun, Hornstein, Lightfoot, and Weinberg (1987), we can also assume that there are distinct locality conditions for phonological and logical structures, and that empty elements which are indexed in phonological structure must be head-governed at that level (see (14c)).[6] Then I assume a standard notion of government, given informally in (14d) and more formally in chapter 2; *b* is taken to be any member of a projection.

(14) a. $_{S'}$[Comp $_S$[NP INFL VP]]

     b. Headless constituents are not maximal.

     c. Empty elements visible at phonological structure are head-governed there.

     d. $a(X^0)$ governs b iff they share all maximal projections.

     e. $a(X^0)$ head-governs b iff a minimally c-commands b.

     f. a minimally c-commands b iff no more than one node dominates b which does not dominate a.

     g. An infinitival marker like *to* may coalesce with a verb that governs it and transmit properties of head-government.

(14e) and (14f) define head-government (ignoring coindexation requirements, which are not relevant here; see Aoun et al. 1987) and incorporate the suggestion of Hornstein and Franks to restrict it to relations between sisters and "step-sisters." So *a* head-governs *b* in structures like [...a...b...], where *a* and *b* are sisters, and a[...b...], where they are "step-sisters," but not in a structure like a[...[...b...]...]. Head-government is a more local relation than government; thus, for example, *saw* governs but does not head-govern *Bill* in (13a). (14g) permits reanalysis of the infinitival *to* marker, as I shall illustrate in a moment.

One can see that *saw* governs and assigns case to *Bill* in (13a) because the S′ contains no lexical INFL and therefore is not a maximal projection (by 14b)). In (13c), however, the S′ does contain a lexical INFL in *to*, therefore is a maximal projection, and thus blocks government of *Bill* by *saw*. The fact that the complement to *see* and such verbs has a nonlexical INFL at D-structure is the lexical idiosyncrasy that children must learn.

The passive sentences have the structures of (15a) and (15b). In the ungrammatical (15a) the trace fails to be head-governed by *seen* because the intervening S′ node blocks minimal c-command. In (15b), on the other hand, the trace is head-governed by its sister *to*; *to*, in turn, is the head of the S′, is therefore governed by *seen*, and thus may coalesce with *seen* and transmit *seen*'s head-government property. This coalescence is quite analogous to the well-known process of *wanna* contraction, whereby *to* may adjoin to certain verbs that govern it, forming a phonetic unit in this case.

(15) a. Bill$_i$ was seen $_{S'}$[$_S$[e$_i$ leave]]
b. Bill$_i$ was seen $_{S'}$[$_S$[e$_i$ to leave]]
c. who$_i$ did you see $_{S'}$[e$_i$ $_S$[e$_i$ leave]]?

(15c) is also well formed: the empty subject of *leave* is governed by and receives its case from *see*, and is head-governed by the coindexed Comp, which minimally c-commands it; the trace in Comp is, in turn, head-governed by its "step-sister" *see*, which minimally c-commands it. Presence of a Comp is crucial in accounting for the asymmetry between *wh* extraction (no *to*) and passivization (*to* required), and this constitutes strong support for treating the complements to these causative and perceptual verbs as uniformly S′.

This provides a principled account of the old puzzle about the distribution of the *to* marker in the complement to causative and perceptual verbs. The complements to these verbs are treated in standard fashion as S′, and we invoke no process of S′ Deletion or Exceptional Case Marking for any of the relevant sentences. Although there may be a nonlexical INFL at D-structure, *to* is required for the S-structure (15b) by principles of Universal Grammar. (An unexplained exception is the verb *watch*: *I watch Jim swim* but **Jim was watched swim*.)

You were expected to win ((8c)), *Kim seems to be happy* ((8d)), and *Kim is certain to win* ((8e)) may be treated in parallel fashion, again with no appeal to a process of S′ Deletion. *To* is governed by *expected*, *seems*, and *certain*, respectively, and may thus transmit head-government to the subject trace. If there were no *to*, the subject trace (which, being indexed, is "visible" at phonological structure) would fail to be head-governed, contravening (14c). Consequently, the corresponding active forms, for which S′ Deletion and Exceptional Case Marking have been generally invoked, may be treated by a natural extension: in *you expect Kim to win* ((8a)) and *who do you expect to win?* ((8b)), *to* is governed by the transitive and case-assigning verb *expect* and thus transmits its case to the subject position.

The infinitival *to* transmits the head-government and case properties of a governing element and does not have these properties inherently. So where it is not itself governed by an appropriate element, it does not license subjects[7]:

(16) a. *[Kim to win] would be a pity
    b. *Kim$_i$ was expected, despite past performances, [e$_i$ to win]

Furthermore, certain elements in Comp block the coalescence of a higher verb or adjective with *to*, for example a *wh* word (as in (17a)) or the *for* complementizer to desiderative verbs ((17b)):

(17) a. *Kim$_i$ was known [what$_j$ [e$_i$ to believe e$_j$]]
    b. *Kim$_i$ was wanted [(for) [e$_i$ to win]]

We shall see in section 4.2 that these facts are not idiosyncratic and have analogues in Brazilian Portuguese. Note here that *want* and other desiderative verbs, in not occurring with passives like (17b), have quite different properties from epistemic verbs: they do not transmit head-government properties to a lower *to*. Chomsky (1981) attributed the nonoccurrence of (17b) to the fact that *for* is deleted in phonological structure after assigning case to *e$_i$*. If so, deletion of the case-assigning *for* is subject to its being head-governed as in (17b); compare (18).

(18) a. (*for) PRO to leave would be annoying
    b. *(for) Kim to leave would be annoying
    c. Jim wanted very much *(for) Kim to come

In (18a), *for* does not assign case and its deletion is therefore not subject to head-government. In (18b) and (18c), *for* assigns case but fails to be head-governed and therefore may not delete.

What I have described here as a coalescence process must take place by S-structure, since it influences the way in which case is assigned. That entails that its effects are available not only to phonological conditions (making the trace in (8f), for example, head-governed by *seen-to*), but also to LF conditions.[8]

This analysis of modern English entails a novel account of the Middle English innovations in (8): *to* came to coalesce with a governing verb and transmitted either head-government properties or both head-government and case. The choice between these two formulations will depend on the parallelism of the innovations: the second formulation will be adopted if (8a) and (8b), which involve transmission of case, entered the language alongside the other forms. This, in turn, is likely to involve understanding the conditions under which the *to* form of the infinitive came to take over from the plain form of the infinitive without the *to* marker. As noted in Lightfoot 1979, this is a difficult matter and has never been properly understood, despite being subjected to much energetic attention by generations of anglicists.

For this reason and because my limited goals here do not require it, I shall not choose between these two formulations. For ease of exposition, I shall write as if there was a single innovation whereby *to* came to coalesce with a governing verb and transmit both the head-government and the case-assignment properties to its local subject. This is a plausible view. It would entail, for example, that (8a)–(8f) were treated in parallel. We know from Kageyama 1975 that (8d) and (8e) were Middle English innovations, and it is quite possible that the same holds for the passive examples (8c) and (8f). Callaway's exhaustive (1913) study showed a very small number of such "objective" infinitives after passive verbs—17, versus 3236 after nonpassives (about 0.5%). Furthermore, of those 17 cases, all but two occur in translations ("subjective" infinitives, on the other hand, occur 48 times with passives and 356 times with nonpassives, about 12% of the total). So it is not unreasonable to say that forms like *Kim was seen/ expected to leave* were not grammatical in the Old English period. In addition, the new coalesced forms discussed here are probably related in some way to the new stranded prepositions (*Kim was spoken to*), which emerged in Middle English; these forms involve the coalescence of the preposition with a verb that governs it, as I shall discuss in section 5.3.

Jim wanted Kim to win has a different analysis from (8a) (*you expect Kim to win*). Here *Kim* is governed by the underlying *for* in Comp (but not head-governed, because only N, A, and V are head-governors), and not governed by a coalesced *want-to*. So the ability of *to* to coalesce with *want* does not suffice to generate such structures, and one is not surprised to find that they have a very different history from the innovations in (8). Visser (1969, section 2064) claims that desiderative verbs manifest the (*for*) NP *to* VP complements only in the twentieth century. He actually provides several examples from the nineteenth century, but they clearly do not represent a Middle English innovation.

If the ability of the infinitival *to* to coalesce with a governing verb and transmit various properties was the crucial Middle English innovation, accounting for the new surface forms in (8), an explanation for the new property has yet to be offered. Recall that it was lack of explanatory force which militated against the accounts discussed earlier. Under the perspective adopted here, any explanation will key the innovations to a parameter which is set by positive data, identifying both the parameter and the relevant triggering experience. So far we have identified the parameter: the ability of an infinitival marker to transmit certain properties of the verb that governs it.

That parameter may have been set positively as a result of another change: the adoption of a system of structural case assignment, which in turn was due to morphological changes. I shall consider that possibility in chapter 5. Here I shall examine an explanation which depends crucially on the notion that parameters are set on the basis of unembedded data, and on the particular definition of "unembedded" given in chapter 2.

Another well-known change that took place during the Middle English period is not usually discussed in connection with the new forms of (8). We have seen that in the Old English period one finds accusative and infinitive forms in the complements to causative and perceptual verbs ((13a)) and to verbs of ordering and persuading ((3b)). However, one almost never finds passive infinitives in these contexts, despite the fact that passive infinitives (*beon/wesan/(ge)weorþan* with a past participle) were free to occur after such pre-modal verbs as *cunnan, motan,* and *willan.* Instead one finds forms like (19).

(19) a. he let cnihtas læran   (*Bede* (Miller 1898), 226)
        he let boys   teach
        'he had boys taught'

    b. ... ðone ic Andreas nemnan herde   (*And.* 1176)
        whom I Andreas call   heard
        'whom I heard called Andreas'

    c. swa we soþlice secgan hyrdon   (*Beowulf* 273)
        'as we truly heard tell'

    d. ðonne heo gehyrdon þine bec rædan & þin godspell sæcgan ...
        then they heard your book read and your gospel say
        'then they heard your book read and your gospel'

    e. þa hie gesawan þa deadan men þiclice to eorþan beran
        (*Orosius* 3.10.138.23)
        '... when they saw the dead men carried so quickly to earth
        [buried]'

In each of these examples one finds an active infinitive with an empty subject which is understood to be arbitrary in reference. This was a common pattern and was often used to translate Latin passive infinitives like *adduci*:

(20) bebead se biscop ðeosne to him lædan   (*Bede* 388.20)
      hunc ergo adduci praecipit episcopus
      'so the bishop bade bring him to him'

Quirk and Wrenn (1955, section 131) say that "a passive infinitive was usually expressed with the active form," and Callaway (1913, pp. 6 and 173) writes of infinitives "used in a passive sense." However, Mitchell (1985, section 942) points out that they "cannot prove that it must be passive in even one example." There is a straightforward analysis along the lines of (21).

(21) a. ic seah turf tredan   (*Riddles* 13.1)
          I saw grass tread
      b. ic seah$_i$ $_{S'}$[Comp $_S$[PRO $_{VP}$[turf tredan]]] e$_i$

Turf is the direct object of the active infinitive 'tread' and occurs in its usual pre-verbal position. Because the subject is arbitrary in reference, it is not governed in this example (see Hornstein and Lightfoot 1987, where PROs that are ungoverned and arbitrary in reference are distinguished from those that are governed and anaphoric). On the other hand, a lexical subject was also possible (*ic seah [John turf tredan]*); since lexical NPs must have case and therefore be governed, this position may also be governed.[9] A trace in subject position must be head-governed, as in (14c), and this is a tighter locality condition than government, involving minimal c-command. This precludes an NP-trace, which would not be head-governed (**John$_i$ was seen $_{S'}$[$_S$[e$_i$ turf tredan]]*), but it would permit a *wh*-trace, which would be head-governed by the coindexed Comp (*who$_i$ did you see $_{S'}$[$_{Comp}$[e$_i$]$_i$ $_S$[e$_i$ turf tredan]]*). As a result, sentences like (21) occur with subjects which are ungoverned (arbitrary PRO), subjects which are governed and case-marked (lexical NP), and subjects which are head-governed by a coindexed Comp. These predictions seem to be correct, and the sentences raise no particular learnability problems.

Now we come to the issue of degree-0 learnability. Consider a Middle English degree-0 learner, as defined above, who has adopted the new setting of the verb-order parameter, as discussed in chapter 3: $_V$[V complement]. On hearing sentences (19) and (21a), the child would be unable to parse the NP between the two verbs, e.g. *turf* in (21a), as the direct object of the lower verb. Even if there were some auxiliary system whereby people make sense of unfamiliar phenomena, perhaps through "marked" or "peripheral" operations, continuing the object analysis of *turf* could not trigger such an operation; it is too deeply embedded to have any effect on degree-0 learners. Furthermore, failure to parse or understand expressions within an existing system might lead children to amend the system, i.e. to set a parameter differently, if two conditions are met: the new parse must yield a reading roughly consistent with the earlier structural analysis in which *turf* was taken as the direct object of the lower verb; and the relevant data must be accessible to the child, i.e. must be unembedded in the appropriate sense, under the hypothesis under examination here.

In this case, the child might take *see* as followed by a nonfinite complement clause, S', in the standard fashion, and *turf* as the subject of that clause (see (22)). This is the important point. Only by being the subject of an infinitive could the properties of *turf* have any effect on parameter setting, as opposed to simply being a by-product of the process. Under that analysis, in view of the context in which (21a) could plausibly be uttered, *turf* would have to be treated as a surface subject but a thematic object of the verb *tread*, i.e. as the subject of either a passive or an "unaccusative" verb. Passive was the option adopted, perhaps because unaccusative verbs are necessarily restricted to certain semantic classes or perhaps for other reasons; this entails the partial structure of (22).

(22) ic seah $_{S'}$[Comp $_S$[turf$_i$ INFL [be trodden e$_i$]]]

Two factors are crucial for the specific notions of degree-0 learnability adopted here. First, the lexical NP must be licensed, i.e. case-marked. In this particular example, case might be assigned directly by the higher verb if the lower clause has no head, as in (14b); otherwise it would have to be assigned indirectly, e.g. by a *to* in INFL coalescing with the higher verb *seah*. Headless clauses are quite restricted across a variety of languages, typically occurring, as in English, as complements to causative and perceptual verbs; it is likely that Universal Grammar is at least partially responsible for that limitation, and I shall assume as much despite having nothing specific to suggest. Therefore, the subject of a complement to *see* might acquire case in one of two ways. However, *persuade*-type verbs are subject to the same reanalysis. So *I order grass cut + infin* would have had the analysis of (23a) for Old English speakers with the verb-order parameter set at [complement verb]. Such an analysis would not be available to a Middle English child with the verb order parameter set at [verb complement]. A degree-0 child would be able to take (23b) as a triggering experience, construing *grass* as an infinitival subject and therefore as case-marked.

(23) a. I order $_{S'}$[Comp $_S$[PRO $_{VP}$[grass cut]]]
      b. I order $_{S'}$[Comp $_S$[grass to ...]]
      c. I order $_{S'}$[Comp $_S$[grass$_i$ to $_{VP}$[be cut e$_i$]]]

Since *order* is not a causative or perceptual verb which may take a headless complement, case could be assigned to *grass* only indirectly; therefore, the coalescence option was invoked and the *to* marker became necessary. Consequently, the parametric option of coalescing the infinitival marker with a governing verb and transmitting its case properties came to be set positively, triggered by the need to license a lexical subject.

The second crucial factor brings us to the central, radioactive core of the argument: the changing form of the lower verb plays no role in setting the parameters and is entirely a by-product of other things. In this example, since grass cannot actively cut, the child would be obliged to treat *grass* as a derived subject, as in (23c). Likewise in (22). Consequently the verb has to be passive. This, however, is an effect and not a cause of anything; specifically, it plays no role in the setting of any parameters. The central point for this argument is that if the earlier active form of the verb were part of what the parameter-setting process responded to, there would have been quite different consequences. If the form of the embedded verb played any role in determining the emerging grammar, there would have been clear evidence that the intervening NP could not be the (derived) subject of a passive infinitive: the infinitive was in fact active in form and therefore incompatible with a passive analysis. If the form of the infinitive had been accessible to parameter setters, it would have demanded a very different analysis.

Furthermore, since the language always had active and passive forms of the infinitive, the new use of the passive in some context cannot reflect *directly* a particular parameter setting specifying active and passive forms. Structural parameters do not have such properties. Rather, the replacement of active forms by passives must be construed as a *by-product* of a structural parameter. The account offered here meets that requirement.

In short, in the grammars of Old English speakers, *grass* received case from *cut* in (23a), and *turf* from *tredan* in (21a), and the empty subject, not being governed, received an arbitrary interpretation. That analysis was not available to a Middle English child hearing the corresponding sentences but having set the verb-order parameter in the new fashion. A degree-0 learner was free to treat *grass* as a subject NP, therefore receiving case indirectly from the higher verb. So (23b) was part of the trigger experience, entailing new possibilities for indirect case assignment. Since the parameter-setting process, being sensitive generally only to unembedded material, could ignore the form of the verb, the child was free to reformulate the verb as required by the sense of the expression, as a passive. This explains the loss of the "active infinitives with passive sense" exemplified in (19), (21a), and (23a), and it explains why their loss coincided with the new verb order discussed in chapter 3. Since indirect case assignment was now required to license *grass* in (23b) etc., that also explains the rise of infinitival subjects in structures like (8a) and (8b), which also receive case through the coalescence of *to* with the higher verb.

This reanalysis could be effected only if children were not influenced by the form of the embedded infinitival. That is, it could be effected only by degree-0 learners.

The central idea of indirect case assignment adopted here is reminiscent of Kayne (1981b), who postulated an abstract preposition in Comp that transmitted case to the subjects of infinitives in English, as in (24).

(24) you expect $_{S'}$[p $_S$[Kim to win]]

However, keying case assignment to the *to* marker in INFL and taking INFL to be the head of the clause has made it possible to offer a somewhat different account, dealing with the complements of causative and perceptual verbs in natural fashion.

This account also makes it possible to understand why Dutch, German, and French did not develop infinitival subjects in a parallel way, and indeed why such forms are generally quite unusual. They arose in English as a result of the convergence of some accidental properties: the existence of "passive sense" infinitives, as in (19), and a distinct infinitival marker *to* at a time when the verb-order parameter was being set differently. These conditions did not exist in Dutch or German (if only because the verb-order parameter never came to be set differently), or in French.

French did show some apparent "Exceptional Case Marking" structures with causatives like *faire* (see (25a)). If new structures arise by "analogical extension," there is no apparent reason why such forms would not have been as good a basis for extension as the causative structures in Old English.

(25) a. s'i fist tuz les vaslets antrer
      'and there (he) made all the servants go in'
   b. fait $_{S'}$[$_{Comp}$[tous les valets$_i$ entrer$_j$] [e$_i$ e$_j$]]

However, such structures manifest the "verb-second" character of early French, by which the verb and some other phrasal category could both occur in an embedded Comp, being analyzed as in (25b). This predicts that such structures should cease to occur as the option of moving verbs and non-*wh* phrases to Comp is lost. This seems to be true for French, but not for English, where, as was seen in chapter 3, verbs could move to "second position" quite productively until the early modern period and there was no correlation between either the rise or the demise of verb-second phenomena and "Exceptional Case Marking" structures.

In this section I have offered a novel account of an old puzzle about the complements to causative and perceptual verbs in modern English, and an explanation of two much-discussed changes in Middle English: the rise of the infinitival constructions of (8) and the replacement of active infinitives by passives in forms like (19). The infinitival *to* came to transmit the head-government and case-marking properties of its governing verb; this was the analysis adopted by children with verb-complement order who were exposed to primary linguistic data like (19), (20), and (21a). The explanation assumes crucially that children are degree-0 learners, and the details of the change show that the formulation of unembeddedness makes some precise and accurate claims about the cutoff point for what makes up the triggering experience: we have found that children must have access to infinitival subjects and, to some extent, to properties of INFL in an embedded clause, but that they do not set parameters on the basis of the form of the embedded infinitival verb. Recall that only finite verbs move to INFL and that infinitival verbs generally do not move out of their VP, where they are inaccessible to our degree-0 children. In chapter 3 it was shown that we cannot assume that children have access to embedded objects if we are to understand how word-order change has taken place. Saying that children have access to unembedded binding Domains predicts exactly this cutoff point: our degree-0 children have access to data from matrix clauses and to the Comp, the INFL, and the infinitival subject of an embedded clause.

4.2   Infinitives in Brazilian Portuguese

The new parameter setting, which allowed more infinitival subjects in Middle English, interacts with the embedded INFL in that the *to* serves to license the subject and assign it objective case. However, until we have a better understanding of the way in which the *to* marker was introduced into the language, it must remain somewhat unclear whether presence of *to* was a precondition for the new parameter setting or, at least in part, a consequence of it. That relationship is difficult to untangle; as a result, one cannot be sure to what extent the *to* in INFL is part of the triggering experience that gave the parameter its new setting.

The formulation of "unembedded" adopted here predicts that degree-0 learners have access to embedded INFLs, which may therefore make up part of the triggering experience; this prediction needs to be investigated. We can sidestep the ambiguity of the Middle English change just discussed by considering a change taking place among speakers of Brazilian Portuguese, which will provide clearer evidence. This will show that embedded INFLs do in fact constitute part of the triggering experience, since changes in the form of an embedded INFL can be shown to set a parameter differently, entailing a variety of surface changes. Taken together with the material already discussed, this change will provide interesting support for the particular limits suggested here for what makes up the triggering experience.

As is well known, Portuguese has inflected infinitives, which vary depending on the person and number of the subject. The forms of the infinitive and the nominative/oblique form of the relevant pronouns are listed in (26).[10]

(26) **singular**   **plural**
  1. eu/mim   vencer   nós/nós   vencer-mos
  2. tu/ti   vencer-es   vós/vós   vencer-des
  3. ele/ele   vencer   eles/eles vencer-em
     ela/ela   elas/elas

These infinitives are like finite verbs and unlike uninflected infinitives in that they co-occur with lexical subjects, which are in the nominative case. However, they are like uninflected infinitives and unlike finite verbs in that they occur only in embedded clauses and are never introduced by a *que* complementizer. Their distribution is restricted. For example, Raposo (1987) notes that they occur as complements to epistemic verbs (see (27a)), to declarative verbs such as *afirmar* 'claim' (see (27b)), and to factive verbs such as *lamentar* 'regret' (see (27c)), but not to volitional verbs such as *desejar* 'wish' (see (27d)). (The verb is moved leftward in the complement to epistemic and declarative verbs obligatorily in European Portuguese, optionally so in the complement of a factive verb; this movement operation is sometimes absent from Brazilian Portuguese, and I disregard it here.)

(27) a. eu penso [terem$_i$ os deputados e$_i$ trabalhado pouco]
          I   think   have + AGR the deputies worked   little

b. eu afirmo [terem$_i$ os deputados e$_i$ trabalhado pouco]

c. eu lamento [os deputados terem trabalhado pouco]

d. *eu desejava [os deputados terem trabalhado mais]

e. eu entrei em casa [sem [os meninos verem]]
   I entered the house without the children see + AGR

f. sera difícil [eles aprovarem a proposta]
   it will be difficult they approve + AGR the proposal

g. *eles não sabem [que crianças convidarem para a festa]
   they don't know which children to-invite + AGR for dinner

h. *eu trouxe a faca [com a qual [eles cortarem o queijo]]
   I brought the knife with which they to-cut + AGR the cheese

i. *esses relogios são difíceis de arranjarmos
   those watches are difficult to-repair + AGR

They occur in an adjunct clause introduced by a preposition ((27e)), and as a subject complement ((27f)), but here generally in "extraposed" position. They do not occur in clauses introduced by overt *wh* words or by null operators—i.e., in interrogative ((27g)), relative ((27h)), or, in European Portuguese, *tough* movement ((27i)) constructions.[11]

Raposo (1987) sought to account for this distribution by claiming that the AGR marker to which the infinitival verb attaches may assign nominative case to its subject only if it has been assigned case itself by a governing verb ((27a), (27b), (27c)) or preposition ((27e)). This is similar to the analysis just offered for English, whereby the *to* infinitival marker may assign features to its subject by coalescing with a verb that governs it. Despite the difference that the Portuguese AGR marker assigns nominative case to its subject whereas English *to* transmits either head government or objective case to its subject, the similarities are so great that it would be surprising if the mechanisms were very different. For example, a governing volitional verb neither coalesces with English *to* ((17b)) nor makes Portuguese AGR a case assigner ((27d)). An intervening *wh* word blocks coalescence in English ((17a)) and prevents AGR from being a case assigner in Portuguese ((27g), (27h)). These phenomena are compatible with both a coalescence analysis and a treatment in terms of case assignment, if one assumes in the latter instance, with Raposo, that AGR must move to Comp in order to receive case. I shall leave aside here the questions of whether the coalescence analysis can subsume the Portuguese material, whether case assignment can be extended to deal with English, whether some third approach is needed to generalize over both English and Portuguese, or whether indeed distinct treatments are needed for the two languages. What is clear is that in certain contexts the agreement marker on an infinitive serves to license a lexical subject.

There have been extensive studies on the loss of various inflectional endings in certain forms of Brazilian Portuguese; see, for example, Guy 1981, Naro 1981, and references cited therein. One such ending is the infinitival agreement marker, which is often absent from the colloquial speech of people from many different regions, particularly among the less educated. Maria Marta Scherre conducted a small survey showing that some children in Rio de Janeiro use infinitives which are inflected in only 18% of the total. The comparable figure for the adults she surveyed is 43%, but there is a strong correlation with educational background: adults who had completed only elementary school inflected 26% of all infinitives, while those who had completed middle school inflected 40% and those who had completed high school inflected 61%. I shall treat the uninflected forms as part of an innovating dialect, while the standard dialect retains the agreement morpheme. Such a bifurcation, of course, glosses over a wider range of variation, mixed forms, and such like, but I shall assume that it is real and that it is an essential ingredient for an understanding of the mixed forms.

Expressions like (28a) and (28b) are typical of the standard dialect of Brazilian Portuguese, where such verbs as *pedir* 'ask', *escrever* 'write', *aconselhar* 'advise', *dizer* 'say', *falar* 'talk', 'say', and *implorar* 'implore' may be followed by *para* and an infinitive with a lexical subject. This use of *para*, which does not occur in European Portuguese in these contexts, was a necessary condition for the reanalysis that I shall describe. (28c) is usual in the innovating dialect (*para* is often phonetically *pra*).

(28) a. ele pediu (para o João) para eu fazer isso
        he asked (of João)   for I to do this
     b. ele pediu (para o João) para eles fazerem isso
        he asked (of João)   for them to do   this
     c. ele pediu (para o João) para eles fazer isso

In (28a) the infinitival subject is in the nominative case and the infinitive has an agreement marker, although it is not morphologically marked. (28b) shows an overt marker on the infinitive, although the third-person-plural pronoun shows no nominative/oblique distinction (see note 11). The innovating (28c) has the oblique form of the pronouns, and the infinitive has no agreement marker. In (28c) there is no overt AGR, and the subject is governed by the preposition *para* (which I assume to be in Comp, although this is not crucial); we shall see shortly that in this dialect AGR is not only not overt in these contexts but also nonexistent. In (28a) and (28b), on the other hand, the infinitival verb, being inflected, adjoins to an overt AGR in INFL, which in turn may govern and assign nominative case to its subject in an appropriate context (see above). The subject in these examples is not governed by *para*, on the standard assumption that if an element has a governor within some domain it cannot be governed by an element outside that domain. So the structures are as in (29), and only in (29c) does *para* govern the subject NP.

(29) a. ele pediu $_S$'[para $_S$[eu $_{INFL}$[fazer + AGR] ...]]
     b. ele pediu $_S$'[para $_S$[eles $_{INFL}$[fazer + AGR] ...]]
     c. ele pediu $_S$'[para $_S$[eles INFL $_{VP}$[fazer ...]]]

This fact alone suggests that the dialect lacking inflected infinitives also lacks AGR as an abstract element in these infinitival constructions. If no AGR governs the lexical subject, one understands why the subject does not have nominative case and why it is possible for *para* to come to govern the subject NP, assigning the oblique case characteristic of prepositions.

Such a hypothesis explains other facts. For example, in the standard dialect it is not possible to raise the subject of an inflected infinitive, and structures like (30a) do not occur (**eles parecem estarem felizes*). However, comparable structures do occur when the infinitive is uninflected, as in (30b). The AGR element in (30a) governs and assigns case to the subject NP, which therefore would need to be a variable and not an anaphor. (30a) also violates the generalized binding theory adopted here: AGR would act as a SUBJECT for the subject trace, obliging it to be locally bound in the embedded binding Domain, which it is not. Such issues do not arise for (30b), where, in the absence of AGR, the subject trace has neither case nor a local SUBJECT.

(30) a. *eles$_i$ parecem [e$_i$ estar + AGR felizes]
           they   seem   to-be   happy
     b. eles$_i$ parecem [e$_i$ estar felizes]

One also finds sentences like (31a) in the standard dialect, where *eles* receives its case from the local AGR which c-commands it. Similarly, one finds questions like (31b), where the subject trace receives case from the AGR (and thus is a variable) and is head-governed and bound by the local coindexed Comp. As one would expect, nothing comparable exists with uninflected infinitives.

(31) a. parece [eles estarem felizes]
     b. que crianças$_i$ parece $_S$'[e$_i$ $_S$[e$_i$ estarem felizes]]

Now consider subject complements. Forms like *eu fazer isso vai ser difícil* 'I do it will be difficult' or the extraposed *vai ser difícil eu fazer isso* occur only in the standard form of the language, where *eu* receives case from the AGR element to which the infinitive is attached. However, forms like *para mim fazer isso vai ser difícil* and *vai ser difícil para mim fazer isso* occur in both forms of the language, but with different analyses. In the innovative language, *para mim* may be construed as part of the embedded clause, *mim* receiving case from the complementizer *para* (see (32a) and (32b)). In the standard form, *para mim* must be a main clause PP, from which *mim* may control the empty lower subject (see (32c) and (32d)).

(32) a. $_S$[para mim fazer isso] vai ser difícil

b. vai ser difícil $_S$[para mim fazer isso]

c. $_{PP}$[para mim] $_S$[PRO fazer isso] vai ser difícil

d. vai ser difícil $_{PP}$[para mim] $_S$[PRO fazer isso]

This predicts that any adverb occurring between *mim* and *fazer* in (32a) and (32b), where *mim* is the subject of *fazer*, is construed as part of the embedded clause, whereas such an adverb in (32c) and (32d), which occur only in the standard form of the language, may be interpreted as part of the matrix clause. This seems to be correct. So structures (33a) and (33b) are characteristic of the innovating language, whereas (33c) and (33d) occur only in standard dialects.

(33) a. [para mim ainda hoje fazer isso] vai ser difícil

for   me   still   today to-do this will be difficult

b. vai ser difícil [para mim ainda hoje fazer isso]

c. [para mim] [ainda hoje] [fazer isso] vai ser difícil

d. vai ser difícil [para mim] [ainda hoje] [fazer isso]

Adjunct clauses with an inflected infinitive, such as (27e), are analyzed as (34). In the standard form, the embedded subject is governed by and receives its nominative case from AGR.

(34) eles entraram em casa $_{PP}$[sem $_S$[eu ver + AGR]]

In each of the constructions discussed so far, there is considerable overlap in the sentences used by both sets of speakers; the differences may be accounted for straightforwardly in terms of the presence or absence of AGR on the infinitives. In many of the cases discussed, as AGR is lost, there is an alternative governor for the lexical subject (namely the prepositional element in Comp), and this has been exploited by the innovative dialect. Where there was no alternative governor, as in the complements to epistemic, declarative, and factive verbs, where *para* does not occur

((27a)–(27c)), the infinitival form has been replaced by a complement introduced by *que* with the verb in the indicative.

It is important to recognize the idealization involved in this account of the two dialects. The loss of inflectional endings in the relevant forms of Brazilian Portuguese is a gradual and complicated process which is not entirely understood; speakers' intuitions are not always sharp. But sometimes they are very sharp: a professor reported that she consciously abandoned the *para* + oblique NP forms because they shocked her husband, and a graduate student was (as a child) reprimanded for using such forms and told not to talk like an Indian. There are speakers who use only the forms characterized here as innovative, and a few Brazilians use only the "standard" forms with the inflected infinitive, even in their spoken language. The bifurcation described here seems to be real and illuminates the mixed forms that are sometimes used.

The innovative dialect reflects a fairly general tendency in Brazilian Portuguese, in which various inflectional endings are being lost (Guy 1981). This is a morphological change, but one with syntactic consequences. It seems that the loss of the morphological agreement markers on infinitives coincides over a significant range with the loss of the abstract AGR element to which an infinitive might move, and loss of AGR predicts different syntactic phenomena: specifically, the rise of alternative forms where there is an alternative governor for the subject NP, and the loss of infinitives with lexical subjects in contexts where there was no alternative governor. Because the new syntactic phenomena can be viewed as manifesting a single change in the grammar (the absence of V-to-INFL movement for infinitives), it is plausible to claim that one parameter setting is involved: presence/absence of AGR with infinitivals. Once that parameter is set, an interesting variety of syntactic phenomena are predicted for each setting.

This account shows that if the INFL properties of embedded clauses vary from one linguistic environment to another, they may entail different parameter settings. This, in turn, entails that the parameter-setting process may be sensitive to an embedded INFL, which must, therefore, be taken to be part of the potential triggering experience. Consequently, the change taking place in some forms of Brazilian Portuguese complements the Middle English changes discussed above and serves to illustrate the extent of the structures to which the parameter-setting process is sensitive.

4.3 Conclusion

The formulation of degree-0 learnability adopted here makes some precise claims about the cutoff point to the child's triggering experience: it claims that there are structural limits to the complexity of the triggering data, and that parameter setting is sensitive only to data from unembedded binding Domains. These will include most data from matrix clauses and certain elements of embedded clauses: the Comp, properties of INFL, and subjects not governed by a local AGR marker. We have seen various reasons to believe that something along these lines is correct, but the historical changes discussed in chapters 3 and 4 suggest that the cutoff point has been drawn quite accurately. In chapter 3 it was shown that the way in which the verb-order parameter came to be set differently in twelfth-century English indicates that children have no access to the position of complements in embedded clauses. Chapter 4 has examined changes in English and Brazilian Portuguese which show that children do have access to the properties of embedded subjects not governed by a local AGR (section 4.1) and to the properties of an embedded INFL (section 4.2), but not to the form of a verb that remains in its VP. The form of the argument has been that diachronic changes would have had to be very different if properties of the embedded VP could shape emerging grammars. Taken together, these historical studies corroborate the hypothesis of chapter 2: that children are degree-0 learners and that degree-0 embedding is best defined in terms of binding Domains.

Chapter 5
The English Case System

Section 4.2 examined some syntactic changes in one form of Brazilian Portuguese which are the direct result of a morphological change: the loss of infinitival agreement markers. So the syntactic structure depends on morphological properties: a change in morphology, i.e. in part of the triggering experience, entails the demise of an abstract element, and new syntactic structures emerge as a result. This chapter examines a similar phenomenon in Middle English, in which a number of syntactic changes may be viewed as resulting from a morphological change: the loss of dative case and the emergence of a purely structural case system. The syntactic changes, therefore, can be explained, like the changes in Brazilian Portuguese, in terms of a close correspondence between morphological and syntactic categories. In being induced by morphological changes, these new parameter settings are examples of a common type of syntactic change, which strongly suggests that morphological properties play an important role in setting certain syntactic parameters. We shall see another example of this when we examine some aspects of the emergence of the English auxiliary verbs in section 6.2.

The first four chapters have examined a particular form of degree-0 learnability, arguing that the child's triggering experience has some precise structural limits. This chapter moves away from that concern and begins to investigate how morphological phenomena may help to set syntactic parameters, again drawing evidence from historical change. We shall need to grind through several derivations, but the reward will be a useful perspective for the changes that will be discussed in chapter 6. After all, the two major changes that occurred in Middle English, the change in the verb-order parameter and the simplification of the inflectional system, had far-reaching consequences. These changes may be interdependent in some ill-understood fashion, but a question that analysts often pose for any Middle English change is whether it is linked to one or the other of these two central changes.

I shall begin by examining how one might explain the emergence of some new passive forms in Middle English.

5.1   An Inadequate Account of NP Movement[1]

Universal Grammar makes available for particular grammars various classes of devices: statements of lexical redundancy, projection types, movement processes, principles of interpretation, and so on. Each class of device has distinct formal properties, given by Universal Grammar. There is now an extensive literature about restrictions on the expressive power of movement processes. I assume, in particular, that they are insensitive to grammatical relations, cannot be annotated for optional versus obligatory application, and may not be sensitive to quantificational statements, dominance relations, semantic features, or the other items familiar from early textbooks on generative grammar; it is also impossible to state lexical exceptions to these rules. So movement processes simply move an arbitrary constituent at some level of representation. Such an operation is constrained by general conditions provided by Universal Grammar and must contribute to an S-structure that can receive a phonetic and a semantic interpretation.

Lexical redundancy rules, however, have quite a different shape and relate subcategorization frames in the lexicon. Redundancy rules, therefore, apply only to base-generated structures and affect particular lexical items (not necessarily all words of a given syntactic category). Since subcategorization frames are local (Chomsky 1965) and refer only to adjacent categories, redundancy rules operate on very restricted domains; however, they are able to mention various categories, relating a noun to an adjective and so on.

Along these lines, a distinction between movement processes and lexical redundancy rules seems entirely plausible. Wasow (1977) accepted such a distinction in Universal Grammar and argued that the grammar of Modern English had both a lexical rule and a movement process for passive sentences. So (1a) was derived from (1b) by movement and could not be related to an active *somebody expected* $_{S'}$[*John to win*] via a lexical rule: the strict subcategorization frame of *expect*, being local, specifies only that *expect* is followed by S' and the frame does not refer to any internal NP.

(1) a. John$_i$ was expected $_{S'}$[e$_i$ to win]

    b. NP was expected $_{S'}$[John to win]

A simple passive like *John was irritated*, on the other hand, might be base-generated and related to the corresponding active by a lexical rule. Wasow did not state the lexical rule that he had in mind, but presumably it was along the lines of (2).

(2)

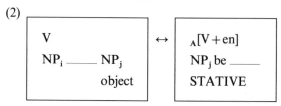

This says that there is a one-to-one relation (subject to lexical exceptions) between verbs that have direct objects and verbs that have participial forms that are adjectives and have a stative semantics; an NP that can occur as the direct object of the active verb can occur as the subject of the adjectival form, and vice versa.

I have noted that some passives, for example (1a), cannot be base-generated and then related to the corresponding active by a lexical rule. But why not the reverse? Why not derive all passives by movement and dispense with the lexical rule (2)? Wasow's answer was that the lexical rule stipulates that the passive participle is an adjective and conveys stative force; not all participles have these two properties, and consequently they are not related to the active by the lexical rule. There are three difficulties with this account.

Difficulty 1

The lexical rule (2), stipulating a semantic feature and a case relation in addition to the subcategorization frame, contains a great deal of information. This information may turn out to be necessary in order to achieve descriptive adequacy, but one wants to know how rules of this type can be attained by a child under normal circumstances, without access to negative data, and so forth. *A priori*, the rule looks suspect.

Difficulty 2

The distinction between adjectival and nonadjectival passive participles is by no means clear. Wasow offered four criteria for adjectivehood: ability to occur after *very*, after the *un-* prefix, as a predicate to such verbs as *seem*, *act*, and *sound*, and in prenominal position. None of these criteria is very persuasive in isolation, and in combination they do not define the correct set of participles.

Several simple passives with stative semantics cannot occur after *very*:

(3) *the door was very closed
    *the house is very owned by Max

Ability to occur with *un-* is not a good diagnostic for adjectivehood, because many clear examples of adjectives do not take *un-*: *unangry*, *untall*, *unfat*. Therefore, one is not surprised that not only movement passives but also several lexical (i.e., adjectival) passives do not occur with *un-*: *the door was unclosed, *Fred was unirritated at John*. In many dialects clear cases of movement passives occur with *seem*: *John seems expected to win*. Finally, the fact that *expected to win* cannot occur prenominally does not make *expected* a nonadjective; an alternative explanation for the nonoccurrence of *the expected to win athlete* lies in the requirement that prenominal modifiers in English must be head-final—hence the unacceptability of *the obvious to everybody solution* and *the interested in genetics linguists*.

Independent of these criteria, Wasow (1977, p. 341) argued, to take *given* and *considered* as base-generated adjectives would entail an otherwise unnecessary phrase-structure rule (or projection type), $A' \rightarrow A$ (NP), for passives such as *John was given a book/considered a fool*. In Lightfoot 1979 it was argued that these forms should be treated as lexical and therefore adjectival passives, if Wasow's criteria are invoked. Moreover, they can be treated adjectivally without complicating the grammar. The allegedly unnecessary projection type is needed for phrases like *near the house* (where *near* is probably an adjective, if only because it has comparative and superlative forms: *nearer, nearest*). This is not surprising if one assumes a strong version of the phrase-structure conventions. If all lexical categories are subject to the same geometrical constraints, the fact that V' can consist of a head (V) and a complement (NP, PP, or S') suggests that N', P', and A' may have a similar complement structure; it would therefore follow that, like a V, an A could be followed by a noun phrase. Such a strong version of phrase-structure conventions was assumed in earlier chapters and seems quite plausible.[2]

Difficulty 3

If Wasow was correct to postulate two ways of deriving passive constructions, there would be massive indeterminacy in the grammar, in that a simple passive like *the door was closed* might be related to the corresponding active by the lexical rule or by the movement process. The only empirical claim here is that it will have a stative meaning when it is base-generated and a dynamic meaning when movement is involved. But if problem 2 is not resolved and if there is no reason to distinguish adjectival and nonadjectival participles, then there is no reason to adopt two *syntactic* analyses. At a more speculative level, if passives have two quite different analyses, one wonders why they look so similar at surface structure.

In earlier work I adopted Wasow's essential framework, ignoring difficulties 1 and 3 and amending the framework to avoid some aspects of difficulty 2. I then argued that the movement passive did not exist in Old English grammars and was introduced at the end of the Middle English period. In Lightfoot 1979 I went further and argued that a device of NP Movement was introduced—that is, a more general device than just a passive transformation; a device affecting other construction types. I took movement to be involved in the derivation of (4) (but, unlike Wasow, not in the derivation of *John was considered a fool*) and argued that there was no motivation for such movement before late Middle English.[3]

(4) a. John$_i$ was expected $_{S'}$[e$_i$ to win]
  b. John$_i$ was given e$_i$ a book
  c. John$_i$ was taken advantage of e$_i$
  d. the bed$_i$ was slept in e$_i$

Also occurring for the first time in late Middle English were sentences like (5), where movement takes place over an active intransitive verb and an adjective. These forms and (4a) were discussed in section 4.1.

(5) John$_i$ seems $_{S'}$[e$_i$ to be happy]
  John$_i$ is certain $_{S'}$[e$_i$ to win]

To say that this movement operation was introduced in late Middle English accounts for the introduction of sentences like (4) and (5), but the analysis is inadequate for two reasons. First, if movement processes are stated in very general form and therefore do not hold of specific construction types, it is implausible to claim that Old English lacked them, because it had fairly free word order and therefore movement processes presumably were operative—although deeper analysis may show that the movement was stylistic and therefore not part of core grammar. (The occurrence of objective genitives, *Rome's destruction*, does not constitute evidence for movement, because the potential source, *the destruction (of) Rome*, seems not to have occurred in the very earliest texts; a common variant was *destruction Rome's*, which could be related to *Rome's destruction* by a stylistic permutation. I am grateful to Anthony Warner for that point.[4])

Second, even if the description had been correct, no explanation was offered for why the Move NP operation should be introduced; one would want to know how the linguistic environment had changed such that a grammar with the operation was triggered by childhood experience. Of course, not every historical change must be explained in this way. But it is not plausible to attribute a set of simultaneous innovations like (4) and (5), or even just (4b)–(4d), to a chance factor, such as foreign influence or stylistic force stemming from a novel expression.

The two inadequacies of the historical account and the three problems with the synchronic framework on which it was based suggest that it may be possible to formulate something better. Wasow (1978) sought to do this by discarding the movement analysis altogether and handling all passives with two kinds of lexical rules. He assumed the "realistic" framework of Bresnan (1978), and extended the definition of lexical rules so that one type can apply nonlocally and does not refer to thematic relations. One could then subsume (4a) under this new kind of nonlocal lexical rule for verbal passives, but there was a high price. In Wasow 1977, the essential localness of lexical rules had been used to explain the nonoccurrence of *John's inexperience showed to be a problem* (cf. *John's inexperience showed* and *Mary showed John's inexperience to be a problem*); now it would have to be attributed to the formulation of the Middle rule in English, which just happens to be local (that is, it happens to apply only to the thematic relations of such verbs as *show*). One wonders how this knowledge could be attained by a child without access to negative data (i.e., information that the relevant sentence is ungrammatical), inasmuch as the rule might have been nonlocal. (Wasow's enriched theory of lexical rules is loose enough for a nonlocal Middle rule to be available.) One is again left with no explanation for why the nonlocal lexical passive rule was introduced in Middle English. Futhermore, lexical rules would have to be subject to some condition to avoid *John was expected would win.*[5]

Lieber (1979) offered an interesting critique, extending the scope of the lexical rule so that it related the base-generated *John was given the book* to the active (unlike Wasow 1977 and Lightfoot 1979, who invoked movement for such sentences). Lieber argued that the lexical passive rule was as in (2) throughout the history of English, crucially applying only to an "objective" NP. In Old and early Middle English, *John* would have dative case in *I gave John the book* and therefore could not be related to *John was given the book* by (2). As the dative case was lost, *John* in such constructions became subsumed under "objective" and was liable to be affected by (2). There is something attractive about this notion—and, I think, something correct, in that Lieber related the emergence of *John was given a book* to a morphological change. Nonetheless, a fundamental flaw is that she assumed a movement analysis for sentences like (4a), (4c), (4d), (5a), and (5b) and gave no reason for why the movement rule did not apply in the Old English period to *John* in *NP was given John the book* to yield the nonoccurring *John was given the book*. She was also open to the objections concerning Wasow's (1977) dual analysis of passives: the lack of reasons to distinguish adjectival and nonadjectival participles, and the resulting indeterminacy. Finally, Lieber dealt with only part of the problem and ignored the other innovative forms.

The moves of Wasow (1978) and Lieber do not represent an advance. The essential difficulty is the dual analysis of passives. What is common to the analyses of Lieber and Wasow is a permissive definition of lexical rules. In contrast, I shall investigate eliminating altogether the lexical rule that relates actives and passives, postulating instead a movement analysis for all passives. In doing this, I do not deny the distinction between movement and lexical rules outlined above (i.e., the distinction assumed in Wasow 1977 and Lightfoot 1979, not in Wasow 1978). That distinction strikes me as plausible, but I no longer think that it is relevant for passives.

I shall argue that the syntactic movement operation has always been part of English grammars and that the lexical rule (2) has never played a role. In that case, one will want to know why the movement process did not yield the sentences of (4), which did not occur before late Middle English. I shall preserve the attractive aspect of Lieber's analysis by relating the innovation to the change in the morphological case system.

Before embarking on this, I draw attention to a methodological point raised by Lieber. In Lightfoot 1979 I noted a small number of Old English sentences like *she was seen to shine*, which Lieber (1979, p. 671) took as a basis for denying that (4a) represented a Middle English innovation. She also denied that passives of complex verbs ((4c)) and prepositional (pseudo-) passives ((4d)) were Middle English innovations, because there were a few examples in OE texts and

it is possible that . . . the gradual increase does not reflect the fact that the construction was actually used more frequently in the spoken language, but rather means that it merely occurred in manuscripts more frequently. . . . If it is the case . . . that occurrence in manuscripts cannot be directly correlated with occurrence in the language, then even a single example from the thirteenth century of a construction such as the pseudo-passive is significant and cannot be discounted [footnote omitted]. There is therefore little basis for the claim that the prepositional passive is a fifteenth-sixteenth century innovation. (p. 672)

Lieber described this as "an important methodological point."

In studying syntactic change, one is bound to one's texts for data about early stages of some language; one should never discount data, but one must interpret the texts with some philological skill. Taking "a single example from the thirteenth century" as evidence that such sentences were grammatical for all speakers of the language may allow one to suppose that there was no change in grammars and therefore nothing to explain, but this does not strike me as sensible. If, in fifteenth-century texts, there is a significant increase in certain sentence types, *rising from near zero* (which Lieber concedes), it is reasonable to suppose that there was a change in many individual grammars, i.e., that many individuals began to set some parameter of Universal Grammar differently from many of their forebears. One would therefore want to explain why that parameter was set differently and precisely what the parameter was. That is the approach I take. I do not suppose that there was an entity "the grammar of Middle English," which changed uniformly and simultaneously for all speakers of English, although it is often useful to abstract away from the kind of variation that Lieber emphasizes.

5.2 A Theory of Abstract Case

Here I take up the idea that Universal Grammar makes available two kinds of cases: those that are assigned only at S-structure and those that are assigned only at D-structure. S-structure cases are assigned to NPs on the basis only of the structural notion of government (see chapter 2), and I shall refer to them as structural: NPs receive nominative or objective case when governed by AGR or by a verb, as in (6).

(6) Structural Case:
   a. NP → nominative iff governed by AGR
   b. NP → objective iff governed by V

Cases are assigned to the S-structures (7) and (8) as follows. In (7), $_{NP}$[John] is governed by AGR but not by *see* and is therefore nominative. $_{NP}$[Mary] is governed by *see* and not by AGR and therefore is objective (AGR does not govern $_{NP}$[Mary] because a VP node dominates $_{NP}$[Mary] and not AGR). In (8), $_{NP}$[John] becomes nominative and $_{NP}$[e_i] becomes objective in the same way as in (7); *who* occurs in an initial position and does not receive any case by these rules.

(7) John $_{INFL}$[AGR] $_{VP}$[see Mary]

(8) who$_i$ $_{INFL}$[AGR]$_j$ $_S$[John e_j $_{VP}$[see e_i]]

These cases are assigned on a purely structural basis, being quite unrelated to thematic roles. So, nominative is assigned to all NPs governed by AGR, even if they carry no thematic role (expletives) or only a thematic role assigned in a lower clause (*she seems to be happy*). Likewise, objective is assigned to any NP governed by a V, even when the verb assigns no thematic role to it (*Jim expected there to be a riot, Poseidon made/saw it rain*). The structural case-assignment procedures of (6) are given in Universal Grammar, and this entails that all individual grammars may distinguish nominative and objective cases in this way. There may be other structural cases, such as the genitive assigned to a NP specifier (*John's hat*).

Other cases are more closely related to thematic roles, less dependent on such structural considerations as government, and assigned at D-structure, remaining at all levels of representation. For example, in Latin and Old English, where particular verbs may subcategorize for a dative or genitive object, these cases would be inherently associated with the relevant NP from D-structure onward. Furthermore, unlike structural cases, inherent cases are assigned even when the verb is contained in a passive participle: *he was* $_A[_V[give] + en]$ *the book* (see the discussion of the government properties of participles below). I shall refer to such cases as "inherent."

In addition, Universal Grammar imposes the following requirements:

(9) a. A variable is inserted into a position containing a case-marked trace, as in (8), but never into any other position.
   b. At LF there is a one-to-one relation between quantifiers and variables.
   c. At S-structure, all lexical Ns except fronted *wh* items (which are quantifiers) have exactly one case.

Under such a theory of case in Universal Grammar, particular grammars may vary according to whether they have oblique and other base-assigned inherent cases. If a verb assigns an oblique case at D-structure, the oblique NP may move to Comp by *wh* movement but it may not become the subject of a passive verb. So the Latin verb *cred-* 'believe' assigns an oblique (dative) case, which must therefore be assigned at D-structure. An initial (10a) would become (10b) by *wh* movement. The case-marked trace becomes a variable linked to the quantifier *cui*. However, an initial (10c) does not yield a well-formed "personal passive" **Marcus creditur*: if the dative NP moves to the subject position, it acquires nominative case, thereby having two cases and violating (9c). In addition, the trace in (10d) has case but cannot be interpreted as a variable, since there is no quantifier present. The only well-formed output from (10c) with a passive verb is the "impersonal" *creditur Marco*, where *Marco* retains its oblique case (which is not "absorbed" by the passive verb). The same phenomenon is illustrated in German and Russian, where oblique NPs do not become subjects of passive verbs.

(10) a. Comp [tu INFL cred- cui]
                  Obl

   b. cui_i [tu credis e_i] 'who do you believe?'
     Obl   Obl

   c. NP INFL cred- Marco
               Obl

   d. Marcus creditur e_i
     Obl   Obl
     Nom

It has been argued that French has structural cases assigned by the procedures of (6) and, in addition, that prepositions in this language assign oblique case at D-structure. However, this addition seems to be unnecessary. An initial (11a) would become (11b) by *wh* movement, with the trace not head-governed. (Recall that prepositions are not head-governors, as first argued in Kayne 1981a.) Consequently (11b) violates the phonological constraint that traces be head-governed (Aoun, Hornstein, Lightfoot, and Weinberg 1987 and chapter 2 above), regardless of whether the trace in (11b) has oblique or objective case.

(11) a. vous INFL parler à $_{NP}$[qui]
   b. qui_i vous INFL parler à $_{NP}$[e_i]

Modern English, however, is different: here the result of *wh* movement is (12b), and a reanalysis process (Hornstein and Weinberg 1981) makes *speak to* into a complex verb.[6] At S-structure (6) assigns nominative to *you* and objective to $_{NP}$[e_i], yielding (12c). Since the trace is now both head-governed and case-marked, a variable must be inserted, yielding a proper quantificational reading: for which *x*, you spoke to *x*.

(12) a. you INFL speak to who
   b. who_i INFL you speak to $_{NP}$[e_i]
   c. who_i INFL [you] $_V$[speak to] $_{NP}$[e_i]
        Nom   Obj

So those languages that allow preposition stranding by *wh* movement have a reanalysis rule: Well-formed structures emerge only if the preposition is reanalyzed in some fashion such that the trace can be head-governed. If prepositions assign D-structure case, the trace following the preposition would have its inherent case and thus a variable (this differs from Lightfoot 1981a). For preposition stranding in passives, therefore, there are two necessary ingredients: (i) presence of an optional reanalysis rule converting a structure like $_A$[speak + en] $_{PP}$[about NP] into $_A$[speak + en about] NP (or some other structure where the NP is head-governed), and (ii) no D-structure case assignment to nouns governed by a preposition. Put in terms of learnability, preposition stranding with *wh* movement (*who did you speak to?*) triggers a reanalysis operation yielding a head-governed trace, and an indirect passive (*John was given the book*) could arise only if there was no inherent case on the trace of *John*; a pseudo-passive (*the bed was slept in*) requires both the reanalysis operation and the absence of inherent case.

Consider an initial (13a). If reanalysis takes place, subsequent movement to subject position yields (13b). The trace has no case: it received none at D-structure, and it is governed by neither AGR nor V at S-structure, and therefore it receives no variable. *John* is assigned nominative by (6a) and a nonquantificational reading is derived. Correct result. If reanalysis does not take place, the result of NP movement is (13c), where the trace receives objective case and therefore a variable in logical form. Now there is a variable but no quantifier, an impossible result by (9b), and the trace fails to be head-governed.

(13) a. NP INFL be $_A$[speak + en] $_{PP}$[about $_{NP}$[John]]

     b. John$_i$ INFL be $_A$[speak + en about] $_{NP}$[e$_i$]

     c. John$_i$ INFL be $_A$[speak + en] $_{PP}$[about $_{NP}$[e$_i$]]

If prepositions assign oblique case at D-structure, *Jean* would receive oblique in (14a). If *Jean* were moved to subject position and received nominative by (6a) at S-structure, as in (14b), it would then have two cases and would be ill formed by (9c). In addition, the case-marked trace could not be treated as a variable, because there is no operator.

(14) a. NP INFL être $_A$[parlé] $_{PP}$[avec $_{NP}$[Jean]]

                            Obl

     b. $_{NP}$[Jean]$_i$ INFL être $_A$[parlé] $_{PP}$[avec $_{NP}$[e$_i$]]

         Obl   Obl

         Nom

However, the trace would also fail to be head-governed, violating our phonological constraint. Therefore (14b) would be ill formed regardless of the case on the trace, and one does not need to claim that French prepositions assign inherent case.

The subject of an infinitive in French generally does not get case, presumably because it is not governed at S-structure by a case assigner: *je crois [Jean être intelligent]. Therefore, something other than case conflict is needed to block *je crois [Jean_i être parlé à e_i], where Jean might carry along its D-structure case, if prepositions assign inherent cases in French. However, the trace would also have inherent case, hence an uninterpreted variable. If French prepositions do not assign inherent case, the structure would still be ill formed, because the trace would also fail to be head-governed.

The different passivizing possibilities of English and French, like the different possibilities for preposition stranding by wh movement, stem simply from the lack of a reanalysis rule in French. But our discussion of Latin showed that a NP with an inherent case at D-structure may not become the subject of a passive verb, regardless of whether there is a reanalysis process.

5.3   The History of NP Movement

I return now to the history of NP movement. I shall argue that English grammars have always had a movement process, but that some verbs once assigned oblique case at D-structure. I shall also consider the possibility that prepositions once assigned oblique case, but there is no strong evidence for this. The reanalysis process invoked above also first emerged in early Middle English, at about the same time. These, then, are the relevant parameters of grammar for which new settings arose in Middle English.

Under the theory of case I have outlined, movement of an NP to another NP position takes place only from a non-case-marked position; if the NP is a wh element moving to an initial position (i.e., a quantifier), it moves only from a position that is case-marked and contains a variable in logical form.

Consider first the complement to an N. Under the strong version of phrase-structure conventions, an N may project to an N' that also contains an XP or a clause as a complement. This allows the structures of (15).

(15) a. Spec _N'[_N[portrait] _NP[Saskia]]
     b. Spec _N'[_N[portrait] _PP[of _NP[Saskia]]]

In (15a) Saskia is not case-marked and the structure is ill formed by (9c); in (15b) Saskia receives case (objective in Modern English, but possibly oblique in early Middle English). Since Saskia in (15a) has no case, it may move to another NP position, giving the objective genitive Saskia's *portrait*; the residual trace has no case, therefore no variable, and therefore no quantificational reading.[7] If, instead of *Saskia*, we had *who*, the trace of *who* would receive no variable, and so no quantificational reading would be possible: **who$_i$ did you see a portrait e$_i$?*

In (15b), movement of *Saskia* to the Specifier position would leave a trace, which would receive structural case in Modern English and therefore would receive a variable; since there is no quantifier binding the variable, the structure is ill formed by (9b): **Saskia's portrait of*. Such structures were also ill formed in early Middle English, but perhaps partly for a different reason: if *Saskia* receives oblique case at D-structure and the possessive case at S-structure through being in a Specifier slot, it would have two cases and would violate (9c) in addition to (9b). Suppose now that we replace *Saskia* by *who*. As *who* moved, its trace (whether oblique or objective) was not head-governed in early Middle English. In Modern English, however, *who$_i$ did you see a portrait of e$_i$* is well formed: *who* receives no case at D-structure, but after movement and reanalysis its trace is head-governed by the complex verb *see a portrait of* and acquires objective case and a variable. Therefore, for all stages of English, this case theory yields correct results for movement from a nominal complement to NP and to initial positions, and we do not need to claim that prepositions assigned oblique case in early English. So far, Hornstein and Weinberg's reanalysis process is all that we need to describe the differences between early and later English.

Continuing with a strong version of phrase-structure conventions, I assume that adjectives have the same projections as other lexical categories, allowing the usual complements, and that in the grammar of modern English A does not assign case to its complement NP—with the exception of *near* (and possibly *like* and *worth*), which does assign case (see note 10). In Old English, however, lexical adjectives could assign dative or genitive case to their complements:

(16) a. þeh hie þæs wyrþe næron   (*Orosius* 104,5)
      though they that + genitive worthy not-were
      'though they weren't worthy of that'
   b. monige sindon me swiðe onlice   (*Cura Pastoralis* 24,7)
      many   are   me + dative very similar
      'many are very similar to me'

Such cases are syntactically oblique and thus assigned at D-structure. The fact that oblique case is inherent predicts that the complement NP may move to an initial position, leaving a case-marked variable, as in (17), but not to a position in which it would receive structural case in addition to its D-structure oblique.

(17) who$_i$ + dative is he [e$_i$ + dative similar]?

Such a treatment of adjectives makes available a convenient analysis of passive participles. The discussions of Wasow 1977 and Lightfoot 1979 conflated two separate questions: (i) Should a passive construction be related to the active lexically or by movement? (ii) Is the passive participle adjectival or not? Both Wasow and I assumed that lexical passives but not movement passives were adjectival. As was noted above, the criteria for distinguishing adjectival and nonadjectival participles were not good, and the distinction may not exist. For English it seems reasonable to treat all passive participles as members of the same syntactic category: adjective.

Adjectives and participles may be coordinated (*the workers are angry and alienated by their work*), and they share many of the same specifiers. Parallelism in coordination is merely suggestive, but overlapping specifiers are stronger evidence for a single category: In general, specifiers are closed-class items which are peculiar to a particular category (Emonds 1986). This parallelism reaches back into Old English, where *swiþe* 'much', *to* 'too', and *wel* 'very much' occurred freely with adjectives and past participles. Indeed, Old English offers further evidence for parallelism: the adjectival inflectional endings, including the strong/weak distinctions, also appear on past participles. This persisted into early Middle English, when the only surviving inflectional ending, -e, also occurred on past participles in the appropriate contexts. Consequently I see no strong reason to distinguish past participles categorically from adjectives at any stage in the history of English. Thus, the initial structure for *the bread was stolen* would be (18) at all stages. I shall assume here that A is the right category label, but this is not crucial. Whether or not [$_V$steal + en] is labeled A, the passive participle "absorbs" structural case (Chomsky 1981), and therefore the complement NP cannot receive structural case by procedure (6b); perfect participles do not absorb structural case in the same way (... *has stolen the bread*), and they may not be adjectival. The trace of *the bread* in (18) does not receive oblique case, because *steal* + *en* is not a lexical adjective.

(18) NP INFL be $_{AP}[_{A'}[_A[_V[$ steal$] + en] _{NP}[$the bread$]]]$

If $_{NP}[$the bread$]$ does not move, it receives no case. If it moves to an NP position, as in (19), it receives nominative at S-structure; again, the trace receives no case and cannot be a variable. This is a good result, and one is not surprised that such passives occur at all stages of English.

(19) $_{NP}[$the bread$]$ INFL be $_{AP}[_{A'}[_A[_V[$steal$] + en] _{NP}[e]]]$

In Old and early Middle English and other languages, some verbs assign dative or genitive case to their object NP. These objects can usually move to an initial position: Latin *cui credis?* 'whom do you trust?', or Greek *tínos deîtai* 'what does he need?'. This fact suggests that a variable can be inserted into the object position, and therefore that a trace in this position has case, as indicated in (10). This follows naturally if these nonstructural cases are inherently associated with their NP. Such cases, however, are insensitive to government and are not absorbed by a passive participle. Consequently, in (20a) *forwyrn-* assigns oblique (dative) case to *him* despite being part of a participle. An oblique object cannot become the subject of a passive verb, and this follows from the theory: in an initial (20a), *him* receives oblique case and therefore cannot subsequently move to subject position and receive nominative at S-structure, where the case conflict would violate (9c).[8] Also, the trace would be case-marked, and hence a variable, but it would have no associated operator (unless *him* was a topic, on the assumption (Chomsky 1981) that topicalization involves operator-variable constructions). Consequently, the oblique/dative is retained, as in (20b), yielding an "impersonal passive." (Here I ignore the underlying object-verb order of Old English.)

(20) a. NP INFL be $_{AP}[_{A'}[_A[_V[forwyrn-] + en]$ $_{NP}[him]$ $_{NP}[ðæs$ inganges]]]

b. and him wæs swa forwyrnad ðæs inganges   Hexameron St. Basil (ed. Norman) 24)

and him was thus prevented the entry

Such impersonal passives do not occur in Old English with a stranded preposition: *him_i was talked to e_i. Such forms could not occur before the reanalysis operation became available, because the trace was not head-governed; they came into the language with the possibility of reanalyzing *talked to* as a complex head governing the trace. The requirement of head-government and the absence of a reanalysis operation also explain the nonoccurrence of topics with stranded prepositions in Old English (*Kim, I spoke to*). *Him was talked to* would also be ungrammatical for independent reasons, if Old English prepositions assigned oblique case: in that event, the trace would be case-marked but not interpretable as a variable.

The existence of inherent case also explains why the indirect passive *John was given the book* did not occur in Old English. In an initial (21), *John* would receive oblique case at D-structure in Old English, and therefore subsequent movement to subject position would result in case conflict and a variable without an operator. Since Modern English has no oblique case, *John* receives no case at D-structure, and subsequent movement to subject yields a well-formed structure where *John* has nominative case and the trace is caseless (and therefore not a variable). So the introduction of *John was given the book* can be viewed as a function of the loss of the thematically based oblique case.[9]

(21) NP INFL be $_{AP}[_{A'}[_A[_V[give] + en]\ _{NP}[John]\ _{NP}[the\ book]]]$

Consider now the passives *the bed was slept in* and *John was taken advantage of*, which did not occur in Old English. The D-structure would be (22), and if reanalysis does not apply to build $_A[sleep+en\ in]\ _A[take+en\ advantage\ of]$, subsequent movement of *the bed* or *John* to subject position yields a trace which is not head-governed. In Modern English, however, with no oblique case assigned at D-structure, the result of reanalysis and movement to subject position is a well-formed structure. Therefore the introduction of these passives is also explained by the introduction of reanalysis.

(22) INFL be $_{A'}[_A[_V[sleep] + en]\ _{PP}[in\ _{NP}[the\ bed]]]$
      INFL be $_{A'}[_A[_V[take] + en]\ advantage\ _{PP}[of\ _{NP}[John]]]$

As prepositional passives developed, so did the possibility of preposition stranding with *wh* movement. This can also be related to the introduction of a reanalysis process. Consider first the straightforward instance of *wh* movement in (23).

(23) a. $who_i\ _S[_{NP}[e_i]\ INFL\ _{VP}[see\ John]]$
      b. $who_i\ _S[_{NP}[John]\ INFL\ _{VP}[_V[see]\ _{NP}[e_i]]]$

In neither instance would *who* receive a D-structure case at any stage of history. In (23a) the trace receives nominative at S-structure and therefore becomes a variable; in (23b) the trace receives objective and also becomes a variable. In Modern English, *who did you speak to?* would be derived as in (12): after reanalysis, the trace following the preposition would be head-governed and would receive objective, becoming a variable. In Old English, a trace after a preposition would fail to be head-governed in the absence of a reanalysis process.

We have cranked through some derivations in this section, and we have a theory that accounts for the continuous existence of forms like *the bread was stolen* and *Saskia's portrait* and for the new passives of (4b)–(4d) (*John was given a book, John was taken advantage of,* and *the bed was slept in*) and for the new possibilities for preposition stranding with *wh* movement (*who did you speak to?*). These innovations are attributed to the loss of base-assigned oblique case and the introduction of a reanalysis process. Clearly verbs like *give* and *forwyrn-* assigned oblique case in Old English, but we still have no compelling reason to argue that prepositions assigned oblique case. All the prepositional innovations may be attributable to the new reanalysis operation.

5.4 Triggering a New Abstract Case System

Because this reanalysis operation constructs a complex verb from adjacent material at D-structure, it could not have been available until the verb-order parameter was given its new setting, by the twelfth century (chapter 3). Before that, when the VP was verb-final, verbs and prepositions were not adjacent: $_{V'}[$ $_{PP}[about\ linguistics]\ speak]$. With the new parameter setting, *speak* and *about* became adjacent and could be reanalyzed into a complex verb: *speak about*. The evidence suggests that the reanalysis option was in fact taken very soon after it became available.

Reanalysis permitted the possibility of *wh* questions with stranded prepositions. Regardless of whether the trace had an inherent oblique case or a structural objective, one would expect to find structures like (24), which result from reanalysis and movement. The trace would be case-marked (either oblique or objective), hence a variable.

(24) who$_i$ did $_S[$Kim $_V[$speak to] e$_i]$

Reanalysis would not permit passives with stranded prepositions or indirect passives, unless also oblique case was lost: if the moved NP had oblique case at D-structure, it could not subsequently acquire nominative case at S-structure without violating the one-to-one relation of NPs and cases ((9c)). This bifurcation is manifested in Icelandic, which allows preposition stranding in *wh* questions but not in passives with nominative subjects; this suggests that Icelandic has a reanalysis operation similar to that of Modern English, but that prepositions assign oblique case.

Old English allowed preposition stranding only by *wh* movement of certain pronouns. Van Kemenade (1987) surveyed the literature on this topic and offered a cliticization analysis. Middle English, however, saw preposition stranding become a much more pervasive phenomenon, as Allen (1977, section 6.1) documented. The first examples of the new types of preposition stranding are found with *wh*-movement constructions in the early thirteenth century. They remain rare through that century, becoming more common in the fourteenth century—particularly, van Kemenade claims, in the prose of the northerner Richard Rolle. It has sometimes been assumed that stranded prepositions in passive constructions came in slightly later, but Denison (1985) provides examples from the thirteenth and fourteenth centuries. Visser (1973, sections 1951 and 1952) cites 24 verbs occurring as prepositional passives for the first time in the fourteenth century, and 57 in the fifteenth century. By the fifteenth century, preposition stranding is widespread in both *wh*-movement constructions and passives. If there is a time difference between preposition stranding with *wh* movement and passives, it is very modest. If there is a real difference, it might indicate that prepositions did assign oblique case. One could then account for the difference by saying that reanalysis became available before the loss of oblique case. Recall that oblique case was compatible with preposition stranding by *wh* movement, but not in passives. But again we have no compelling reason to say that prepositions assigned oblique case.

Only with the loss of oblique case could prepositional passives arise. Under our analysis, this loss would be manifested by the loss of transitive adjectives and the emergence of indirect passives. Visser (1963, p. 327) notes the rapid decay of transitive adjectives, which were very frequent in Old English (and in most modern European languages) and which were replaced in early modern English by prepositional forms (*similar to, worthy of*, etc.). The transition seems to begin in the thirteenth century, when new prepositional forms first emerge, and Visser cites several new forms from the fourteenth century. Visser gives (25) as the last attestation of a transitive adjective, although there is some evidence that *like, near,* and *worth* persisted in the old form.[10]

(25) enough is me to paint out my unrest   (1579 Spenser *Shep.* Cal. 79)
    'it is enough for me to paint out my unrest'

However, new adjectives borrowed from French seem not to have occurred transitively, and this may suggest that transitive adjectives ceased to be grammatical in any productive sense long before their last gasp in the sixteenth century.

Indirect passives are slightly more complex. Handbooks sometimes cite early examples which turn out not to be genuinely indirect passives, and editors have sometimes emended impersonal passives like (20b) so that the initial dative NP is replaced by a nominative. This is discussed in Lightfoot 1979 (p. 259ff.), where it is argued that the first indirect passives date from the fifteenth century.

Lieber (1979) claimed to have found four earlier indirect passives:

(26) a. he cuað ðæt he haten wæs   (Ælfred, *Bede* (Miller) 388, line 29)
        'he said what he was commanded (to say)'

b. swa ic eom forgifen fram þam ælmihtigan gode nu þyssere byrig
   siracusanan eow to geþingienne... (Ælfric's *Lives of Saints*
   (EETS nos. 76, 82) and ch. IX lines 136–138)
   'so now am I given by the almighty God to this city of Syracuse,
   to intercede for you'

c. he was iȝefen Arþure to halden to ȝisle... (Layamon's *Brut*,
   Brook and Leslie edition, line 11372 (EETS no. 277))
   'he was given to Arthur to hold as hostage'

However, Russom (1982) argued persuasively that none of these were
indirect passives. In active sentences with *hatan*, the person commanded is
regularly in the accusative; consequently the passive in (26a) does not
involve a passivized indirect object. Lieber cites (26b) twice, confused by
the fact that secondary sources cite Old English examples sometimes by
volume and page and sometimes by chapter and line. It is actually just one
sentence. Russom examined its context: noting that *forgiefan* 'give' sub-
categorizes for a direct object (the thing given) and an indirect object
(usually a person), she found that here the person *ic* was what was given
to the city, hence the underlying direct object. In (26c) Russom shows that
Lieber (and Visser (1973)) omitted the macron over the final *r* of *Arþur*,
which indicates inflectional endings in the Madden edition; the EETS
edition spells the macron out as a dative ending. Consequently *he* represents an underlying accusative and (26c) is no indirect passive. More
generally, Mitchell (1979, p. 539) argued that "none of the Old English
examples cited by Visser in his discussion of the passive (iii, sections
1905–2000) breaks the general rule that only verbs which can take an
accusative object in the active voice are used personally in the passive,"
despite Visser's claims to the contrary. Van Kemenade (1987, p. 211) cites
two genuine examples from the fourteenth century, but indirect passives
seem to become productive only in the fifteenth century, as I claimed in
my first discussion of these forms. Some early examples are given in (27).

(27) a. as þow in thy vision was opynly schewede   (c. 1400, *Morte
        Arthure*, 827)
        'as you were openly shown in your vision'
     b. he shuld be alowyd mor   (1422–1509, *Paston Letters*
        (Gairdner), vol. 1, p. 252)

Many of the earliest examples are found in the Paston Letters. Consequently, new indirect passives became productive as transitive adjectives
came to be replaced productively by prepositional forms.

If this is correct, it can now be argued that Old English prepositions did not assign oblique case. As was noted above, there seems to be no compelling reason to take them to assign oblique case; the idea is simply redundant. However, if indirect passives like *John was given the book* did not become productive until the fifteenth century, 200 years after prepositional passives like *John was spoken to*, then it is plausible that oblique case was lost after the reanalysis operation became available and that prepositions never assigned oblique case. If English prepositions have always assigned objective case, then the availability of the reanalysis operation would suffice to permit prepositional passives, while indirect passives could emerge only with the loss of oblique case, which seems to have occurred some 200 years later.

As has been noted, there are some difficulties in interpreting the texts, and one cannot regard the matter as clear and settled. It is my tentative conclusion that oblique case was lost as a syntactic entity by the fifteenth century. This was manifested by the emergence of indirect passives and the obsolescence of impersonal passives. The change was distinct from the earlier emergence of the reanalysis operation forming complex verbs. That change may be related to the change discussed in chapter 4, whereby an infinitival *to* came to coalesce with a governing verb.

I have spoken so far mostly of abstract cases, but the loss of oblique followed the loss of the morphological dative case in early Middle English. Distinct case endings on nouns had disappeared by the thirteenth century, but pronouns were more conservative, losing the three-way distinction (see (28)) during the Middle English period; the original dative was retained as the non-nominative in most forms.

(28)		1sg	2sg	3sg:m	f	n	1pl	2pl	3pl
	nom.	ic	þu	he	hio	hit	we	ge	hie
	acc.	mec	þec	hine	hie	hit	us	eow	hie
	dat.	me	þe	him	hire	him	us	eow	him

It is often claimed that the breakdown in case endings was at least a partial consequence of vowel reduction in unstressed final syllables, whereby the distinctive vowels of the case endings (mostly *a* and *u* in nouns) were reduced to a schwa. The reduction in case endings is manifest in the *Peterborough Chronicle*, where, for example, the plural is standardized as *-(e)s* for most noun classes. Interestingly, the dative forms persist most as the complement to prepositions. Even in the pronoun system, the accusative/dative distinction is obliterated in the last section of the chronicle (which dates from the first half of the twelfth century).

This kind of morphological decay typically takes place over a long period, spreading from one dialect area to another, as is illustrated by Jones' (1988) study of the loss of grammatical gender. It is generally supposed that case was first lost in northern English dialects, as first attested in the tenth-century Northumbrian *Lindisfarne Gospels*, and that the loss spread gradually to the south. Van Kemenade (1987) sketches this spread by briefly examining inflections in the continuations of the *Peterborough Chronicle* (northeast Midlands, early twelfth century), the slightly less reduced *Sawles Warde* (west Midlands, early thirteenth century), and the most retentive *Kentish Sermons* (south, mid-thirteenth century). She notes that Richard Rolle (Yorkshire, mid-fourteenth century) used an almost modern noun morphology. However, although the loss began in Northumbria in the tenth century and was complete in Yorkshire by the fourteenth, there is almost no extant northern prose literature from the intervening 300 years. This makes it difficult to make precise correlations between syntactic oblique and morphological dative case. Nonetheless, there are some correlations: van Kemenade (1987, p. 229) points to Rolle as the first writer to manifest fully reduced morphological case and the first to use indirect passives and preposition stranding quite freely (p. 209).

Although the textual evidence is not as rich as one might have hoped, there is enough to permit a venture to relate abstract and morphological case systems. French also manifests this relation, in having a three-way morphological distinction (manifested in the pronoun system: *il, le, lui*) and nominative/objective/oblique at the abstract level. The parallelisms suggest that grammars have symmetry between morphological and abstract case systems: children may postulate three abstract cases if there is a three-way morphological distinction, and two abstract cases if there is a two-way morphological distinction (ignoring possessive). This may hold as an absolute restriction on grammars or it may reflect the unmarked situation. That choice can be determined only by investigating other grammars; languages in which the morphological case system is undergoing a change would be of particular interest.[11]

Whether the symmetry between morphological and abstract case holds absolutely or only at the level of markedness, one can relate the syntactic changes in English discussed here to the loss of the dative case in Middle English. The changes are therefore explained by the theory of grammar I have outlined and by the fact that English lost its dative case. Because the linguistic environment at some point ceased to distinguish accusative and dative, oblique case was no longer triggered, with the syntactic consequences that I have discussed. Such a correlation provides a better explanation for the syntactic changes than reversing direction and keying loss of oblique case to the introduction of the new passives. That account, treating the new passives as the cause of the changes in case rather than as the effect (van Kemenade 1987, p. 96; Roberts 1985b, p. 155), leaves mysterious how and why the new passives emerged. Passives, furthermore, would be an unreliable trigger for the existence of oblique case: as was noted above, Old English and other languages often tolerate passivizable verbs that, when active, assign either accusative or dative, genitive, or some other case to their complement. It is reasonable to say, as above, that the passive corresponds to the active form that assigns accusative case. Indeed, this would be required by the theory of case outlined here. However, if passives were the trigger for the structural nature of objective case, it is hard to see how the dative and genitive forms would ever arise with verbs that also may assign accusative and occur in the passive. Such coexisting forms represented an unstable and transitional state of affairs; this can be understood most naturally in the context of an obsolescent case system, as will be discussed further in section 6.1.

Thus, I postulate that oblique case was lost from the syntax of late Middle English as a result of the loss of morphological dative case. This, then, is another example of the close relation between abstract syntactic devices and morphological properties: morphological properties play a role in triggering the syntactic devices. Of course, there is no reason to stop here. One could ask why the dative case was lost, perhaps relating the loss to phonological changes involving word stress, to the reduction of vowels in final syllables, or to Scandinavian influence. But that is another story.

Chapter 6 will examine another consequence of the changing case system (section 6.1) and another example of syntactic changes resulting from morphological shifts (section 6.2).

Chapter 6
Obsolescence and Lexicalism

In chapter 3 we saw how statistical shifts in surface instances of object-verb order in unembedded binding Domains entailed a new setting of the verb-order parameter. This entailed, directly or indirectly, new syntactic patterns in embedded Domains (chapter 3), new passive infinitival complements, and new accusative subjects (chapter 4). It also entailed the disappearance of object-verb order in embedded Domains and of active infinitival complements to verbs such as *order*, *see*, and *make*. In general, this is the right kind of explanation for obsolescence: obsolete forms must be shown to have disappeared as an indirect consequence of something else. It could hardly be otherwise.

A new form, appearing for the first time at some historical stage, might arise for one of a number of reasons: it might represent a borrowing from some contact language (Lightfoot 1979, pp. 381–384), it might be a creative innovation introduced for the expressive force that novel expressions often have and then being perpetuated through more extensive use by other speakers (ibid. pp. 384–385), or it might result from a new parameter setting, such as the new passives (discussed in chapter 5) that arose when oblique case was no longer triggered. The first two factors could not explain directly why a form disappears from a language, although, of course, the obsolescence of a form may be an indirect result of foreign influence or of the introduction of new stylistically motivated types. This simple fact has important consequences for historical work, although they are not always properly appreciated.

For example, historians often like to adopt heavily lexical descriptions of the various stages of a language, wherein individual words may be annotated richly to account for their distribution. The attraction is obvious: one can provide descriptions reflecting textual attestation quite precisely. So, if a given verb is last attested in some grammatical environment in, say,

1152, one can say that grammars after this date contained an appropriate lexical annotation on the verb. If another verb is last attested in that environment in 1206, it may be said to have acquired the relevant annotation from that date on. Obsolescence is handled in the same way, by changing a lexical feature. The problem is that such descriptions, with an accretion of lexical features each capturing what ceased to occur at various stages, are unlearnable, hence not psychologically plausible, and therefore have no explanatory force (see chapter 7): since children have no access to negative data (see section 1.3), the nonoccurrence of a form for some generation of speakers cannot be said to trigger a lexical feature or anything else. As a result, obsolescence requires a more indirect approach and thus an analytical framework of some abstraction—certainly of greater abstraction than a purely lexical model.

Thus, obsolete (i.e., newly nonoccurring) forms are not part of the triggering experience. If children are degree-0 learners, setting their parameters on the sole basis of simple data, the obsolescent structures discussed in chapters 3 and 4 and drawn from embedded Domains (object-verb order, etc.) were never part of the triggering experience, and their obsolescence is indeed a consequence of something else (namely the new setting of the verb order parameter). In this chapter I shall examine the loss of some simple unembedded structures, with a view to finding what they reveal about the triggering experience. I shall investigate two sets of changes, whose analysis in Lightfoot 1979 gave rise to extensive discussion: the loss of certain "impersonal" verb forms and the emergence of a class of auxiliary verbs. Many interesting questions have been raised about these changes. I shall not address all of them here; my goal is more limited, focusing on the nature of the triggering experience. I shall argue that the highly lexicalist treatments that have been offered are defective and that more explanatory accounts are available.

There is, after all, an important point of logic for the central hypothesis of this study: if simple, unembedded structures may disappear from a language and thus not be part of the triggering experience at some stage, then perhaps the obsolescence of object-verb order in embedded clauses is of the same type and does not show that the parameter-setting process is generally independent of data from embedded binding Domains. The main point of this chapter will be to show that principled accounts must and can be offered for the loss of simple, robust construction types, and that no comparably principled account can explain the loss of embedded forms discussed in chapters 3 and 4, unless parameter setting is never influenced by embedded data.

6.1 Impersonal Verbs

In section 5.1 of Lightfoot 1979 I examined changes involving impersonal verbs, which often did not have an apparent (nominative) subject in Old English and did not agree in person and number with any subject NP, being invariably in the third-person-singular form. These impersonal verbs included examples like (1).

(1) a. sniwde 'it snowed'
    b. gelomp þæt an swiþe wis mon ... 'it happened that a very wise man ...'
    c. him[dative] hungreð 'he is hungry'
    d. me[dative] thynketh I heare 'I think I hear'
    e. him chaunst to meete upon the way A faithlesse Sarazin (1590, Spenser, *FQ* I ii 12)
    f. mee likes ... go see the hoped heaven (1557, *Tottel's Misc.* (Arber) 124)
    g. him[dative] ofhreow ðæs mannes[genitive] 'he pitied the man'

It is difficult to give an accurate pretheoretical definition of "impersonals"; for example, *sniwde* often occurred with the neuter pronoun *hit*, which is generally taken to be nominative (although not overtly distinct from the accusative). Anderson (1986), therefore, distinguished a subclass of "quasi-personal impersonals." Also, *lician* 'like' is often classed as an impersonal, despite not fitting the definition given: it could have a nominative subject, although often not in the usual position and invariably (in Old English) corresponding to the theme NP and not to the experiencer. Nonetheless, if one ignores problems with these intuitive classifications, one can see that there was a productive construction type. In Old English there were over forty verbs occurring in contexts like (1g), with two NPs but no nominative subject. Indeed, some new verbs were added to this class during Middle English, in some cases having been borrowed from personal verbs in French or Old Norse. However, several of the verbs occurring in sentences like (1) disappeared from the language altogether by the end of the Middle English period, some developed an expletive subject (*it*), and some were apparently reanalyzed in such a way that one NP came to act as a structural subject with nominative case. Consequently, impersonal verbs had effectively disappeared by the early modern period, no longer triggering any grammatical device which might have served to generate them and keep them productive.

In earlier work (Lightfoot 1979, 1982, 1988a) I focused on the verb *like*

and attributed the loss of certain forms with postverbal nominative subjects to the loss of case distinctions and the new verb-object order at
D-structure. Children with the new parameter settings, exposed to sentences like *the king liked pears* and *him like pears*, could analyze them only
as subject-verb-object, which in turn meant that *him like pears* became
obsolete, having been replaced by *he likes pears*. It also meant that the
nominative NP came to represent the experiencer instead of the theme of
earlier grammars, and that the dictionary meaning of *like* was therefore
changed from "cause pleasure for" to "derive pleasure from". This was an
appropriate kind of explanation, although I considered only a narrow
range of facts and not the true impersonals. Indeed, Allen (1986) showed
that the object-verb-subject order was a minority pattern even with *lician*
in Old and Middle English. This does not invalidate the explanation, but
it does show that its scope is limited and that it fails to account for the
obsolescence of other structures which in fact seem to have died out at
roughly the same time.

Here I shall broaden the perspective and build on an analysis offered by
Belletti and Rizzi (1988). This will make it possible to see the changes in
these verbs as instantiations of the loss of oblique case, discussed in chapter
5. I shall draw on ideas of Fischer and van der Leek (1983) and Anderson
(1986), amending them in a small but important way and adopting a
diglossic analysis.[1]

The impersonal verbs under discussion do not make up an arbitrary
class but are, in most cases, verbs of psychological or sometimes bodily
states—"psych-verbs." It has been noted for several languages that such
verbs often reflect thematic roles in unusual syntactic configurations. This
is true of Italian, where one finds patterns like (2).

(2) a. Gianni teme questo
      'Gianni fears this'
   b. questo preoccupa Gianni
      'this worries Gianni'
   c. a Gianni piace questo
      'to Gianni pleases this'
   d. questo piace a Gianni
      'this pleases to Gianni'

Belletti and Rizzi (1988) distinguish the straightforward transitive, (2a),
from (2b)–(2d), which are derived from a D-structure where the initial,
subject NP is empty and the theme and experiencer NPs are arrayed as
shown in (3).

(3) $_S$[NP INFL $_{VP}$[$_{V'}$[verb theme] experiencer]]

Temere, preoccupare, and *piacere* are each subcategorized in the lexicon to occur with experiencer and theme NPs. For *temere* the experiencer is specified as the NP becoming the external argument, which gives rise to a simple transitive D-structure such as (2a). *Preoccupare* and *piacere* each assign an inherent (D-structure) case to the experiencer (accusative and dative respectively), as discussed in chapter 5, and they have no external thematic role. Nothing further is specified in the lexicon. Indeed, Belletti and Rizzi's theory of lexical entries would prevent specifying anything beyond the thematic roles with which a verb might occur, the cases manifesting those thematic roles, and an indication as to which (if any) of these roles might be externalized. A set of principles guides the mapping of lexical representations into D-structure configurations. Two principles are relevant: (a) V assigns structural case only if it has an external argument, which is an interpretation of "Burzio's generalization," and (b) an experiencer must be projected to a higher position than a theme NP. This entails that (3) is the only possible D-structure for these verbs and that for no psych-verb can the string *this V John* have the properties of a simple transitive structure. In (2b) the theme NP *questo* is a derived subject and *Gianni* is adjoined to VP and not a direct object dominated by V'. The experiencer with *piacere* may move to the empty subject position in (2c), but it may not receive nominative case (which would clash with the inherent case already assigned at D-structure). Instead nominative is assigned by INFL to the theme after it has adjoined to the VP (Belletti and Rizzi 1988, p. 339).

Belletti and Rizzi argue for an analysis along these lines by showing that the surface subject of (2b) has a cluster of properties typical of derived subjects, and that D-structures like (3) permit a straightforward account of otherwise mysterious binding properties found with psych-verbs. The arguments depend on negative data, on the interpretability of empty subjects, on relatively exotic data about the behavior of psych-verbs in the complements of causative verbs, and on the distribution of long-distance anaphors. Such data are typically not available to children, or to investigators of dead languages. This means that it is probably impossible to argue for the appropriateness of D-structures like (3) for early stages of English, except in the most speculative and incomplete fashion. However, it is also the case that, since Belletti and Rizzi's arguments are not based on the kind of data generally available to children, the analysis must be dictated in large part by the demands of Universal Grammar.[2] In that case, it might be productive to assume the most fundamental aspects of their analysis also for Old English: the verbs under examination are subcategorized to occur with an experiencer and a theme, and the lexical entries may specify a D-structure case and an externalization option. I shall now devote a few pages to showing that there is indeed some profit in adopting such an analysis for Old English. This will enable me to offer a diglossic account for what is observed during the Middle English period and to give an explanatory account of the diachronic changes.

The most striking feature of psych-verbs in Old and Middle English is the wide range of syntactic contexts in which they appear—sometimes occurring impersonally with an invariant third-person-singular inflection, sometimes with a nominative experiencer, sometimes with a nominative theme. These verbs also show idiosyncrasies of verb agreement, sometimes occurring in the third person singular but with a plural or a first- or second-person nominative NP: *þu ne þearft sceamian* 'you need not be ashamed'. However, an analysis along the lines of Belletti and Rizzi 1988 predicts the range of psych-verbs attested in earlier English with appropriate accuracy. The verbs would be subcategorized to occur with experiencer and theme NPs, like the comparable verbs in Italian, and this would yield D-structures like (4), with the experiencer NP higher than the theme. (After the change in verb order, the theme and the experiencer would be arrayed to the right of the verb.)

(4) $_S$[NP INFL $_{VP}$[experiencer $_{V'}$[theme verb]]]

In (5) I list two lexical entries which typify several Old English psych-verbs.

(5) a. hreowan: experiencer-dative; (theme-genitive)
    b. lician: experiencer-dative; theme

Hreowan 'pity', *þyrstan* 'thirst', and several other verbs sometimes occurred just with an experiencer NP in the dative case (*me hreoweþ* 'I felt pity'), or they might assign two inherent cases, yielding surface forms *him[dative] ofhreow þæs mannes[genitive]* 'he was sorry for the man'. (5a) must be interpreted in such a way that the theme is assigned genitive case when realized by a NP; generally, the theme might alternatively be manifested by a clause or, with increasing frequency through the Old English period, by a PP; in the latter event, no case is assigned. *Lician* 'like/please' usually occurred with an experiencer in the dative case and a theme in the nominative. With a lexical entry as in (5b), the theme would receive no inherent case at D-structure. Nor could it receive the objective structural case, because Vs assign structural case only if they have external arguments (a nominative subject, in this instance); this would be impossible because the experiencer, having dative case inherently, could not acquire a second case at S-structure. Therefore the theme could receive nominative case at S-structure. It might be adjoined to VP and receive nominative in that position, as Belletti and Rizzi require for (2c). Alternatively, the theme might move to the subject position and receive nominative case under government by AGR, as with Italian *preoccupare*.

The verbs differ in what cases they assign. So the verb *lician* worked just like Italian *piacere* and assigned dative to the experiencer NP in (5b); the theme acquires nominative either by adjoining to VP or by moving to the subject position. Since in main clauses one of the NPs and the verb are fronted, one would expect to find either the order experiencer[dative]-verb-theme [nominative] or theme-verb-experiencer. In embedded clauses, with no verb movement to an initial position, the theme might adjoin to VP to receive case, and one would expect the order theme-experiencer-verb or experiencer-verb-theme. The movement of the experiencer to the subject position would entail the additonal possibility of experiencer-theme-verb. So far our treatment is similar in its general outline to those of Fischer and van der Leek (1983) and Anderson (1986). Fischer and van der Leek initially postulate three subcategorization frames for *of-hreowan* but then show that only one is needed if an option of deriving surface subjects is allowed.

Belletti and Rizzi (1988, section 4.2) argue that a dative NP in (2c) may move to subject position, carrying along its inherent case and therefore not receiving nominative at S-structure; instead, nominative is assigned to the theme NP, which is adjoined to VP. Again the arguments are based on negative data; therefore, the analysis would not be learnable by children not having access to negative data, and it would have to be dictated by Universal Grammar if D-structures like (3) or (4) are available. This, in turn, suggests that a dative experiencer could also move to the subject position in Old English. In Lightfoot 1979 I noted that such dative experiencers could show some properties of subjects: they sometimes determined the person and number of the verb, as in (6a), and they could behave like regular subjects in reduced conjoined structures, as in (6b) and (6c), controlling the empty subject in (6c).

(6) a. me think we shall be strong enough   (1534, More, *Works* (1557))
    b. but moche now me merueilith, and well may I in sothe   (c. 1405, *Mum and the Sothsegger* (EETS) ii I)
    c. us sholde neither lakken gold ne gere, But *e* ben honoured whil we dwelten there   (c. 1374 Chaucer, *Troil.* IV 1523)

The examples cited were from the late Middle/early Modern English period and were taken as transitional forms, illustrating elements of the earlier and later grammars. (Warner (1983, pp. 204–206) is skeptical.) The editorial practice deplored by Jespersen, which emended objective pronouns in structures like (6a) for nominatives, makes it harder to date these constructions, but it is possible that they manifested the movement of the dative NP to subject position and occurred earlier. In fact, Allen (1986, section 4.1) pointed to early examples like (7) and argued that they manifested a process of coordinate-subject deletion under identity with a preceding subject.

(7) ac gode[dative] ne licode na heora geleafleast[nominative] ... ac
     asende him to fyr of heofonum   (Ælfric, *Homilies* xx.71)
     'but their faithlessness did not please God, but (he) sent them fire
     from heaven'

Allen also argued that in early Middle English sentences with NP[dative]-verb-NP[nominative] order (where, I have argued, the postverbal NP is adjoined to VP) it is the preverbal dative NP that agrees with the verb and therefore acts as a "quirky" subject:

(8) a. and ðat hem[dative] likede here lodliche sinnes[nominative]
        (*Old English Homilies of the 12th Century*, ed. Morris, II, p. 7)
        'and that they liked their loathsome sins'
    b. ne rewe[sg.] him[dative] nauht ane his sennes[nominative]
        (*Vices and Virtues*, ed. Holthausen, p. 121)
        'let him not only regret his sins'

A grammar along the lines of what has been described so far generates a good sample of the bewildering range of contexts in which these impersonal verbs may occur. However, there are other possibilities. Some of these, noted by Anderson (1986), require only minor modifications: with some verbs the experiencer NP is optional (*gelomp þæt an swiþe wis mon* ... 'it happened that a very wise man ...'; *gif him gelimpe þæt he þearfa beo* 'if it befalls him that he is destitute'); other verbs develop the option of a *hit* variant in late Old English (*hit me ofþincþ* 'it grieves me'; *sore hit me forþynkeþ of þe dede* 'I repent sorely of the deed'). Others are more systematic. Fischer and van der Leek (1983) noted some alternative forms where the experiencer appeared in the nominative.[3] This happened with some verbs in an "absolutive" construction with no object: *ic licige* 'I am pleased', *ic hreowe* 'I am sorry', *ic sceamige* 'I am ashamed', etc. Alternatively, an object might be present: ... *þæt þu[nominative] Gode[dative] licie* 'that you please God'. Furthermore, the theme might occur in the nominative case. Anderson (1986) gathered three examples from Ælfric, one showing the verb *hreowan* being used impersonally, one with the theme as nominative, and one with the experiencer as nominative:

(9) a. him[dative] ofhreow þæs mannes[genitive]
       'to-him there-was-pity because-of-the man'
    b. þa ofhreow ðam munece[dative] þæs hreoflian
       mægenleast[nominative]
       'then brought-pity to-the monk the leper's feebleness'
    c. se mæssepreost[nominative] þæs mannes[genitive] ofhreow
       'the priest because-of-the man felt-pity'

Anderson suggested plausibly that *hreowan*, in showing all three possibilities, represents the typical case, and that many verbs manifesting only one or two of these possibilities in fact are revealing only accidental gaps in the texts. Certainly it would require a rich lexicon to express the distributional limitations found in the texts.

Adopting Anderson's strategy, one still needs to account for the variation found with *hreowan* and other verbs. One could complicate the lexical entries for all verbs manifesting the nominative forms, such that the experiencer might be dative or might have no case; similarly, the theme might be genitive (or a PP), or might lack case. Any NP lacking case at D-structure would have to acquire a case by S-structure, perhaps moving to a position in which it might be assigned nominative. This predicts that experiencer and theme NPs may not both receive nominative in the same clause, if AGR may only assign its case once. Since nominative is not an inherent case assignable at D-structure, it cannot be specified in a lexical entry; consequently one does not need to block the possibility of lexical entries' assigning nominative to both the experiencer and the theme, which is a problem for analyses that treat nominative as an inherent case (Allen 1986; Brody 1989; Roberts 1985b). It also predicts the absence of nominative-accusative forms. Although case assignment is optional, Burzio's generalization precludes the possibility that neither NP receives lexical case. In that event, one NP would have to move to subject position and receive nominative case at S-structure, the other receiving structural objective case. This would violate the restriction that a verb assigns structural case only if it has an external argument (see above), and this nominative-accusative pattern is not attested in the earliest stages (see the paradigm in (9)).

The above is, effectively, the proposal of Fischer and van der Leek, who make it a defining property of these impersonal psych-verbs that they assign their lexical cases only optionally, whereas non-impersonals assign their cases obligatorily (p. 357ff.). This does not hold in Italian and so cannot be dictated by Universal Grammar; instead, it represents parametric variation—as Fischer and van der Leek point out, a marked option. One is left wondering how such a marked option could have arisen in the language, a question to which we shall return. More seriously, it is unclear how the existence of such an option could be learned under normal childhood conditions. Presumably, optional case assignment is determined by the variation seen in paradigms like (9). Crucially, the triggering experience would be a paradigm set, and perhaps a certain kind of paradigm set; no single structure like those involved in (9) could trigger anything other than a simple lexical entry or subcategorization frame, resulting in a total of three entries. It is only the fact that the sentences of (9) are perceived as a paradigm set that triggers optional case assignment. This makes their optional case assignment quite different from, say, the optionality of an indirect object with *give*. There the child effectively learns two subcategorization frames: theme and theme-goal. This can be stated economically in one frame with the goal optional: theme (goal). Fischer and van der Leek, on the other hand, are not dealing in optionality arising from economy of statement. For them, one assumes, the existence of the variation determines that case assignment is optional. It may indeed be necessary to attribute this capacity to language learners, that they can construct paradigm sets which in turn establish certain parameter settings. However, before making that move, one should note some other difficulties with this account.

First, given this analysis for Old English, Fischer and van der Leek are forced to treat the subsequent historical changes as item-by-item lexical reanalyses, which enables them to account for the presumed fact that "different verbs developed along different lines and often at a different pace" (p. 367). However, since we are dealing here with obsolescent structures, this approach reduces to vicious circularity: if one element of a paradigm set like (9) drops out of the primary linguistic data, optional assignment of lexical case is no longer triggered for that verb. But why should that element have been lost, except by loss of the optionality of case assignment? The obsolescence fails to be a by-product of some parameter setting determined by positive data, which is a fundamental requirement (see the introductory paragraphs of this chapter). As a result, Fischer and van der Leek must say that a series of unrelated accidents led to the loss of impersonal constructions with an NP in an oblique case, which leaves them far from the announced insight that the loss of these forms was due to the change in the morphological case system.

Second, a particular difficulty for this account, noted by Allen (1986), is that it fails to generalize to the causative-to-receptive change affecting *like*—and it was Fischer and van der Leek's initial goal to explain this change. They are reduced to claiming (p. 364) that "it is the theory of change which must be held responsible for the disappearance of one or the other type ... [because] any re-analysis resulting in the survival of both construction-types for the same verb would have been a genuine threat to communicability." This won't do, because they note elsewhere, correctly, that there can be no independent theory of change. Rather, it is for the theory of grammar to show how one or other of the construction-types with *like* became unattainable. Fischer and van der Leek provided a good account of the loss of the impersonal verbs, keying it correctly to the loss of morphological dative case. The account, however, sought to be too accurate and to provide too close a representation of what the texts showed at various stages. This entailed putting too much information into individual lexical entries and thus attributing the loss of the impersonal form of any particular verb too directly to a change in that lexical entry, thereby sacrificing any kind of explanation. There is, after all, no reason to suppose that there exists a single grammar of Old English, least of all a single grammar generating exactly what is found in the extant texts from any year, decade, or century.

So, an alternative account is needed. One can avoid these difficulties by attending to the methodological points noted and making a small but important change. One can adopt the essentials of Fischer and van der Leek's analysis, couched now in terms of Belletti and Rizzi's (1988) general theory of psych-verbs, and view the nominative forms as reflecting the general loss of oblique case discussed in chapter 5. Rather than build the option of dative or no case into various lexical entries in a given grammar, which suggests a wide range of possibilities with certain verbs having the option and others not, one might treat the situation as diglossic. Two grammars coexisted in the speech community, one with lexical entries with dative and other cases and the other with no such inherent case specifications for the verbs under discussion. Together the two simple grammars account for the range of data generated by the single grammar with the built-in variation.

In fact, the two simple grammars would yield a greater range of data. A grammar with oblique case would generate "impersonal" forms like (1c)–(1g). Lexical entries would be along the lines of (5), and NPs assigned a lexical case would not surface with a structural case, as I have indicated. A grammar lacking morphological dative case, under the hypothesis of chapter 5, would also lack oblique lexical cases. Therefore the lexical entries would specify no D-structure cases. As a result, NPs would have to acquire cases structurally, under government by some case assigner. No dative experiencers would be generated, but these verbs would occur with NPs in the objective case. Such a diglossic account would predict that once a grammar without dative case (and thus without truly impersonal verbs) is attested, one might find any of the impersonal verbs with nominative and accusative NPs. Given the haphazard and fragmentary attestation for any given period, one could not expect to find all the relevant verbs attested in both construction types at a certain time. Similarly, as dative cases ceased to be attested anywhere, one would expect to find no more verbs used impersonally and lacking a nominative subject. Beyond these outer limits, this diglossic account does not predict what the texts will manifest at any particular time while the two grammars coexist. The account is less ambitious than that of Fischer and van der Leek, but appropriately so; excessive ambition is not always a good thing, as Macbeth taught us.

A striking property of the loss of the impersonal verbs is its gradualness. The two grammars coexisted for several hundred years. The first nominative-objective forms are found in Old English, but impersonal verbs with dative subjects continue to exist until the middle of the sixteenth century. The gradualness of the change is expected if the loss of lexical case is a function of the loss of morphological dative cases. Jones' (1988) study of the loss of gender markers, which seem to carry no functional load, makes clear how gradual morphological change can be, spreading in that instance over at least 300 years. The loss of the impersonal forms coincides appropriately with the novel forms discussed in chapter 5 and attributed there to the loss of inherent case. However, the disappearing impersonals provide a more precise probe into the chronology and geography of the change in case systems, by virtue of the fact that the new system entails the obsolescence of certain structures; the syntactic changes discussed in chapter 5 were manifested mostly by new passives and not by any kind of obsolescence except that of impersonal passives. Clearly there is scope for detailed checking of this hypothesis, investigating the extent to which the predicted correlations hold of individual texts and authors.

Our notion that the existence of lexical cases, assignable at D-structure, is triggered by the occurrence of oblique morphological cases predicts that grammars manifesting a dative case would not manifest impersonal verbs with structural objective case, nor would they manifest the indirect passives discussed in chapter 5. Conversely, grammars manifesting no dative case morphologically are expected to show impersonal verbs with structural objective cases, hence passives with such verbs (see below), PPs instead of former genitives, and indirect passives quite generally. These correlations seem to be roughly correct, but the coexistence of two grammars may influence the writing of any individual and certainly the scribal and editorial transmission, and it is not always possible to distinguish the two systems as cleanly as one would like; it is clear that individuals can operate with more than one grammatical system in a kind of internalized diglossia, although the limits to this capacity are not understood.

The particular theory of lexical case adopted here makes some accurate predictions about the nature of these changes. For example, it predicts that the new grammar would be manifested first by new nominative cases and only then by new objective cases. On the version of "Burzio's generalization" adopted above, objective case may be assigned only by a verb with an external (i.e. nominative) subject. Consequently, if a verb assigned dative case to its experiencer, the NP could not be externalized to a position in which it would receive a second case and so the verb could not, in turn, assign objective case. Only when dative no longer occurred in a lexical entry might the experiencer NP be externalized, and only then would the verb be able to assign objective case.

The theory adopted here also predicts that an impersonal verb assigning lexical case to its NPs would not occur in the passive agreeing with an externalized nominative NP; such constructions would occur only after the loss of lexical case. Before that, lexical case would be assigned to the NP even if the verb were in the passive form, and thus the NP would not be able to acquire a second, nominative case. The reason is that assignment of lexical case does not depend on government (see section 5.2): although a passive verb "absorbs" its structural case when it fails to govern its complement, it cannot absorb a lexical case in the same way. This is what generally blocks passivization of dative NPs, as was discussed in chapter 5; it similarly blocks passivization with the datives of impersonal verbs. Belletti and Rizzi (1988) discuss why this must be so, illustrating with examples of Italian psych-verbs and showing why verbs like *preoccupare* do not occur with personal passives. Denison (1990) shows that although some Old English impersonal verbs occur in what look like passive constructions, they are not in fact so. Instead one finds "impersonal passives" like (10).

(10) ac him næs þære bene getiðod   (Ælfric, *Catholic Homilies* II 35
302.115.)
but to-him[dative] not-was that prayer[genitive/dative] granted
'but he was not granted this request'

The fact that passives are necessarily impersonal with these verbs is,
incidentally, quite incompatible with Fischer and van der Leek's notion
that the verbs assign lexical case optionally. If that were so, an NP not
receiving lexical case would be expected to be able to occur as an S-
structure subject of a personal passive, acquiring nominative case.

Where does this leave us with *like*, which remained a difficulty for Allen
(1986) and for Fischer and van der Leek (1983)? With the lexical entry of
(5b), the innovating grammar would simply lack any reference to dative
case. Consequently both NPs would have to acquire structural case. In
such a context, one NP would have to be externalized, and the lexical entry
would automatically be changed to include such a specification. We have
seen that by far the most common pattern for *like*, certainly after the verb-
order change, was experiencer[dative]-verb-theme[nominative], with the
theme acquiring nominative case by adjunction to VP. *Lician* was a common verb, with over 400 citations in the *Concordance to Old English*, and
Denison (1990) notes that the type with a dative experiencer and nominative theme made up "the overwhelming majority, to the extent that it is
doubtful whether the others are grammatical at all." The child without
morphological dative case would perceive such forms as experiencer
NP–verb–theme NP, with no lexical cases. Since the experiencer NP often
had subject properties, as was noted above, and actually was the subject
despite the dative case, the most natural analysis for the caseless child
would be to treat the experiencer as the externalized NP. How could it be
otherwise? This in turn would permit the verb to assign objective case to
the theme. If the experiencer did not externalize and nominative were
assigned to the theme in the old fashion, by virtue of its being adjoined to
VP and so governed by AGR, AGR would thereby assign its case and the
experiencer would have no way to acquire a case and would thus violate
the case filter. Consequently, externalization of the experiencer is the only
viable option in the new grammar, and assignment of nominative to the
theme in an adjoined position is automatically eliminated. Unlike Fischer
and van der Leek, I do not need to postulate an independent change
whereby grammars lose the ability to assign case by chain government; it
would simply not be needed under the new analysis, and thus it would not
be triggered. As a result, the change involving *like* is subsumed under the
more general treatment of impersonals, which was the original goal of

Fischer and van der Leek, and neither the Transparency Principle nor the Trace Erasure Principle is a necessary component of my explanation (see Lightfoot 1979, 1981b).[4]

This account of the obsolescence of the impersonals is of the right type. If Universal Grammar imposes a correlation between lexical and morphological case, essentially treating overt morphological case as the manifestation of abstract, syntactic case, then one can say that the loss of morphological oblique cases entailed the loss of cases in lexical entries like those of (5). This, in turn, entailed that the experiencer NP had to be externalized, and thus it entailed the rise of nominative-objective forms and the automatic loss of the nonexternalized or "impersonal" forms. So, as the primary linguistic data changed so that they no longer triggered morphological case distinctions, the impersonals could no longer exist. By lowering my sights and not seeking to account for the alternations found in the texts through a single grammar, I have postulated two coexisting grammars without needing to attribute highly marked and unlearnable properties to Old English. This, in turn, permitted a natural account of the changes taking place.

Although I made only a small technical move, eliminating Fischer and van der Leek's property of optional assignment of lexical case and postulating coexisting grammars, my account differs fundamentally, and I do not need to view the change as a sequence of unmotivated changes in various lexical entries. This is also true *a fortiori* when this account is compared against the avowedly lexicalist treatments of Allen (1986) and Denison (1990). These accounts can be made extremely accurate, because they postulate new lexical entries as new forms are attested, but, in so doing, they do not meet the basic requirements of an explanation for obsolescent forms (see the introduction to this chapter).

Roberts (1985b), Allen (1986), and Brody (1989) offer related analyses based on a similar cluster of ideas, holding not only that lexical cases were lost but that, before they were lost, they were the only cases available: for these writers, Old English lacked structural cases. This cannot be right, unless very different definitions of lexical and structural case are adopted. For example, the existence in Old English of simple passives, such as *the bread was stolen*, entails that the empty object of *steal* not have case; this is possible only if case is "absorbed" because of failure of government. Government, however, is relevant only for structural case, and it is the fact that lexical case is assigned regardless of government that blocks absorption of case and thus blocks personal passives of verbs assigning dative or genitive case to their complement.

Furthermore, if nominatives and accusatives, which existed in Old English, could be lexically assigned, it is hard to see how there could be a straightforward correlation between morphological and syntactic case—particularly if, as for Brody, individual lexical entries can specify structural cases. In that event, one could not attribute the introduction of structural case to the loss of morphological oblique cases. The question why lexical case was lost and structural case introduced would then arise. Roberts (1985b) attributes the loss of lexical case to the new passives discussed in chapter 5 above and to the changing patterns with impersonal verbs. In other words, he adopts the reverse of the causal chain adopted here, where the new case system entailed new passives and new forms for the old impersonal verbs. For Roberts, "the development of pseudopassives was a *cause*, not an *effect*, of the loss of oblique case" [Roberts' emphasis]. The problem with this is that one is left wondering why the new passives were introduced. No account is offered, and it is hard to imagine one.

In summary: Impersonal forms lacking a nominative subject dropped out of the language as a function of the loss of lexical cases assigned at D-structure. This, in turn, was a function of the loss of oblique morphological cases. The Middle English period witnessed a coexistence of conservative grammars with lexical cases and innovative grammars with no cases assigned inherently at D-structure. One can therefore understand the loss of the impersonal forms as a by-product of other changes in the primary data: the losses of oblique cases. As these cases were lost, Universal Grammar dictated that forms like (1c)–(1g) could not be analyzed as in earlier grammars and therefore had to be reanalyzed in certain ways.

6.2 Auxiliary Verbs

In Lightfoot 1974 (revised in 1979) I argued that certain expressions, including those of (11), dropped out of the language simultaneously, revealing that *can, could, do, did, may, might, must, shall, should, will*, and *would*, formerly treated as main verbs, were now being treated as manifestations of INFL ("Aux," in the earlier formulation) and were "auxiliary verbs." Hence, in current terminology, some parameter had been set differently.

(11) a. I shall can do it
   b. I am canning do it
   c. I have could do it
   d. I want to can do it

No real explanation was offered, but the change was keyed to a mounting "opacity" in the grammars of earlier generations, whereby those verbs steadily became more and more exceptional as they developed the characteristics of (12), which emerged slowly during the Middle English period. As their exceptionality reached a certain point, children attained a different grammar, which assigned these verbs to a new category. If the theory of grammar could define attainable levels of exceptionality, it would explain why a new grammar was triggered at a certain stage.[5]

(12) a. These verbs lost their ability to take direct objects.
     b. They became inflectionally distinct after the loss of other preterite-present verbs.
     c. With the loss of the subjunctive mood, the relation between their present and past tenses became non-temporal in certain senses.
     d. They were never followed by the *to* form of the infinitive.

There has been extensive discussion of this and of analogous changes, most usefully by Warner (1983), and some revision is called for. Warner argued that (12a) probably belongs with the loss of (11) and was not a causal factor, and he suggested that the structures of (11) did not disappear as suddenly as was supposed in Lightfoot 1979. Warner 1990 argues for a lexical treatment and for placing the reanalysis earlier. However, the persistence of the old inverted and negative forms (*came John?* and *John came not*) indicates the opposite, that the change was later. A curious feature of my earlier treatment was that the reanalysis of these verbs was dated as complete by the early sixteenth century, the simultaneous loss of the structures in (11) providing the evidence, but that the old inverted and negative forms persisted much later, being attested quite robustly until the late seventeenth century. The persistence of these forms suggests that at least some critical part of the reanalysis took place later, toward the end of the seventeenth century, with the new inverted and negative forms manifesting the new analysis.

Warner's discussion suggests that there were two crucial stages to the change. In the first stage, the modal verbs gradually acquired the properties of (12b)–(12d), which entailed a reanalysis whereby they came to be generated under INFL. This was manifested by the loss of their nonfinite forms (see (11)) and their direct objects (see (12a)). Technically, the reanalysis consisted in a reassignment of category membership: the items in question were formerly categorized in the lexicon as verbs, but came to be categorized as INFL markers. This change may not have been as cataclysmic as I claimed in Lightfoot 1979. Nonfinite forms of *can, may,* and *will* are found in the sixteenth century, but it seems that nonfinite forms of *must* and *shall* were absent earlier. Arguments *ex tacito* must always be treated cautiously, but it is possible that some verbs were recategorized before others. Even if one allows for this possibility, it does not seem unreasonable to say that the recategorization was effectively complete by the sixteenth century. Allan (1988) offers a careful examination of the last attested nonfinite form for each of the individual words, and shows (p. 142) that almost all of the last attestations are drawn from the sixteenth century, with just a few residual examples from later periods. The data are actually more dramatic than he claims, because his statistics include nineteenth- and twentieth-century poetic occurrences of *ought*, which does not fall into the relevant class (*ought Kim do that?*, *Kim ought not do that*), and also include the verb *will* with a direct object.

The second stage is manifested by the obsolescence of the old inverted and negative form. It seems to have been completed only at the end of the seventeenth century, significantly later than the loss of the nonfinite forms (see (11)) and the direct objects (see (12a)). First let us ask what the change consists in, how grammars changed, and which parameter came to be set differently. If INFL is the head of a clause, then it is the key element for inversion and negation processes: inversion applies to INFL, moving it to some initial position (see chapter 3), and negatives occur immediately to the right of INFL in English. Let us assume that the earlier change consisted in a recategorization whereby a set of verbs came to be base-generated under INFL, i.e., categorized in the lexicon as instances of INFL and not of V; to be precise, they were generated as a sister to AGR in the position *v* in (13).

(13) $_{S'}$[Comp $_S$[NP $_{INFL}$[v AGR] $_{VP}$[... V ...]]]

In that case, the seventeenth-century structural change would be that the nonmodal verbs lost the ability to move up to the *v* position in INFL and thus to interact with inversion and negation properties. Roberts (1985a) developed one account along these general lines. If they cannot move to INFL, they cannot occur to the left of *not*. Also, they cannot move to the initial position unless they move first to INFL, because the empty V would then not be head-governed; recall that all empty elements visible in phonological structure must be head-governed there, and that head-government includes a relation of minimal c-command (section 4.3). As a result, forms like *came John to London?* and *John came not to London* ceased to occur.

Also ceasing to occur, and thus providing further evidence for this structural change, are forms in which a tensed verb is separated from its direct object by an intervening VP adverb:

(14) a. he touched gently her shoulder

     b. she sought always the best for her servants

Such V-adverb-NP forms occur freely in languages with the V-to-INFL operation, including the Romance languages and earlier English, where the verb moves across Specifiers of VP and sentential elements which are sisters to INFL and VP:

(15) a. j'aime toujours les portraits de Rembrandt
        *I like always Rembrandt's portraits

     b. il finit heureusement les travaux
        *he is finishing happily the jobs

     c. ils regardent tous la télévision
        *they watch all television

The position of these adverbial elements did not change in sentences with auxiliary verbs: forms like *Kim can always visit London* stayed grammatical after (14) became obsolete.

The net result of the seventeenth-century change was that the INFL position was appropriated by a subclass of verbs: the modals and *do*. As a result, the V-to-INFL operation no longer applied generally to all tensed clauses. Eventually, true verbs could no longer move to the v position in INFL and the V-to-INFL operation was lost.

So I revise the earlier account by claiming that two major changes were involved. First, the changes in the distribution of the modal verbs, completed by the sixteenth century, reflected a recategorization in the lexicon as instances of INFL. Second, the late-seventeenth-century change in the distribution of verbs reflected the loss of their ability to move to INFL. This refines the account of Lightfoot 1974 and 1979 but retains its essential features: in each case I invoke changes that are purely syntactic in the sense that they consist of a recategorization and the loss of a particular (V-to-INFL) movement operation.[6] The changes affect structures, and lexical features play no central role. What will be important for the claims made here is that each of these structural changes was manifested primarily by the obsolescence of various forms. However, before I consider why these changes took place, and thus offer an explanation for the obsolescence of (11), let me consider some alternative accounts which have been offered.

Critics of Lightfoot 1979 fall into two classes, some arguing that the premodal verbs were auxiliary-like in Old English and others arguing that they have been verbs throughout their history, undergoing changes in lexical features but no structural change. Denison (1989) and Warner (1990) point to some auxiliary-like behavior of the premodal verbs in Old

English but do not actually argue for full auxiliary status. The most important data, noted independently (Denison and Warner are divided by the Pennines, which have blocked all forms of conspiracy and collaboration since the Wars of the Roses), involve the occurrence of premodals with the impersonal verbs discussed in section 6.1:

(16) a. mæg þæs þonne ofþyncan ðeodne Heaðobeardna   (*Beowulf*, ed. Dobbie, 2032)
        may of-that[gen] then displease prince[dat] of-the-Heathobards
        'that may then displease the prince of the Heathobards'
    b. his me sceal aþreotan for Romana gewinnum   (*Orosius* 115.30)
        it[gen] me[dat/acc] shall weary for Romans' conflicts
        'I must weary of it because of the conflicts of the Romans'

Warner notes that in such examples, which occur quite frequently in the texts, the premodal acts as a "sentence-modifier," having no nominative subject of its own, and therefore is some sort of auxiliary. He adopts notions from the work of Eleanor Rosch and takes such data to motivate a subordinate category which later evolved into a basic-level category in the sixteenth century or shortly before, which in turn led to a further shift in the nineteenth century, mostly relating to *be*. If the sixteenth-century changes manifest the emergence of a full-fledged "basic-level" auxiliary category, then it is not clear what status a "subordinate" category had in the earlier grammar. However, there are other ways of approaching these data, particularly after the discussion of impersonal verbs in section 6.1. First, the data show clearly that the premodal verbs did not necessarily assign a thematic role to their subject NP, which could therefore be empty, as with *seems* and *snows*. Denison suggests that this happened only with impersonal verbs, but Warner shows instances of the occurrence of premodals without subjects as epistemics, as in (17).

(17) eaðe mæg gewurdan þæt þu wite þæt ic nat   (Apollonius of Tyre, ed. Goolden, 1958, 21.10)
        '(it) easily may be that you know what I do-not-know'

Second, it was noted in section 6.1 that a dative NP could move to subject position and act like a "quirky subject." If so, it could presumably also move to the subject position of a higher clause, even though Old English generally did not have the usual kind of subject-to-subject raising (see section 4.1). Recall that subject-to-subject raising did not occur before the infinitival *to* marker came to transmit the case-assigning and head-government properties of the governing verb; until then the empty subject would not have been head-governed and hence would not have been licensed at S-structure. However, the impersonal verbs assign inherent case at D-structure, and an NP with inherent case is free to move as long as it does not acquire a second, structural case, presumably because its trace is identifiable through its inherent case. If an analysis along these lines can be maintained, these data do not provide any motivation for treating the premodals as anything other than verbs in Old English.

As far as I know, nobody has gone beyond Warner and argued that the premodals were full-fledged auxiliaries in Old English. On the other hand, others have argued for stasis (i.e., that no structural change took place), on the grounds that the premodals remain verbs throughout the history of English. So Allan (1988) and Lieber (1982) claim that these verbs have simply acquired more and more exceptional lexical features. Allan, in fact, revives the generative-semantics approach to diachrony and adopts the view that the rules of the base are invariant except with regard to "word order changes" (p. 143).[7] He illustrates his approach with the development of *cunnan* (his example 2.23):

(18) cunnan   [+ ___ NP]
     [+V]   + ___ V
     [+non part]   [+non part]
     [+part 1]
     [+part 2]   ⇒ [−part 2] ⇒ [−part 1] ⇒ [−non part]

(18) codifies that *cunnan* first loses the ability to appear in a present participle ("part 2"), then loses the ability to appear as a past participle ("part 1"), and eventually fails to appear as an infinitive ("non part"). Allan writes that "the introduction of these features allows us to capture the time spread over which the changes occur and to capture the exceptions," and he adds an air of mystery by telling us that his lexical-diffusion model "makes claims about preservation of communication between generations" (p. 143). The problem lies precisely in that "these changes in the features attached to the lexical entry reflect the increasingly restricted distribution of *cunnan.*" As *cunnan* becomes more restricted in its distribution, a feature changes. The obsolescence of a particular form, however, is a negative datum: if the form ceases to occur for a particular generation, its nonoccurrence can scarcely be said to trigger anything, unless novel claims are to be made about the experiential basis of language acquisition. The resulting grammar, including a compendium of lexical features, may reflect the historical evolution of the language (or, rather, one view of it), but it could not have been attained in that form by young children of, say, the seventeenth century, who knew nothing of the earlier history of the

language. So at best Allan and Lieber (who adopts the same approach) offer a means of codifying changes which are quite unexplained. If different forms had become obsolete, there would have been different lexical features. Since the changes affecting the premodal verbs were manifested overwhelmingly by obsolescence (e.g., of forms like (11)) rather than by innovative forms, an account in terms of lexical features does not meet basic requirements. Consequently it is not surprising that no account can be offered for why so many of the relevant lexical features should have changed at one time, during the sixteenth century.[8]

The first change, whereby the premodal verbs came to be classified as instances of INFL and to be generated under INFL, was a change in lexical specifications and therefore may have affected some items earlier than others. The claims of Warner (1983), Plank (1984), and Allan (1988) that the changes progressed gradually may help to illuminate the actual sequence of recategorizations, although the claims must be treated with some caution (see below). What is important here is to establish what changes in the primary linguistic data triggered the recategorization. To establish this, one needs to know what changes took place in triggering experiences before the recategorizations occurred.

The consequences of some morphological changes that took place gradually through the Middle English period are listed as (12b)–(12d). The preterite-present inflectional class, to which all the premodals except *willan* belonged, became much smaller during Middle English (see (12b)): some preterite-present verbs were reassigned to other, more regular inflectional classes, and others (the least common[9]) disappeared from the language altogether. There was some variability, and some forms survived as instances of INFL only in northern and Midland dialects, including *dugan* 'avail', *þurfan* 'need', and *munan* 'intend'. After the general simplification of verbal inflection, the surviving members of this class were inflectionally distinct, lacking the distinctive third-person-singular -s ending. Furthermore, the surviving members of this class were the premodals, which had not been inflectionally distinct. It has sometimes been hinted that semantic factors determined which of these verbs were lost, but these factors have never been properly articulated. So Plank (1984), putting the cart before the proverbial horse, claims that elements with grammatical meaning occur in smaller, semantically more coherent word classes than elements with purely notional meaning, and that they do not tolerate extensive synonymy (p. 312); no evidence is offered for these generalizations, nor is any reason given to view the premodal verbs (before their recategorization) as "elements with grammatical meaning."

Being preterites in origin, the preterite-presents developed a new past tense, which was phonetically identical in many forms to the subjunctive (modern *could, might, should, would*). As the subjunctive mood was lost as a general inflectional category, so *could* etc. preserved certain subjunctive senses, carrying no past-tense sense; see the modern *she could be here tomorrow* and *she might be a student*. So the relations *can: could, may: might*, and so on were not necessarily temporal (see (12c)).

Finally, the emerging *to* form of the infinitive, discussed in section 4.1, never occurred with the premodals (see (12d)). This also held for the active forms of perception and causative verbs; thus, it is not entirely definitional of the premodals, but presumably it helped to distinguish them as an emerging class.

These three changes had the effect of isolating the premodals, but it is sometimes claimed that other factors were involved. Allan (1988) and Plank (1984) claim that changes in meaning were crucial, but their claims are not convincing. They point to the particular meanings that the premodals had in association with direct objects, and they note that these meanings were lost: *sculan* meant 'have to pay', *cunnan* 'know', and so forth. However, as was noted above, the loss of these meanings was too late to be a causal factor and, in any case, was entirely a by-product of the recategorization: once *shall, can*, etc. were classed as INFL, they could not occur with direct objects, and consequently the meanings they had in association with direct objects were automatically lost. Similarly, the development of nonpast meanings for *could, might*, etc. is a by-product of the homophony of the old subjunctive and past-tense forms and of the loss of the subjunctive mood as a distinctive morphological class; no independent semantic change is implicated here. Of course, there were independent semantic changes affecting the premodals, many of which were noted in Lightfoot 1979: *should* used to mean 'was under an obligation to', and *may* used to mean 'have physical capability to'. However, the loss of these meanings seems unrelated to the recategorization; certainly nobody has shown how such changes made the linguistic environment more likely to trigger the new classification of the premodals. That is what would be needed in order to show that semantic factors were crucially involved, and this has not been shown, despite contrary protests by Allan and Plank.

Consequently, it is reasonable to hold that it was the morphological changes of (12) that led to the recategorization. These changes had the effect, in many ways accidental, of making the premodals into a small and distinctive class. In fact, the class was so small that it must have looked to language learners like a closed class, consisting of items which were not heads in the sense of our phrase-structure conventions (section 1.2) and not special kinds of verbs. It seems that such morphological factors are crucial for determining category membership, and here one sees another instance of syntactic changes determined by prior morphological changes. The syntactic changes are characterized by obsolescence (see (11)), and we have the right kind of explanation, keying their loss to the emergence of a new morphological system, which in turn entailed a reclassification of a set of verbs. This casts some light on how words are assigned to syntactic categories, which is not well understood. It also casts light on the nature of the triggering experience: the obsolescent forms (11), heard by children who had classified *can* as INFL, ceased to trigger any grammatical property that would ensure their survival.

If something along these lines is plausible, then from the sixteenth century on, in the standard language, the verbal position in INFL was appropriated by the modal verbs and *do*. For some 200 years verbs could continue to move to this position, if it was empty, and thus perpetuate the old surface patterns. At this stage one found S-structures like (19), where the verb has moved to the empty v position in INFL.

(19) a. $_{INFL}$[come$_i$ AGR] John $_{VP}$[e$_i$ to London]
      b. John $_{INFL}$[come$_i$ AGR] not $_{VP}$[e$_i$ to London]
      c. John $_{INFL}$[read$_i$ AGR] $_{VP}$[often e$_i$ newspapers]

However, this V-to-INFL operation did not apply if the v position was already filled by a modal:

(20) a. $_{INFL}$[can AGR] John $_{VP}$[come to London]
      b. John $_{INFL}$[can AGR] not $_{VP}$[come to London]
      c. John $_{INFL}$[can AGR] $_{VP}$[often read newspapers]
      a'. *$_{INFL}$[can AGR come$_i$] John $_{VP}$[e$_i$ to London]
      b'. *John $_{INFL}$[can AGR come$_i$] not $_{VP}$[e$_i$ to London]
      c'. *John $_{INFL}$[can AGR read$_i$] $_{VP}$[often e$_i$ newspapers]

The V-to-INFL operation was then lost altogether. This second change was also manifested primarily by obsolescence: the loss of inverted forms like *came John to London?*, negatives like *John came not to London*, and postverbal adverbs like *John read often newspapers* (see (19)). Again one finds a discrepancy between experience and production: some children heard the old forms but did not produce them, because no grammatical device had been triggered which would ensure their survival. Why should these forms have dropped out of the language when they were robust and frequently attested in the linguistic environment? The inverted and negative forms came to exploit the periphrastic *do* in modern English (*did John come to London?*, *John did not come to London*), and it seems natural to try to explain the obsolescence of the old forms in terms of the new periphrastic forms.

Ellegård (1953) argued that in Old English *do* was a causative verb and did not take on a periphrastic usage until the late thirteenth or early fourteenth century. It occurred characteristically in a biclausal structure and could be followed by either a *þæt* or, increasingly, an infinitival complement clause. However, there were noncausative uses with an empty VP:

(21) reced weardode unrim eorla, swa hie oft ær dydon   (*Beowulf*, 1238)
    'innumerable men guarded the building, as they often did'

The rise of the periphrastic took place, Ellegård claimed, under the special conditions of the southwestern dialect of the thirteenth century, in which the embedded infinitive almost always lacked a lexical subject: *he dude writes send* 'he caused to send writs'. Out of context such sentences might have a causative ((22a)) or a periphrastic ((22b)) interpretation.

(22) a. he did $_{S'}$[PRO $_{VP}$[writs send]]
    b. he $_{INFL}$[do AGR] $_{VP}$[writs send]

Here *did* is an element in INFL carrying the tense marker. Ellegård showed that the periphrastic *do* was exploited first by poets, for rhythmical purposes and rhyming, since it often permitted the infinitive to occur at the end of a line; he pointed to some writers who used the periphrastic in verse but only the causative in prose. As the periphrastic use became more common, the causative gave way to *make* and *cause*. We saw in section 4.1 how structures like (22a) became obsolete as an indirect result of the new verb order. Presumably the reclassification of the premodal verbs, such that there arose a class of lexical items which could be base-generated in INFL, also played some influence in favoring the analysis of (22b). Only at the end of the fifteenth century did the *do* form become widely used in prose texts. From then on it spread rapidly for about two generations (Ellegård 1953, p. 209). At this stage, *do* was used "exuberantly" as a tense carrier, particularly in learned writings, occurring even with modal elements: *hit you behouith ... behold ho [= who] shall doo gouerne* (c. 1475, Partenay (EETS) 2385). This usage survived until St. Thomas More: *now if I would then doe ... tel him that ...* (1534 *Works* [1557] 1192 F4). The fifteenth century marks a watershed; from then on the use of *do* was more strictly confined to its present-day contexts, and this state was reached in the seventeenth century in most dialects. Contemporary grammarians viewed *do* as a tense carrier with no other meaning of its own. In 1633 Charles Butler (*English Grammar*, p. 45) wrote: "The Present tense is

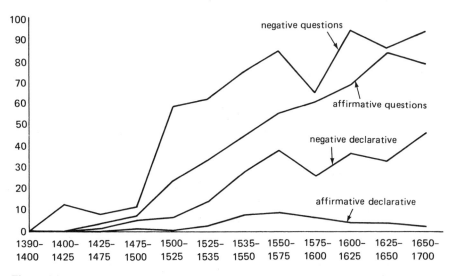

Figure 6.1
Rise of periphrastic *do*.

formed ... either with the sign, or without the sign: '*I love, thou lovest, hee looveth* ...; with the sign: *I doo loove, thou doost love, hee dooeth loove* ...'" In 1685 Christopher Cooper noted in his *Grammatica Linguae Anglicanae* (Part III Cap. 4 Section 5) "*I did learn* discebam et *I learned* aequipollent."

Ellegård (1953) examined various construction types and calculated the percentage using *do*, presenting his results in a graph on page 162; that graph is presented here, in redrafted form, as figure 6.1. From the end of the fourteenth century, as the causative *do* was disappearing, the overall frequency of the *do* forms rose quickly. These statistics have been examined by Kroch (1989a, b), who showed that the *rate* of increasing usage of *do* is virtually identical through 1560 in the four relevant construction types, although the change occurs first with negative questions and last with affirmative declaratives. That is, the graphs rise essentially in parallel over that period. This parallelism is strong evidence that there was a grammatical change underway, as Kroch discusses, and he argues that the rise in periphrastic *do* was related to the change in verb order discussed above in chapter 3. After 1560, the frequency of *do* in affirmative (nonemphatic) declaratives drops steadily; by the eighteenth century, the modern restriction against the use of *do* in this context is established.

The distribution of periphrastic *do*, as reported by Ellegård, varies within the writings of individual authors, and therefore the data cannot be interpreted only in terms of a mixture of dialects. A better interpretation is that there was no change in the relevant aspects of individuals' grammars before 1560. Grammars incorporated the V-to-INFL operation and allowed *do* to be classified in the lexicon as INFL with no distinctive meaning of its own; this represented a change from the earliest grammars, in which *do* was arguably only a main verb with some kind of causative or factitive meaning. For any utterance, then, *do* might or might not occupy INFL at D-structure; if not, the verb would move to this position and carry the AGR features. There was much variation in whether or not *do* occurred, but some structural factors seem to have favored its occurrence—for example, at any time before 1560 *do* was more likely to occur with negative than with affirmative questions. Throughout this period the grammar did not change in any relevant way, but the relative frequency of the competing forms varied; as noted, the *do* forms increased steadily.

According to Ellegård's figures, however, 1560 marks a turning point. From this point, *do* dropped in frequency in three of the four contexts measured, and in one context (affirmative declarative sentences) it never recovered from the drop. Thus periphrastic *do* became restricted to contexts where the v position in INFL was separated from the verb by intervening lexical material at S-structure. This marks the beginning of the loss of the V-to-INFL process. It is not enough to say that V-to-INFL failed to apply across intervening material and continued to operate elsewhere, because that would predict that *came John to London?* should have continued to occur (V-to-INFL followed by movement of INFL to an initial position). Now it must be explained why V-to-INFL was lost, which forced *do* to occur in INFL (hitherto just one of two options).

It is hard to imagine that this is not related to the fact that a class of lexical items, the former premodals, were now base-generated in INFL. This was the context in which periphrastic *do* emerged, being another manifestation of INFL. These were essentially changes in category membership, in the lexical classifications (not in lexical features, however), which had many consequences for what was generated by the grammar but no effect on the *structural* properties of individuals' grammars (no new movement operations, for example, were introduced or lost at this stage). As a result of these changes, the v position in INFL was now, for the first time, associated with particular lexical items, and hence constituted a lexical category.[10] That seems to be the context in which a structural change, the loss of the V-to-INFL operation, occurred. Because affixes must be attached to lexical categories, as the V-to-INFL operation was no longer available, so an INFL lowering process was activated, whereby inflectional elements could be attached to a lower verb (the familiar "affix hopping"). Somehow Universal Grammar must enforce a connection between the new lexicalness of INFL and the loss of V-to-INFL in order to explain the obsolescence of *came John to London?* and the like.

Problems of this kind have often elicited functional solutions. The loss of V-to-INFL eliminated rampant violation of bi-uniqueness relations between D-structures and S-structures: the pairs *John did leave*: *John left* and *John did not leave*: *John left not* had effectively identical D-structures, differing only in whether INFL contained the dummy element *do*. So one might ascribe the loss of V-to-INFL to a need to eliminate such dysfunctional multiplicity. However, as is usually the case with such functional accounts, one is left wondering why periphrastic *do* should ever have emerged in the first place, if it created such dysfunctional violation of bi-uniqueness relations; its emergence seems to have served no particular need.

Chomsky (1988) invokes a novel kind of functionalism. He argues, developing work by Pollock (1989), that modern English AGR is "weak" and thus cannot "attract" true verbs, which assign thematic roles.[11] He provides an analysis of verbal inflection based on the principle that raising of V is necessary if possible, because shorter derivations are preferred to longer ones by a kind of "least effort" principle. The lowering of INFL onto verbs in modern English leaves an improper trace, which necessitates raising of the inflected verb back to the trace position at LF—a two-step derivation. The *do* option avoids such two-step derivations: inflectional endings attach to *do* without lowering to V with subsequent raising at LF. However, as Chomsky notes, this device also permits **John did write books* (*do* unstressed), which should be not only available but (arguably) obligatory if shorter derivations are always preferred. Consequently, writes Chomsky, "the 'least effort' condition must be interpreted so that UG principles are applied wherever possible, with language-particular rules [e.g., *do*-support—DWL] used only to 'save' a D-structure yielding no output.... UG principles are thus "less costly" than language-specific principles. We may think of them, intuitively, as 'wired-in' and distinguished from the acquired elements of language, which bear a greater cost." (p. 9) This means that selection of *do*-support is a reflex of parameter setting, i.e. choice of weak AGR under Chomsky's analysis.

Given the historical material discussed in this section, Chomsky might say that some property of "weak AGR" emerged as a result of the morphological changes isolating the premodal verbs, and that periphrastic *do* developed as a result of this new parameter setting. However, his functional account then runs into difficulties: initially, as we have seen, *do* developed quite generally, occurring in affirmative declaratives alongside negative and inverted sentences. This permits short derivations, but such derivations were already ensured by the V-to-INFL operation, which persisted after the recategorization of the premodals and the initial rise of periphrastic *do*. The question then arises: What could have induced language learners in the mid-sixteenth century to begin not to select the V-to-INFL operation, and at the same time not to use forms like *John did write books*? If a functional account is invoked to explain the general, across-the-board rise of periphrastic *do*, it is hard to see how such an account can also treat the subsequent restrictions that characterized the use of *do* from 1560 on.

What is needed from Universal Grammar, rather, is an account of why the option of having lexical items classified as manifestations of INFL should preclude the option of moving verbs up to that position, although both options could coexist for some 200 years. Because the changes are characterized by the obsolescence of various forms, an account cannot be provided in strictly language-specific terms; Universal Grammar must play a role. For the moment I shall leave the matter there, having defined a problem fairly clearly but having offered no solution. A proper formulation of the relevant principle(s) will depend on the examination of other grammars permitting a lexical manifestation of INFL at D-structure and disallowing the V-to-INFL operation.

6.3   Conclusion

The last two sections have examined the conditions under which some simple (degree-0 complex) and robust structures became obsolete in earlier English. The mere fact of obsolescence shows that the triggering experience (i.e., the *primary* linguistic data) did not include such simple expressions, even though they are robustly attested in childhood experience: they had no shaping effect on the new emerging grammars. No data are simple or complex until given at least a partial analysis, and, as we saw earlier, the triggering experience at all stages of a child's development does not consist only of words or sentences; it also includes partially analyzed expressions, with various structures assigned. The point of this chapter has been to show that no analysis was available for such expressions at the time that they became obsolete. For this reason, they were not part of the triggering experience for seventeenth-century children, and they had to be reanalyzed.

We started from the assumption that cases of obsolescence require a type of explanation very different from that required by the introduction of novel forms, being viewed as a by-product of other changes. What is distinctive about the cases of obsolescence discussed in this chapter, apart from their evident simplicity and robustness, is that prior changes in the triggering experience (the loss of dative case endings discussed in section 6.1, and the morphological isolation of the premodals discussed in section 6.2) made conservative analyses unavailable under certain assumptions about Universal Grammar. So those hypotheses about Universal Grammar would explain the obsolescence, given the prior changes identified. Regardless of whether children are degree-0 learners or whether they set their parameters on the basis of complex structures, the forms discussed could no longer occur with their earlier analyses and, in many cases, had to drop out of the language.

These scenarios are quite different from those discussed in chapters 3 and 4. There I examined changes affecting embedded clauses, showing that they were by-products of new parameter settings induced in turn by new patterns in *unembedded* Domains. There was no reason to believe that the obsolescent forms could not have been perpetuated by analyses consistent with what is known of Universal Grammar, *if* children were sensitive to data from unembedded Domains. There are two relevant cases: the loss of object-verb order in embedded clauses (chapter 3) and the loss of active infinitives in forms like *I ordered grass to cut* (section 4.1). First, after children came to set the verb-order parameter such that verbs preceded their complements at D-structure, they could have preserved the old object-verb order of embedded clauses by a trivial application of the widely employed adjunction operation, adjoining the object NP to its VP as in (23) and yielding the surface object-verb form (for such adjunction operations, see Chomsky 1986).

(23) Kay said $_S'$[Comp $_S$[Ray $_{VP}$[Jay$_i$ $_{VP}$[met e$_i$]]]]

Not only is such a strategy available; it would be expected if children set their parameters on the basis of data from embedded Domains. Second, after adopting a verb-complement setting, if children were sensitive to the active form of an embedded infinitive, they would have been expected to perpetuate forms like *I ordered grass to cut* either by treating *cut* as a middle form (if such an analysis is permitted by Universal Grammar) or by treating *grass* as adjoined to VP, as in (23). These would be trivial consequences if children were not degree-0 learners. The fact that they did not occur suggests strongly that children are indeed degree-0 learners.

So, although many matters have been left unresolved, it is clear that the obsolescence discussed in this chapter is different in kind from the obsolescence involved in the changes discussed earlier: the obsolescent forms here simply could not be analyzed by children equipped with an appropriate form of Universal Grammar. However, it seems that it would be impossible to invoke aspects of Universal Grammar to account for the obsolescence of object-verb sequences and active infinitives in embedded clauses. If Universal Grammar cannot explain the obsolescence of these embedded forms in anything like the way that it has served to explain the obsolescence of the simple, unembedded forms discussed in this chapter, then something else is needed. If children set their parameters entirely on the basis of unembedded data, then we have the principled account that we need, and there is no reason to invoke Universal Grammar for the obsolescence of such embedded forms.

Chapter 7
Chaos, Catastrophes, and Creoles

7.1 Chaos and the Gradualness of Change

Anybody who has attended a performance of *Richard III* or read the King James version of the Bible knows that English has changed over the last 400 years. Shakespeare's sentence structures were not like those of today's English, although few of them are difficult to understand. Difficulties do arise, however, if one goes back 200 years more to Chaucer's *Canterbury Tales*, where the language is a good deal less familiar. Go back much further, to *Beowulf*, and one may as well be reading a foreign language. Large-scale changes that one can perceive over centuries reflect, in some way, smaller changes. A middle-aged person who has kept letters or tape recordings from twenty years ago may well have evidence that there have been changes in the kinds of expressions used, and sometimes in aspects of pronunciation. Such changes may accelerate if a person moves from one linguistic community to another in which a significantly different form of the same language is used. They may also accelerate if somebody comes under the influence of speakers of another language. The most striking changes in an individual's speech involve the use of idiomatic phrases, which may change substantially over a lifetime. So linguistic change affects languages and individuals quite generally, and the study of its generality formed the basis of modern linguistics, revealing productive methods of description and analysis, types of change, and more.

Not only are languages in a state of constant change, but any individual speaker is liable to be exposed to different forms of that language through changes of circumstances. There may also be statistical changes, with certain forms being heard more frequently as one moves to a new home or job or takes up with a new circle of friends. In fact, the linguistic experiences of any two speakers are almost certain to be different, if only in terms of the statistical frequency of some construction types. Everything is in flux.

As historical linguists have sought to record and understand this flux, they have been impressed by the apparent gradualness of change. Indeed, they have often been overimpressed, inventing or "reconstructing" unattested stages mediating between two attested forms and thus creating a "gradual" change from one to the other.

Harris' (1980) concern for gradualness led her to analyze Old English sentences such as *þam wife [dative] þa word[nominative] wel licodon[plural]* (*Beowulf* 640), which she glossed as 'the woman liked these words well', with *wife* as the underlying subject and *word* as the underlying object. An optional "inversion" rule demoted the subject to indirect object for certain verbs, and an obligatory "unaccusative" rule advanced the direct object to subject. Harris offered no evidence for this analysis of these sentences, and did not suggest how a child might be led to treat the dative NP as the underlying subject and the nominative NP as the underlying direct object. She considered no alternatives, and she did not mention the change affecting the thematic roles of the NPs associated with the verbs occurring in these contexts (see section 6.1); nor did she ask why the change took place. Instead, the goal was to discuss the gradualness of the loss of the putative inversion rule, as if this took place independently. Harris represented the change as a process whereby three "coding rules" of Word Order, Subject Agreement, and Case Marking, which formerly applied to the output of Inversion, gradually and one by one came to apply to the input to the rule, rendering the rule redundant and inapplicable in an unexplained way. It is not clear what might have triggered the reordering of each of these rules with respect to Inversion, but Harris was satisfied that intermediate stages must have existed, even though they were inherently "unstable."

Commitment to the gradualness of change has a long pedigree. It was a crucial element in the "typological" view of change, which dominated discussion of diachronic syntax in the 1970s. The typologists held that languages progressed from one "consistent" type to another, losing and acquiring harmonic word-order properties in a prescribed order. So "diachronic universals" were stated in terms of "continua" or "hierarchies" by which, say, a SOV language might acquire all the harmonic properties of a SVO language; so the new verb-object order was said to emerge before the new noun-determiner or noun-adjective order, etc. The hierarchies were quite elaborate, sometimes involving 15–20 word-order properties, but no single language's history was ever shown to record more than one or two changes in these relationships. This entailed postulating many unattested stages to account for such changes as those deriving the modern Romance languages from Latin, where a fairly complete typological change was thought to have taken place. That change was broken down into many constituent parts, but many of those constituent parts were not attested and, where attested, sometimes differed from what was found in other languages undergoing parallel typological shifts. It was perhaps not surprising that the most elaborate work was conducted on reconstructed histories, where problems of attestation did not arise. Lightfoot (1979, p. 387ff.), Smith (1981), and Coopmans (1984) offer critical discussions of the general approach which demonstrate that the commitment to the gradual acquisition of the new harmonic properties was much more an article of faith than a empirical result based on investigation.

A defining characteristic of gradualness was also inherent in earlier approaches to syntactic change. For example, Traugott (1969) formulated diachronic processes mapping one grammar into its successor, and Hausmann (1974), who held that successive grammars could differ from each other only minimally, described the rise of periphrastic *do* as a sequence of rule reorderings and reformulations of conditions on transformational rules. Gradualism is also inherent in more traditional approaches that ascribed change to a series of analogies between surface structures, or sought to break down large-scale changes whereby a language moved from being globally "synthetic" to generally "analytic." As with the typological analyses of the 1970s, many of the intermediate stages had to be "reconstructed" in the absence of any attestation, and there were no reliable methods of internal reconstruction (Lightfoot 1980).

A less procrustean way of modeling gradualness is through the use of a rich set of lexical features. As a particular verb is recorded in a new syntactic environment, a feature in its lexical specification is changed accordingly. This model has been formulated in different ways. Proponents of "abstract syntax" or "generative semantics" in the 1960s annotated lexical items with features indicating which transformational rules they could or could not undergo (Lakoff 1968). Allan (1988), Lieber (1982), and many others annotated items with features specifying which morphological forms they may or may not manifest at any given time (see chapter 6). Such models, with fairly unconstrained systems of features, permit accurate codifications of what occurs in the historical texts at any period. However, they cannot be construed as representations of a person's mature linguistic capacity, because they are demonstrably not attainable. This can be seen particularly clearly in cases of obsolescence, where the loss of a construction with some verb is codified by a new lexical feature on that verb. The problem is that this new feature is a response to the *absence* of some syntactic form, and there is no reason to believe that children set grammatical parameters on the basis of negative data. Such models have been popular with historians because they are powerful enough to state even the narrowest generalization, but they are not grammars in the sense of being models of a person's mature linguistic capacity, attained through normal childhood experience. Although they can be made to be observationally accurate, systematizing what is recorded in the texts at an arbitrary time by ever-changing lexical features, these models characteristically offer no explanations for the changes being recorded.

If the gradualness of change has been overemphasized, one may wonder where its limits lie. If grammars assign different structures to expressions from one generation to the next, then at least some changes will be abrupt: if syntactic structures are topological entities, as assumed here, they are not generally amenable to incremental modification. However, the triggering experience and grammars may change gradually in certain ways.

First, some changes take place while grammars remain constant. For example, a particular construction type may become more frequent, perhaps as a result of taking on some expressive function (a greatly underestimated source of linguistic change). So dislocation structures such as *George, I like him* may vary in frequency as a matter of fashion as groups of speakers adopt different means for focusing on different NPs. As another example, we saw in chapter 3 that Old English could conjoin clauses at the level of IP or an extra YP projection. If the second conjunct was YP, then the verb occurred in Comp; if the second conjunct was IP, there was no pre-S position to which the verb could move, and it typically remained in clause-final position. Both analyses were possible, but the second option gradually became less frequently attested in the texts through the Old English period. This reflected a change in the performance of speakers in terms of the likelihood of choosing one or other of the available analyses, but there was no reason to say that the gradual change observed in the texts manifested a change in individuals' grammars. The same would be true if one observed a gradually changing ratio of active and passive sentences whereby, say, passives became somewhat more common. Although they do not reflect changes in grammars, such changes nonetheless affect the triggering experience. The declining frequency of object-verb order in conjunct clauses may interact with other factors to help set the verb-order parameter differently, as we saw in chapter 3. At that point an abrupt change takes place, but it was preceded by gradual changes affecting triggering experiences but not grammars.

Second, lexical items may be categorized differently, and this recategorization may affect some words before others, progressing gradually. We saw in chapter 6 that the premodal verbs were recategorized as instances of INFL as a result of a number of morphological changes simplifying the verb classes of Old English. Not only were the morphological changes gradual, affecting certain verbs before others according to the evidence of the surviving texts; in addition, the recategorization may have been gradual, affecting certain premodal verbs before others. Similarly, *do* came to be classified as an instance of INFL, being base-generated in that position, and this new classification may have preceded or followed the recategorization of specific premodal verbs. Since the recategorization of the premodal verbs took place, on the analysis of section 6.2, in response to prior morphological changes, one would expect variation in the time of the morphological shifts to entail variation in the time of the recategorization of any specific verb. Such recategorizations may affect classes of lexical items gradually by a kind of diffusion process. They may affect the structure of any given expression, such that *John can sing* is analyzed as (1a) instead of (1b), but they need not affect the total set of available structures; that is, they need not involve a change in the form of phrase-structure rules or in the definition of available projection types.

(1) a. John $_{INFL}$[can AGR] $_{VP}$[sing]
    b. John INFL $_{VP}$[can $_{S'}$[Comp $_S$[PRO INFL sing]]]

Third, the nature of the acquisition process ensures a certain kind of gradualness to change under usual circumstances, although circumstances are not always usual. Normally the output of a parent's grammar is a significant part of the linguistic environment that triggers the emergence of a child's grammar. This militates against major discontinuities in the class of expressions and their associated meanings. However, if such things could be quantified in some appropriate fashion, there would be no one-to-one relation between similarities at that surface level and similarities in the underlying system. Because grammars are abstract objects, grammars with quite different structural properties might generate sets of sentences which were more similar to each other, and grammars differing in just one parametric setting might generate wildly different outputs. Correspondingly, two slightly different sets of primary linguistic data might set some parameter(s) differently, entailing significantly different outputs. Furthermore, there are unusual circumstances where, because of population shifts, the output of a parent's grammar is not a significant part of a child's triggering experience.

Fourth, a new parameter setting may spread gradually through some speech community. That is, there may be a discrete change in the grammars of some individuals before the new parameter setting affects the grammars of others. This is expected if triggering experiences may change gradually in the ways that we have seen and if an individual's speech may change in the course of a few years. Consequently, my child's triggering experience is unlikely to be identical to the output of my grammar, and highly unlikely to be identical to the output of my grammar at the time that my parameters were first set (let us say up to 10 years of age). As somebody adopts a new parameter setting, say a new verb-object order, the output of that person's grammar often differs from that of other people's. This in turn affects the linguistic environment, which may then be more likely to trigger the new parameter setting in younger people. Thus a chain reaction may be created, which may gradually permeate the speech community. The spread of a new parameter setting through a speech community is typically manifested by categorically different usage on the part of different authors rather than by variation within the usage of individuals, although the data are sometimes not as clean as that idealization would suggest, because a writer often commands more than one form of a language.

This type of spread has often been misconstrued because of a failure to understand the limits to a useful idealization. Observers note some apparently gradient historical data and interpret it in terms of a gradual shift in "the grammar of Old English." The grammar of Old English, however, is a convenient fiction permitting the statement of certain generalizations and ignoring certain types of variation. It no more exists than there is such a real object as the French liver, the American brain, or the Irish wit. These fictions idealize the livers of Frenchmen and the brains of Americans and abstract away from much of the variation that one could observe if one considered the individual entities. So it is with grammars: grammars are individual constructs existing in the minds of individual speakers, just as livers and brains exist in individual bodies. There is no such thing as "the grammar of Old English"; rather, there were thousands of speakers, all of whom had internalized grammars, some differing from others. That *set* of grammars generated much of the Old English corpus, and much more that went unrecorded. If the grammar of English does not exist, then there can be no gradual shift in that grammar, in the same way that there could be no gradual shift in an aggregate French liver if alcohol ceased to be available.

So gradualness exists: triggering experiences may change gradually, lexical classifications may change gradually, and new parameter settings

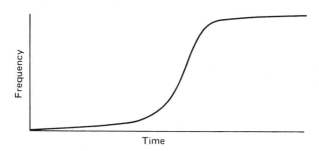

Figure 7.1

may gradually permeate a speech community. Much of this gradual change may have no immediate effect on the setting of *structural* parameters, which are reset only when the triggering experience has changed in some critical fashion. If one aggregates across dialects, genres, and time periods, one can study the global changes in much the same way that population geneticists study variations in the populations of species under various conditions.

The analogy with population genetics was taken up by Kroch (1989a), who considered some models of linguistic change, all of which could be expressed mathematically by the logistic function. When graphed against time, Kroch notes, the logistic function has a characteristic S-shape growth curve, familiar from much discussion on language change (figure 7.1). Kroch points out that "the logistic function expresses a number of basic growth relationships in population biology and genetics," such as the rate of replacement of one species by another where the two compete for the same resources with differential reproductive success. He goes on to show that it is also useful in understanding the development of the periphrastic *do* in English. In general, one might expect structural changes (reflecting new parameter settings) to show S-shape curves, and other changes (such as the loss of gender markings, discussed in Jones 1988) to show straight-line patterns.

In population biology and linguistic change there is constant flux; the changes are often slight and have no significant consequences. If one views a language as a totality, as historians often do, one sees a dynamic system that seems never to find a steady state. A slight perturbation may be followed by more perturbations, and in time the system may look quite different. Such systems are chaotic and have engaged the attention of chaos theoreticians (Gleick 1988). Chaotic systems are random and unpredictable, epitomized by the so-called Butterfly Effect: the weather may be so sensitive to tiny variations that the beat of a butterfly's wing in Beijing today may be the cause of a hurricane in upstate New York next month. In that case, there is no hope of making long-term weather forecasts, but simple mathematical equations can provide computer models of such chaotic systems. Widely separated observations of a chaotic system may appear random, but more closely spaced observations often reveal regularities. It is believed that there is order behind chaos, at least some chaos, and that the techniques of chaos theory may reveal simple causes for complex and unpredictable effects. Chaotic systems may be random and unpredictable, but they are governed by mathematical laws and have fractal or strange "attractors." Edward Lorenz, constructing a weather model in 1963, saw "order *masquerading* as randomness" (Gleick 1988). He saw weather as a system that almost repeated itself, but never exactly, and that this "aperiodicity" was what made it unpredictable. His computer models locked into repetitive cycles, but he eventually put in an equation that varied the amount of heating from east to west and destroyed the repetition. He mimicked both the nonrepetitiveness of weather and its sensitivity to slight variations in initial conditions, and then he sought simpler ways to produce this kind of complex behavior. He found one in a set of three nonlinear equations which generated a shape like an owl's eyes: a swirl of lines which most of the time circled one or other of the "eyes," meaning that the system had settled into a pattern of behavior that would repeat itself periodically. From time to time, however, the line would break out of its circle and move over to circle the other eye (corresponding to a marked change in wind patterns). Crucially, there was no way of knowing in advance when the line would switch over. Further, the fractal nature of Lorenz's attractor meant that an otherwise identical line might not cross over at the same point. Lorenz's system "always stayed within certain bounds, never running off the page but never repeating itself, either. It traced a strange, distinctive shape, a kind of double spiral in three dimensions, like a butterfly with its two wings. The shape signalled pure disorder, since no point or pattern of points ever recurred. Yet it also signalled a new kind of order." (Gleick 1988, p. 30; Gleick shows the trajectory on p. 28).

These developments are worth noting because they make clear that some general properties of language change are shared by other dynamic systems in the natural world, namely its aperiodicity and unpredictability in a context of underlying order. There even exist mathematical models which can simulate these properties in certain areas. Conspicuously, these models have been more successfully applied by physicists than by biologists. Techniques for analyzing chaos are "data-hungry," and it is hard to determine whether fractal attractors exist for some body of data unless there are enormous quantities of data. Though it may be hard to verify chaoticness in biological domains, the ideas of chaos theory have influenced the way in which problems are viewed. For example, it used to be assumed that populations might either remain essentially constant or fluctuate regularly around some equilibrium point, thus being essentially regular—with exceptions. Where erratic behavior was observed, it was assumed that that behavior had nothing to do with the mathematical models postulated; some missing feature, it was thought, could always explain the discrepancy. Alternatively, others took populations to fluctuate wildly—with exceptions. These opposing camps also differed over the application of mathematical models to biological questions, not surprisingly. Researchers who believed that populations were essentially regular in their behavior argued that they must be regulated by deterministic mechanisms; those who believed that they were erratic claimed that they must be bounced about by unpredictable environmental factors, which wipe out whatever deterministic properties might exist. Now, however, it is acknowledged that chaotic behavior may indeed exist. Simple deterministic models can produce what looks like random behavior. Behavior may have a fine structure, even though any part of it may be indistinguishable from noise. Analogously, from certain perspectives the basic phenomenon of language change is surprising, and one would expect languages to stabilize around "a consistent type" or "a set of unmarked parameter settings"; and, when one notes the variations in primary linguistic data, one might be surprised that grammars do not change at a faster rate. Somehow one needs to be able to model the order within the apparent chaos.

The Butterfly Effect acquired the technical name *sensitive dependence on initial conditions*, which Gleick related to old notions in folklore: "For want of a nail, the shoe was lost; for want of a shoe, the horse was lost; for want of a horse, the rider was lost; for want of a rider, the battle was lost; for want of a battle, the kingdom was lost." A chain of events can have a point of crisis that can magnify small changes. In the domain of linguistic change, this point is identifiable with a new parameter setting. Under the constant, chaotic flux in the linguistic environment, one can observe points where the data shifted in such a fashion as to entail a new parameter setting. Where that has happened, different and more catastrophic clusters of changes typically have taken place.

7.2 Catastrophes

The linguistic environment, then, changes constantly, and often in ways which are independent of the structural properties of individuals' grammars. Nonstructural changes do not require and could not receive explanations in terms of a theory of structural parameters. So a theory of grammatical parameters should not seek to explain all the changes that a language might undergo. After all, the history of a language is not determined by the properties it shows at some arbitrary starting point and by the properties of the mental genotype. Many changes are due to other things, which relate to the ways in which grammars are used rather than to their internal structure.

A moment's reflection will show that this must be the case, because a language may split in two and then pursue different courses, diverging more and more. Latin, for example, developed into French, Rumanian, Spanish, and several other identifiable languages. Most European languages and several languages spoken in India descend ultimately from a Proto-Indo-European language, for which there are no direct records. Although the parent language is usually supposed to have had an underlying word order of subject-object-verb, its descendants have quite different orders: Hindi has retained subject-object-verb, English has developed subject-verb-object, Welsh and Irish have verb-subject-object. Owing to the possibility of divergent development, historical changes cannot be fully determined by the properties of Proto-Indo-European and the (invariant) demands of Universal Grammar, the relevant part of our genetic endowment. The theory of grammars cannot prescribe a universal path for languages to slide along at various rates, acquiring properties in a predestined order; it cannot prophesy what changes a language will undergo in the future, because it cannot predict which chance factors will operate or when, and so it cannot predict what statistical shifts will take place in the linguistic environment.

Nonetheless, languages do not change in completely arbitrary ways; many changes recur in one language after another. Despite the role of nongrammatical factors and chance, some changes and the manner in which they arise can be explained and they occur as a matter of necessity, reflecting new parameter settings and often being somewhat catastrophic in nature.

In earlier chapters we examined six new parameter settings in the history of English: the new verb-complement order at D-structure (chapter 3), the ability of the infinitival *to* marker to transmit case-marking and head-government properties of a governing verb (chapter 4), the loss of the inherent D-structure oblique case (sections 5.3, 5.4, and 6.1), the emergence of a reanalysis operation (section 5.3), the recategorization of the premodal verbs, and the loss of the ability of verbs to move to a governing INFL position (section 6.2). Each of these new parameter settings has some distinctive characteristics.

First, each new parameter setting is manifested by a cluster of simultaneous surface changes, and this is one element of their catastrophic nature. For example, the loss of the V-to-INFL operation entailed the predominance of forms like *Kim always reads the editorials* instead of the earlier *Kim reads always the editorials* and the obsolescence of inversion and negative sentences like *reads Kim the editorials?* and *Kim reads not the editorials*. The same was true for all verbs, and there is no reason to believe that the change affected certain verbs before others. Similarly, the loss of inherent oblique case permitted the development of new personal passives with former dative-assigning verbs (such as *obey*), new prepositional passives (e.g., *Kim was spoken to*), and the loss of a variety of constructions with psych-verbs (*him like pears* and many others).

Second, not only are new parameter settings typically manifested by clusters of changes, but they also sometimes set off chain reactions. The clearest example of this from our studies is the establishment of verb-complement order at D-structure. We have seen that this entailed indirectly the analysis of the infinitival *to* as a transmitter of properties of its governing verb and the introduction of an operation analyzing *speak to, spoken to*, etc. as complex verbs. Such chain reactions can be understood through the acquisition process: a child with the new verb-complement setting is forced by the constraints of Universal Grammar to analyze expressions like *I ordered the grass cut + infin* differently from the way they were analyzed in earlier generations, with *the grass* coming to be analyzed as the subject of the embedded clause, as discussed in section 4.1.

Third, changes involving new parameter settings tend to take place more rapidly than other changes, and they manifest Kroch's S-curve. For example, grammaticalization and morphological change, involving the loss of gender markers (Jones 1988), the reduction in verbal desinences, or the loss of the subjunctive mood, generally take place over long periods, often several hundred years. In the transitional period, individual writers and speech communities show much variation in the forms they employ. This kind of gradual cumulativeness is generally not a hallmark of new parameter settings. The new verb-complement setting of the verb-order parameter was manifested primarily by the introduction of verb-object order in embedded clauses and the loss of object-verb order. Almost every scholar who has examined this change over the last hundred years has commented on the remarkable speed with which it proceeded, contrasting sharply with the much slower and more variable loss of object-verb order in matrix clauses. In chapter 3 I noted the statistics of Gorrell (1895), which showed object-verb order used 80–90 percent of the time in embedded clauses throughout the Old English period. There was no steady decline, but an abrupt elimination of the old order. Similarly, the old inverted and negative patterns (*reads Kim the editorials?* and *Kim reads not the editorials*) were quite robust and widely attested in the texts until their demise, which was rapid. And forms like *I ordered to go* were richly attested and then disappeared quickly, with active Old English forms like *I ordered [PRO the grass cut + infin]* being replaced with passives like *I ordered the grass to be cut*, as discussed in section 4.1. Of course, residual forms are found in archaistic texts, but the changes are generally characterized by sharp S-curves: the change may be foreshadowed in various ways, but there is a short period of rapid change, followed by a longer period where occasional residual forms gradually disappear. The fast spread of new parameter settings is not surprising if one thinks of it in the context of language acquisition. Once the linguistic environment has shifted in such a way as to trigger a new parameter setting in some children, the very fact that some people have a new parameter setting changes the linguistic environment yet further in the direction of setting the parameter in the new fashion. That is, the first people with the new parameter setting would produce different linguistic forms, which would in turn be part of the linguistic environment for younger people and so contribute to the spread of the new setting.

Fourth, obsolescence manifests new parameter settings. When structures become obsolete, it is hard to see how to attribute their obsolescence to the ebb and flow of nongrammatical changes in the linguistic environment. A novel form may be introduced for expressive reasons, to focus attention on some part of the expression by virtue of the novelty of the form, but a form can hardly drop out of the language for expressive reasons or because of the influence of another language. At least, that cannot be the direct cause. On the contrary, obsolescence must be due to a structural "knock-on" effect, a by-product of something else which was itself triggered by the kind of positive data that are generally available to children (see chapter 6 for discussion).

Fifth, any significant change in meaning is generally a by-product of a new parameter setting, for much the same reason that the obsolescence of a structure must be the indirect consequence of a more abstract change. Consider the psych-verbs discussed in section 6.1. Such changes affecting the thematic roles associated with particular NP positions could hardly arise as idiosyncratic innovations that somehow became fashionable within the speech community. It is hard to see how the variation in meaning could be attained by children on a nonsystematic basis, and even harder to see how the variation could have been introduced as a set of independent developments, imitating properties of another language or serving some expressive function through their novelty. Rather, such changes must be attributed to some aspect of a person's grammar which was triggered by the usual kind of environmental factors—in this instance, the existence of only structural cases.

Sixth, a further defining property of new parameter settings, if my central hypothesis is along the right lines, is that they occur in response to shifts in unembedded data only. They are not sensitive to changes or continuities in embedded domains. Embedded domains will be as likely as unembedded domains to reflect the usual toing and froing of the chaotic linguistic environment, but they have no effect on parameter setting. We saw this most clearly in the adoption of the new verb-complement order in early Middle English. This took place when embedded clauses had remained steadfastly object-verb; if children had been free to attend to them, these embedded clauses would have provided much evidence for an underlying object-verb order at D-structure.

Historians have always been aware that languages sometimes undergo a period of particularly rapid change, then settle into a time of relative stasis. From the perspective adopted here, it is natural to try to interpret such cascades of changes in terms of a new setting for some parameter, sometimes having a wide variety of surface effects and perhaps setting off a chain reaction. Such "catastrophic" changes have the distinctive features just discussed and are quite different from the piecemeal, gradual, and chaotic changes which constantly affect the linguistic environment.

These environmental changes, on the other hand, typically do not result from the genetically determined acquisition process, whereby something triggers some structural property with systematic effects. Rather, they are induced by contact with other languages and dialects or introduced for stylistic reasons, some being novel forms that achieve stylistic effect purely through their novelty. In each case these innovations either mimic or are independent, but they do not involve poverty-of-stimulus properties whereby elements of the input have wide-ranging systematic effects that go beyond the actual input data. For such environmental changes we have no systematic explanations, and as far as grammarians are concerned they may as well be attributed to chance: they are unlikely to tell us much about the nature of grammars, grammatical theory, or trigger experiences (except perhaps illustrating the structural limits within which borrowing and stylistic innovation may take place), and grammatical theory could never and should never explain why English speakers borrowed from French and not from Spanish in the Middle Ages.

This, of course, is not to say that such changes are unimportant, or that they are entirely random. They have the effect of changing triggering experiences for future generations, and this may entail a new setting for some parameter. So, for example, it is a fact of biological necessity that languages always have devices to draw attention to parts of sentences, and people may speak more expressively by adopting a novel or unusual construction, perhaps a new word order. When they first occur, these novel forms may not be part of the output of a grammar but may be quite irregular, specially learned accretions, in the way that formulaic expressions such as *Good morning*, *Hi*, and *Wow* are part of my language but quite idiosyncratic and not a function of any general rule.[1] There are limits, of course, but one cannot forecast which novel forms will be introduced or when; least of all can one forecast which novelties will catch on and be perpetuated. Chance or nongrammatical factors are at work. At a later stage the forms originally introduced as novelties may become "grammaticalized" and have a general, predictable, and rule-governed distribution. This would reflect a parameter's having been set in such a way that these forms are generated by the grammar.

Dislocation sentences fall under this rubric: for example, *Mingus, I heard him* and *he played cool, Miles*. These forms, they have been attested from Old English onward (Visser 1963, sections 67ff., 598ff.), but they have a distinct stylistic force, focusing attention on the NP. They have become common in Yorkshire dialects, among British sports commentators, and in the speech of many Jewish Americans. As they are commonly used, such expressive forms characteristically become bleached and lose their novelty value. This can be illustrated by the parallel dislocation sentences in French: *Pierre, je le connais* and *je le connais, Pierre* were originally stylistically marked alternants of *je connais Pierre*, but now they have lost much of their special force and have become relatively unremarkable construction types, to the point that in simple, affirmative main clauses they are the norm and the former *je connais Pierre* is vanishingly rare.

This process is familiar in lexical change, where, to the constant dismay of the purists, adjectives are regularly "devalued" by a kind of linguistic inflation: *excellent* comes to mean merely 'good', and *enormous* to mean 'big', and *fantastic*, *fabulous*, and other adjectives lose their original force. As this happens, new superlatives must be invented to describe the endpoint on some scale; hence novel forms such as *ginormous* and *fantabulous*, which have developed in some teenager speech. Similarly, metaphors become standard through frequent use, requiring a constant effort on the part of speakers to find new forms that have surprise value.

So in syntax new constructions are introduced which, by their unusual shape, have novelty value and are used for stylistic effect. The special stylistic effect slowly becomes bleached out, and the constructions lose their particular force, become incorporated into the normal grammatical processes, triggering some new parametric settings as they are grammaticalized, and thereby require speakers to draw on their creative powers once more to find another new pattern to carry the desired stylistic effect. So sentences such as *Mingus, I heard him* have a special focusing effect in most dialects; in other dialects, notably those of North Americans with a Yiddish background, the construction has already become bleached of its special effect, like the dislocation sentences of French.

These changes are grist for the mill of historical change. Without them linguistic change would be less interesting, in fact nonexistent; languages would be stable. They show the folly of trying to construct lengthy "drag chains," whereby the development of a language over millennia is construed as an inevitable consequence of some single innovation. A drag chain may involve two or three links, but there are no lengthy drag chains recorded so far which do not depend on the intervention of language-specific novelties. These phenomena are ubiquitous and indispensable to linguistic change; however, in contrast with new parameter settings, they do not necessarily cast light on grammatical theory, and they properly remain beyond grammatical explanation.

On this view of language history, parallel changes affecting several languages independently are not surprising. It is sometimes a matter of chance, nongrammatical factors that the linguistic environment should change in a particular way, perhaps incorporating a new kind of expression for a focusing effect. It is a matter of biological necessity that the grammar should be readily attainable, that surface strings should be processible with minimal perceptual difficulty, and that the ouput of one generation's grammars make up a large part of the triggering experience for the next generation. Such necessities force reanalyses at certain points and restrict the possibilities for any particular grammar. This explains the partial similarity of developments in French, English, and Lithuanian.

The properties of Universal Grammar and the way in which grammars are triggered shed light on catastrophic historical changes reflecting a new parameter setting, because the old parameter setting is no longer attainable. Conversely, the point at which parameters are set differently illustrates the limits to attainable grammars. A grammar is not an object floating smoothly through time and space, but a contingent object that arises afresh in each individual. An individual's grammar may differ significantly from that of her father; that constitutes a new parameter setting. If changes over time can inform us about the limits to grammars, the study of diachronic change can show how idiosyncratic properties may be added to a grammar without affecting its internal structure, and diachronic study may show what it takes to drive a grammar to reanalysis, with a parameter set differently. Examining historical reanalyses illuminates what kinds of triggering experiences elicit grammatical reanalyses and what kinds are not robust enough to have that effect. The point at which reanalyses take place sheds light on the load that can be borne by grammatical operations; the limits are manifested by the occurrence of the reanalyses; the reanalyses are manifested by the simultaneity of various surface changes and the other properties of parametric change (above). In this way research on historical change informs work on a restrictive theory of grammar and is fully integrated with that general enterprise.

Not only does the mere occurrence of a reanalysis suggest things about the proper shape of the theory of grammars, but the particular cluster of properties that the reanalysis encompasses is informative. Universal Grammar includes parameters which are set on exposure to relevant experience. Setting a parameter one particular way may have elaborate consequences for the form of somebody's knowledge—that is, for the range of possible surface structures. We have seen several examples of this, and research aims to define the parameters as accurately as possible. If in historical change a parameter comes to be set differently, the precise definition given by Universal Grammar for that parameter will have implications (often far-reaching ones) for what exactly will change in the surface structures. Examining the cluster of properties encompassed by particular reanalyses sometimes suggests things about how parameters should be defined. This is illustrated by the changes discussed in section 4.1, which suggested a new formulation of the parameter permitting lexical subjects to infinitival clauses, as in *I expect Kim to win*.

It may be objected that this approach to language history accounts only for some changes and not for others. Typically a theory works where it works and has no principled basis for not dealing with certain phenomena.

In this particular domain one *must* allow a role for nongrammatical factors; historical developments cannot and should not be totally predictable, for the reasons given earlier. Moreover, one cannot know in advance precisely which changes are due to chance, nongrammatical factors and which are prompted by the theory of grammars. I have adopted a typology of parametric change, identifying six characteristics, and it is reasonable to suppose that changes involving major semantic innovations or the loss of certain sentence types must be due to principled factors. However, there are gray areas, and we do not have enough firm guidelines to decide in advance of analysis exactly which phenomenological changes directly manifest a parametric change and which do not.

A theory of Universal Grammar casts light on historical changes by explaining new parameter settings. If a given theory explains change x and not change y, then x is a predictable reanalysis and y is due to nongrammatical causes. If a theory aims only to explain historical changes, there is a problem of indeterminacy; there is no independent way of knowing which changes were due to grammatical and which to nongrammatical functions, and thus no way to choose between theories that explain different changes, attributing others to chance. In fact, a theory of Universal Grammar, being a theory of part of the psychological makeup of human beings, must meet many more demands, and at this stage of research it is hard to imagine having to choose from a variety of theories which met the various empirical demands we are making, differing only in how they handle some change in the history of Spanish. The problem, rather, is to find one adequate theory.

The picture of language change that emerges is one of "punctuated equilibrium." Languages are constantly changing gradually and in piecemeal fashion, but meanwhile grammars remain in equilibrium, unchanged in their structural properties. From time to time, however, they undergo more radical, catastrophic restructuring, corresponding to new parameter settings. A process of gradual, piecemeal, and chaotic change punctuated by periodic structural change is reminiscent of current models of evolutionary change, but what is interesting about linguistic change of this type is that it requires a particular kind of explanatory model: one couched in claims about the genetically determined makeup of part of our cognitive capacity and about the way language acquisition proceeds. It is the definition of the parameters that accounts for the shape of the catastrophic changes. A coherent notion of what kind of linguistic experience sets these parameters will account for the timing of the structural changes.

7.3   Creoles

Sometimes new parameter settings may arise in rapid succession. This might happen under an especially heterogeneous triggering experience consisting of expressions from various languages, including perhaps a "pidgin" language. For example, creoles are acquired, at least in their early stages, under unusual conditions: the linguistic experience of one generation of children is quite different from that of the preceding generation, and, more important, the linguistic input for that generation differs quite dramatically from the capacity the children eventually attain. If we can discover some properties of the grammars that emerge in these people, and if we know something of the childhood experience that triggered those properties, we may be able to learn something about triggers in general and about the limiting cases. The particularly dramatic contrast between the input and the mature capacity of the first creole speakers might make it easier to identify which elements of their experience acted as triggers for the emerging grammars, if we can take advantage of the experiment that nature has provided.

If the triggering experience is a subset of a child's total linguistic experience, consisting only of some data from unembedded binding Domains, then the total experience involves considerable redundancy in the "information" available to the child. From this perspective, the restrictedness of the input to creole-speaking children does not look as dramatic as when one is concerned with children's total experience. That is, the difference from the non-creole cases is not as extensive. The question now arises: To what extent does the creole child lack *relevant* input for setting the parameters provided by the linguistic genotype? The answer to this question might be: not at all, or not very much. This would explain how children with apparently quite impoverished input nonetheless attain a mature capacity virtually as rich structurally as that of children with a more extensive and more uniform input; it would simply mean that children with apparently impoverished input are not exposed to as much redundant information. Answering the question, of course, requires fairly detailed knowledge of the input to the first creole speakers. This kind of information is sometimes available, and this is one reason why Sankoff's work on Tok Pisin is so important (see Sankoff and Laberge 1973). Usually, however, the triggering experience of the original creole speakers is covered by layers of historical mist, and written records of early stages of creole languages are meager. This is not to say that no information is available. Derek Bickerton has done interesting detective work on the early context of

Saramaccan; Singler (1984, 1988) discusses relevant demographic material for other creole languages, which indicates roughly which languages were available as potential triggers and to what degree; and Hilda Koopman (1986) derived some interesting results by considering properties of various West African languages which might have made up part of the trigger for the early stages of Haitian.

Under a research program seeking to find how children acquire their mature linguistic capacity, creole languages can be studied profitably in the context of unusual triggering experiences, and one can expect that the sharp contrast between the input and the eventual mature capacity, at least in the early stages of creole languages, will provide a useful probe into the nature of triggering experiences in general. However, one finds claims in the literature that go far beyond this. It is sometimes claimed that creolization is the key to understanding language change in general. Bickerton (1984a) expected the study of plantation creoles to yield "special evidence" about the nature of genetic principles, particularly about the value of the unmarked settings of parameters of Universal Grammar.

The particular form of Bickerton's claim has changed somewhat, which is no bad thing. In his articles published around 1984 he argued that the grammars of creoles were genetically given; this was his Language Bioprogram Hypothesis. He drew an analogy with Herodotus' story about the king who isolated a child and waited to hear the first word the child produced; the child produced a Phrygian word, which convinced the king that this was the oldest language. Bickerton's idea was that children who had no real triggering experience would have to rely almost entirely on their bioprogram, which would thus be manifested directly in creole grammars. Now, there have been many occasions when I have been baffled as to how some aspect of English could be attained, and I was tempted to say that it was genetically wired in. After all, if the language I am working on is genetically given, the language you are working on is just your problem.

This position has been abandoned in Bickerton's more recent work in favor of a weaker but perhaps more tenable position: every parameter has an unmarked setting, and the unmarked setting is adopted unless experience instructs the child differently; creoles emerge as children select the unmarked setting for every parameter, or sometimes the setting of the superstrate language (Bickerton 1984b).

Markedness values, like most other aspects of Universal Grammar, have been postulated on the basis of arguments from the poverty of the stimulus. For example, Rizzi (1982a, chapter 2) argued that S or S′ might be a bounding node for Subjacency (see chapter 2 above). He further argued that S must represent a less marked setting than S'. The reason was that if the English child had to "learn" that S was a bounding node, this could be done only on the basis of knowing that certain sentences were ungrammatical; since such information is not available to children, such a property could not be learned and must represent the unmarked case. The Italian child, on the other hand, could "learn" that S' was a bounding node as a result of hearing certain sentences which in fact occur in Italian—perhaps Rizzi's complex sentences, such as *tuo fratello, a cui mi domando che storie abbiano raccontato, era molto preoccupato* 'your brother, to whom I wonder which stories they told, was very troubled', or perhaps the simpler, unembedded triggers discussed above in chapter 2.

Bickerton's prime example of a "radical creole," Saramaccan, has a marked setting for at least one parameter. Some languages do not allow *wh* items to be extracted from a subordinate clause, and they have been analyzed as having both S and S' as bounding nodes, not permitting the movement in (2); this must represent the least marked case.

(2) who$_i$ $_S$[did Kim say $_{S'}$[e$_i$ $_S$[Jim saw e$_i$]]]

An English child goes to the next level of markedness (where only S is a bounding node) on hearing evidence that the least marked case does not hold; an Italian child goes to a higher level of markedness (where S' is a bounding node), again on exposure to evidence that requires this. In this respect Saramaccan is like English: Bickerton has informed me that *wh* items can be extracted from subordinate clauses, as in English.

Supposing that we had no evidence along these lines from Saramaccan, I would see no reason to expect only unmarked settings in "radical" creoles. Such an expectation presupposes that marked settings require access to more extensive experience, and perhaps to fairly exotic data, and that this is not available to the first speakers of a creole. This presupposition seems to me to be unwarranted. It is not hard to imagine a parameter that could have the marked setting on the basis of readily available data, even in the first forms of a creole. For example, suppose that Bickerton is right and every parameter has an unmarked setting. One parameter, under the hypothesis of (7) in chapter 1, is that a NP consists of a Spec and an N', with the order to be fixed depending on the language to which the child is exposed. Suppose, with Bickerton, that one of those orders is marked. The marked setting (say, N' Spec) would be established on the basis of data which would be available almost every minute—expressions such as *horse that* and *trees two*.

But that raises the question of why one would want to say that either of the two settings for this parameter, Spec N′ and N′ Spec, should represent a marked value. The same point could be made for the parameter that puts a complement in front of its verb or behind it, object-verb or verb-object; why should one of these values be marked? Why are they not equipotential? It is hard to see that specifying that one value is marked would contribute to solving any poverty-of-stimulus problem, which is the rationale for all properties of the linguistic genotype, as we saw in the case of the bounding nodes for Subjacency.

There are other approaches that treat creoles as a special type of language. One treats them as directly reflecting universal semantic structures; another treats them as the crystallization of some stage in the development of second-language learning, because the first creole speakers do not have sufficient access to a model and thus arrive at an approximative system; another regards them as reflecting a simplified baby talk provided by speakers of European languages; another derives the similarity among different creole languages from the common communicative requirements imposed by the plantations on the slaves, who did not have a common language of their own. These and other approaches are surveyed in Muysken 1988.

Muysken points to some general properties of creole languages: preverbal particles, a simple morphology, and subject-verb-object order, as in (3).

(3) a. wanpela man i bin skulim mi long Tok Pisim   (Tok Pisin)
    one man PR ANT teach me in Tok Pisin
    'a man was teaching me in Tok Pisin'

  b. sō mō ka ta toka pálmu   (Senegal Kriol)
    one hand NEG HAB touch palm
    'one hand can't touch its palm'

  c. m te pu bay lazā   (Haitian)
    I ANT MD give money
    'I had to give the money'

The prevalence of preverbal particles in creole languages played an important role in shaping Bickerton's Language Bioprogram Hypothesis. Where these particles do not exist in the source languages but represent innovations in the creole, they may be supposed to reflect some sort of ill-understood tendency on the part of children to analyze primary data in terms of preverbal particles. Where the particles reflect properties of one of the source languages, one may ask why these items are attainable but elements of inflectional morphology are not. Put differently: why do elements of inflectional morphology require a more robust triggering experience than is generally available to the first speakers of a creole language? There are no illuminating answers to such questions as yet.

However, if we do not understand why inflectional morphology is so impoverished in creole languages, we do understand some of the consequences. In earlier chapters it was noted that morphological properties help to set various parameters with widespread syntactic consequences. As Muysken discusses, the absence of inflectional morphology entails that creoles based on Spanish and Portuguese show no null-subject option and no subject-verb inversion, which are dependent on a rich morphology (Rizzi 1982a). Consider (4).

(4) a. e ta kome   (Papiamentu)
       he ASP eat
       'he is eating' (cf. Spanish *él está comiendo*)
   b. *ta kome
       ASP eat (cf. Spanish *está comiendo*)
   c. *ta kome maria
       ASP eat Maria (cf. Spanish *está comiendo Maria*)

The uniformity of subject-verb-object order is interesting, particularly when it does not reflect properties of the source languages. It is not surprising that English and French creoles have subject-verb-object order, since that order occurs in the superstrate languages. However, some explanation is required for creoles based on Spanish and Portuguese, which show frequent verb-subject-object order, and for those based on Dutch, which has subject-object-verb order at D-structure. The explanation might be found in the substrate languages, if they show subject-verb-object order. But Hilda Koopman (1984) has argued that many of the relevant languages of the West African peoples from which the slaves were drawn had subject-object-verb order, like Dutch, along with a verb-fronting operation. A particularly challenging case is the Guyanese creole Berbice Dutch, which is based on two subject-object-verb languages—Dutch and the Kwa language Eastern Ijo (Smith, Robertson, and Williamson 1987)—but which nonetheless has a subject-verb-object order.

The word order of Berbice Dutch has been treated as something of a mystery, but the notion of degree-0 learnability may cast some light on it. Dutch is the lexifier language for this creole (i.e., the language that has provided most of the vocabulary), but Ijo provides a high proportion of the basic vocabulary, some morphological material (including the verbal ending -*te* 'past' and the nominal ending -*apu* 'plural', and some syntactic pat-

terns (e.g., locative postpositions such as *war ben* house in; 'in the house').
Recall that Dutch has object-verb order at D-structure but that verb-object
order often occurs in matrix clauses because of a verb-movement operation that moves the verb to INFL and then to an initial position. Our
degree-0 learner sets the verb-order parameter, I argued in chapter 3, on
the basis of unembedded data concerning the position of separable particles and negation elements and perhaps clause-union structures like *Jan
moet Marie bezoeken* 'Jan must visit Marie'. Ijo has similar properties,
often showing subject-verb-object order in matrix clauses, despite having
object-verb order at D-structure (Kouwenberg 1989). In each language
children set the verb-order parameter on the basis of indirect evidence in
unembedded Domains. If that indirect evidence is obscured in some way,
as it was toward the end of the Old English period, children may not be
able to attain the old parameter setting and may set the verb-order parameter differently. In the case of Berbice Dutch, if the first speakers did
not have robust evidence about the distribution of the separable particles,
or if negative elements were no longer retained in their D-structure position
(marking the D-structure position of the verb), or if the verb-raising (clause
union) operation was not triggered in the same way as in Dutch, then there
would arise a situation comparable to that of late Old English: there would
no longer be adequate data to trigger the object-verb setting. Negation,
for example, works differently in Ijo and Dutch. In Dutch the negative
element occurs to the right of an object NP, marking the position from
which the verb moves, but in Ijo the negative particle "is adjoined directly
to the verb in its proposition-negating role" (Smith et al. 1987) and moves
with it, as in Old English:

(5) á nimi-γá
    I know not

Ijo provided the negative marker for the creole, *kane*, although it is a
free-standing morpheme in Berbice Dutch and not a clitic. Because Ijo
provided the basis for negation patterns, one of the Dutch indicators of
underlying object-verb order was obscured.

We do not have good records of the early stages of Berbice Dutch, and
therefore it is difficult to be more precise and to spell out exactly how the
available data did not contain adequate triggers for the object-verb order.
However, the negation example shows that one indicator of underlying
object-verb order may be nullified if the other language is dominant in the
relevant aspect. Similarly, Dutch may have been dominant in an area of
grammar that provided keys to underlying object-verb order in Ijo. If chil-

dren are degree-0 learners, the creole's verb-object order is less mysterious: parameter setters who are degree-0 learners are insensitive to embedded Domains where there would otherwise be much evidence for object-verb order in each of the languages to which they were exposed. Instead they rely on indirect evidence from unembedded Domains, and minor shifts in those patterns must have entailed a different setting for the verb-order parameter. Consequently, one can understand how a creole language might emerge with quite different properties from both the languages on which it is based, if one assumes that the *relevant* data for language acquisition are structurally limited and that some of the simple data might be analyzed differently by children as a result of the contact situation.

Although we know little of the primary data to which early creole speakers had access, there is no reason to believe that there is a qualitative difference in the acquisition of the first stages of a creole and the acquisition of Dutch and Ijo under usual circumstances. For example, Koopman (1986) considered various aspects of Haitian and showed that they reflected properties either of French or of a cluster of West African Kru and Kwa languages. She thereby argued against the notion that creoles are not influenced by the structural properties of substrate languages, and by focusing on general West African properties she avoided the danger of postulating substrate influence by arbitrarily invoking one particular language, like Yoruba, when one could not show that its speakers were dominant among the slave communities as the creole emerged.

Koopman argued that although the phonetic shapes of Haitian verbs are clearly derived from French, many of their selectional properties differ from those of French and are strikingly similar to those observed in West African languages. For example, one finds double-object constructions in Haitian and the West African languages but not in French; Haitian and the West African languages lack subject-raising verbs, which occur in French (e.g. *sembler*); Haitian and the West African languages lack infinitival indirect questions and infinitival relatives, in contrast with French; French modal verbs (*pouvoir, devoir*, etc.) are followed by an infinitive, whereas the corresponding verbs in Haitian and some West African languages may select either an infinitive or a tensed complement (although the Kru languages have only tensed complements to modal verbs). Koopman also points out that some Haitian verbs, for which there are no equivalents in the West African languages, have the same properties as French verbs. Also, the order of heads and their complements coincides with that of French and not with those of West African languages, which often have mixed or head-final properties. Haitian numerals occur prenominally, as in French, whereas West African numerals uniformly occur postnominally. Koopman found only one way in which Haitian resembled neither French nor the West African languages: besides the pleonastic pronoun *li*, Haitian has a zero pleonastic pronoun for certain contexts, in contrast with French and the West African languages.

The earliest form of Haitian was presumably a pidgin, a contact language, which made up much of the triggering experience for children as they set their parameters and acquired some form of the language. This pidgin was spoken by African slaves, by fugitives, and by some of the free population, as a second language, alongside their native African languages. Koopman notes that a well-known strategy in second-language learning and in language-contact situations is relexification: the transfer of lexical properties from the native language to the target language. So if the primary data which made up the triggering experience for subsequent forms of Haitian contained West African properties, via relexification, one can understand the correspondences between Haitian and the West African languages that Koopman observed.

This scenario, accounting for lexical parallelisms, does not explain the absence of infinitival relatives and indirect questions. One must claim that devices generating such forms were not triggered by the contact language. It is likely that the primary data that served as input to the formation of Haitian lacked such infinitival forms: these constructions do not occur in the West African languages and are not very frequent in French. Consequently, it seems plausible to claim that they would not have been robust enough in children's experience to have any long-term effect.

If one views the genesis of creole languages in this way, focusing on familiar properties of Universal Grammar and trying to tease out likely properties of the structurally simple input data, there is no need to invoke any special procedures or devices. In particular, there is no reason to believe with Bickerton that the parameter settings in creole languages are generally unmarked or determined by the superstrate language. It may, of course, be true that creole languages have failed to incorporate oddities like historical relic forms or infrequent constructions, which require a lot of exposure for learning, but that is a very different claim. The properties of Haitian suggest that there was a fairly well-developed contact language, influenced on a continuing basis by the substrate languages. This conforms to the findings of Sankoff and Laberge (1973), who pointed to an increasing complexity in the pidgin Tok Pisin before it was acquired by native speakers (i.e., before it served to set children's parameters). Also, Koopman notes that "because of the high mortality, low birthrate, mass suicides, and mass desertions on the labour intensive sugar plantations, massive importation of slaves took place. New speakers of African languages were thus arriving all the time. . . . These circumstances leave plenty of space and time for African languages to be spoken and learned." (1986, pp. 253–254) This would account for the extensive influence of the substrate language.

The early stages of creole languages are particularly interesting in that sharp contrasts between the triggering experience and the mature capacities attained show how normal, rich systems of knowledge may arise on exposure to quite impoverished input. This is quite surprising for somebody who believes that children need access to rich and complex structures for a normal grammar to emerge, but less so for somebody arguing that the emergence of normal grammars depends on access only to simple, unembedded structures. From this perspective, there is no reason to invoke special learning strategies for creole languages, or to argue that creoles have some special status, reflecting Universal Grammar in some privileged fashion.

7.4   Conclusion

Alongside creolization contexts, there are other unusual triggering experiences that shed some light on the way in which parameters may be set. Sometimes there is no triggering experience, as with "wolf children" such as Genie (Curtiss 1977) or the wild boy of Aveyron portrayed in François Truffaut's *L'enfant sauvage*, or deaf children raised in nonsigning homes. Sometimes the triggering experience is more diverse and heterogeneous than usual, as when children are raised in multilingual homes. Or there may be an exceptional amount of degenerate input, as in the case of children raised monolingually by immigrant parents who do not fully command the language in which the children are being raised. We will understand more of these unusual conditions as due attention is paid to the less unusual, more regular conditions.

Since the triggering experience is a subset of the total linguistic experience, the research program followed here will gain little from costly experiments in which tape recorders are strapped to the backs of children for long periods, recording what kinds of expressions are uttered around them. I have argued that much can be learned from studying the way in which languages change historically by considering how expressions cease to trigger grammatical devices under certain conditions, becoming obsolete, and how changes arise which appear only to affect embedded clauses. Properly construed, this material can illuminate the way in which parameters are set and under what conditions they come to be set differently. There is much more to be said about the chaotic elements of the environment, about catastrophes that follow from new parameter settings, about creolization, and about the parameter-setting process in general, but studying the way in which new parameter settings arise suggests that data from embedded binding Domains are not relevant for parameter setting and that the primary data that serve to set parameters are drawn entirely from unembedded binding Domains.

If something along these lines proves to be correct, it will explain the old observation that "what happens downstairs also happens upstairs, but not vice versa"—the "penthouse principle" of Ross (1973). The structure-preservation principle can also be seen as an epiphenomenon of the way in which parameters are set. Each of these principles sought to capture the limited range of operations affecting embedded domains. More marked operations require specific learning and therefore, under the hypothesis of degree-0 learnability, must be instantiated in unembedded Domains.

Like all hypotheses, this may turn out to be incorrect and to be too strong. My goal here has not been just to air a new hypothesis about language acquisition, showing degree-0 learnability to be a plausible and productive notion, but, more broadly, to focus attention on the least-examined element of our tripartite account of language acquisition. There are many rich and interesting ideas about Universal Grammar, and about particular grammars, but much less has been written about the triggering experience and about how parameters are set. Since there is such a close relationship among the three elements in our explanations, this must be rectified lest our hypotheses lose touch with reality. I hope that this book will encourage more thought about this component. But first you have to tell me why children are not degree-0 learners.

I have tackled the matter of the triggering experience very much from a linguist's perspective, being concerned with consequences for claims about Universal Grammar, evidence from language variation and change, and so on. However, the matter obviously relates to many aspects of language acquisition not touched upon in this book, and other perspectives may be able to tell us more about the true nature of the trigger.

Notes

Chapter 1

*Chapters 1 and 2 are adapted from Lightfoot 1989 and from my response to the commentaries on that paper.

1. (3b) provides only one possible structure for a noun phrase consisting of a head noun followed by a preposition phrase, whereas (3a) provides more than one structure: *student from NY* can (and must) have the structure $_{N'}[_{N'}[_N[$student$]]$ $_{PP}[$from NY$]]$, while *student of physics* is $_{N'}[_N[$student$]$ $_{PP}[$of physics$]]$. The pronoun *one* refers to a preceding N'. *Student* is a N' in (5b), hence a referent for *one*, but not in (5a). In (6a) both *suit* and *old suit* are instances of N' and thus possible referents for *one*, hence the ambiguity. For details and the reasons why *student from NY* and *student of physics* must have different structures, see Lightfoot 1982.

2. Travis (1987) considers possible word orders within VP and postulates three parameters to generate eight possible word orders, two of which she takes to be nonexistent (her 18c and 18f). The variety that she studies is exaggerated by taking adjunct PPs into account. In fact, the single parameter of (7b) suffices to generate the attested range of possibilities. Travis' system predicts the possibility of $_{VP}[$PP V NP$]$ as a D-structure, but she is unable to cite any attestation.

3. The rules of (3a) allow an adjective to occur before an N or an N', but the convention (7) says nothing about possible adjective positions. This is appropriate because the convention (7) stipulates the basic geometry of categorial structures; this basic geometry may be supplemented in response to experience. The position of adjectives is fully determined by a normal child's experience; exposure to phrases like *the tall student* will suffice to show that an English N' may have an adjective at its front. There is no poverty-of-stimulus problem for such adjectives which would require a richer convention in Universal Grammar, as far as I can see.

4. While there is evidence that a reduced *is* is *syntactically* attached to a following word, its voicing assimilates to the preceding segment, suggesting that *Jim's* in (10b) is a constituent in phonological structure, perhaps as a result of some reanalysis operation. For other discrepancies between the syntactic and the phonological dependency of clitics, see Klavans 1985.

5. Young children are known to have great difficulty in detecting for themselves the absence of forms, even when confronted with carefully prepared paradigmatic

sets of patterns (Sainsbury 1971, 1973). Grimshaw and Pinker (1989) offer a good discussion of the nonavailability and the uselessness of negative linguistic data. They point out that linguists, with access to as much negative evidence as they need, are significantly less successful at grammar discovery than children are. If children's success is attributed to their reliance on Universal Grammar, this also obviates the need for negative data.

6. The notion of "markedness" has led to much confused discussion. Universal Grammar includes a theory of markedness that leads to the preference of one parameter setting over another and permits "core grammar" to be extended to a marked periphery (Chomsky 1981, p. 8). So the unmarked parameter setting is adopted in the absence of contrary evidence, but specific evidence will be required for a marked setting.

7. Baker (1979) discusses a transformational movement rule relating *John gave the book to Alice* and *John gave Alice the book*, which does not generalize to *report* and *say*. The fact that the rule is not entirely general suggests that negative data are needed to establish the limits to the generalization. Baker goes on to show that a lexical relationship is preferable to a movement analysis and circumvents the apparent learnability problem if children are conservative in establishing the lexical properties of verbs, generalizing only within narrowly prescribed limits. However, children are not entirely conservative in this regard and they do, in fact, over-generalize double objects to certain verbs. For further discussion, see Mazurkewich and White 1984 and Randall 1986.

8. Sentences like *Kirsten has* NP[*a blue cup*] *and Heidi has a red one* show that *one* must also be able to refer to something smaller than an NP.

9. This was pointed out to me by Jim McCawley.

10. Lebeaux (1988, p. 330ff.) distinguishes "kernel" and "non-kernel" verbs, where only kernel verbs head-govern more than one complement. Pinker (1989) discusses this problem extensively and well, making it the central element of his "learnability paradox."

Chapter 2

1. Friends with my interests at heart have pointed out that configurations like (1), using S and S′, have an old-fashioned flavor and may be quite unfamiliar to anybody whose linguistic education began after 1986. Chomsky (1986) took Comp and INFL to be subject to the phrase-structure schema (7) of chapter 1, projecting to CP and IP respectively. This quickly became standard usage, eclipsing the previous record for speedy convergence on one point set by the gregarious Gadarene swine. As far as I am aware, no arguments have been presented for the projection Comp and INFL in the manner of lexical categories. If they do project in that manner, they also have several exceptional features, as is noted in Chomsky 1986 and discussed in Lightfoot and Weinberg 1988. I shall not offer counterarguments here to a position which has not been argued for, but I shall adopt the old-fashioned formulation, and not entirely for reasons of middle-aged boneheadedness. It will be important later to be able to treat INFL as the head of a clause and to treat Comp as a position which, when indexed appropriately, may govern or bind ele-

Blundell (Mary Whitlock)

Helping Friends and Harming Enemies: A Study in Sophocles and Greek Ethics

Camb UP, 1989

Wid PA4417 .B54 1989   +Lamo (scan)

ments internal to S; such a government relation would not be possible if the intervening node were a maximal projection (IP)—unless it had exceptional properties, which is the position of Chomsky 1986. Of course, these exceptional features may turn out to be independently motivated, and the IP analysis may gain plausibility. In the interests of liberalism and open-mindedness, I shall occasionally use the CP-IP formulation, but I stress here that this issue needs more careful examination than it has received so far. For a brief discussion see Lightfoot 1990.

2. If there are grammars which generally prevent extraction from an embedded clause (as is claimed for Russian), then there is a setting for this parameter that is less marked than the English value: both S and S' are bounding nodes. This would block the second movement in (i), from the embedded Comp into the higher Comp.

(i) who$_i$ $_s$[did Jay say $_s$·[e$_i$ [Kay saw e$_i$]]]

The English-speaking child is confronted with specific evidence that this default value does not hold—i.e., sentences corresponding to (i). The Italian child is driven to a still more marked value when confronted by (2a).

Since direct questions like *quel livre Jean sait à qui offrir?* 'which book does John know to whom to offer?' occur in French (but not in Italian), a trigger with one level of embedding can be specified.

For more discussion of the Italian case and alternative analyses, see Adams 1984, Grimshaw 1986, and Rizzi 1989.

3. Since (5) requires that S not be a bounding node in French, structures like (4b) will also be well formed. This is the right result, because French shows none of the English-type phenomena that Hornstein and Weinberg used to motivate the reanalysis rule. That is, there is no positive motivation in the primary linguistic data in French for an English-style reanalysis rule yielding a structure like (4c). (This kind of extraction is not possible from a subject NP (*de qui$_i$ est [[le frère e$_i$] peintre]?), for reasons other than the Subjacency Condition).

There is a closely analogous extraction process in Dutch, which seems not to set S' as a bounding node. Bennis (1983) analyzed sentences like *wat heb je voor kinderen?* 'what kind of children do you have?' as involving a restructuring operation splitting up the NP ("wat voor Split") and then movement of the NP to Comp. Thus, a D-structure, such as (i), is mapped into a S-structure, such as (ii):

(i) je heb $_{NP}$[wat voor kinderen]
(ii) $_{NP}$[wat$_i$] heb je e$_i$ $_{PP}$[voor kinderen]
    what have you for children?

The major evidence offered for the restructuring operation is that it permits a derivation that does not violate Subjacency. Bennis does not address the question of why such sentences do not set S as a nonbounding node, as in French. It is assumed that S is a bounding node in Dutch because of the absence of long-distance *wh* movement comparable to (2).

There are various ways to square the Dutch and French material: (a) to find triggers for *wat voor* Split in the primary linguistic data (but Dutch colleagues have been unable to suggest any); (b) to allow sentences like *wat heb je voor kinderen?* to set S as a nonbounding node and to attribute the absence of long-distance *wh* movement in Dutch to something other than Subjacency (Peter Coopmans and

Riny Huybregts, personal communication); (c) to treat *wat* as the head of a *wat voor NP* phrase; (d) to attribute the choice of S as a nonbounding node in French to something other than *combien* extraction, perhaps something along the lines of the Italian extractions in (27) below.

4. The Comp indexing convention is given by Universal Grammar and permits Comp to take on the index of an element that it contains. An indexed Comp (but not an element inside Comp) is "high" enough to act as a head-governor at PF and as an antecedent for an anaphor at LF. See Aoun et al. 1987 for details. It is important that S not be taken as a maximal projection (like Chomsky's IP), in order that the indexed Comp may govern the subject position.

Rouveret and Vergnaud (1980) propose a coindexing relation between a NP and the item from which it receives a theta role, and so a verb is coindexed with and thus head-governs its direct object, as in (10a). In exactly the same sense, a Comp head-governs a coindexed subject in (10c), (11), and (12).

5. In (13) I have shown the auxiliary verb moving to Comp, but this might not be correct; it may move to some other pre-S position, perhaps adjoined to S, as in Lasnik 1981. Similarly for the Dutch case in (12). Under this analysis English and Dutch would differ in terms of whether an element in Comp could head-govern an empty subject across intervening material. This relates to questions about the status of verbal traces; for example, do they need to be head-governed, as nominal traces do? It also relates to the formulation of "verb-second" properties, to be discussed in chapter 3. I shall not take up these complex questions here, because they do not affect the limited matter of the acquisition of the forms under discussion. What might affect the analysis is the fact that *of* 'whether' (unlike *of dat*; cf. (11b)) does not permit percolation of indices to Comp: *$*wie_i$ vraag je [of e_i het boek geschreven heeft]* 'who are you asking whether has written the book?' (Peter Coopmans, personal communication).

6. This analysis assumes that a *wh* word moves first to its local Comp, as in (10c). This is required by the Subjacency Condition if S is a bounding node in English (see above in the main text). So movement from the lower subject position to the higher Comp in (10b) would cross two bounding nodes, in addition to violating the binding theory ((7a)) and the PF condition that empty items be head-governed.

7. The "obviation" properties of Romance subjunctives might also be viewed as problematic *prima facie*: the subject of a subjunctive complement must be disjoint in reference from the higher subject:

(i) je veux que Pierre/*j'aille à Paris
    I want that Peter/I should go to Paris

These phenomena suggest that the Romance subjunctive has the effect of making the binding Domain for the embedded subject the next clause up, as an infinitive does. Germán Westphal (personal communication) suggests that this may be part of a more general "transparency" of subjunctive clauses. So in Spanish the negative particle *no* may license a negative phrase nonlocally if the verb is subjunctive:

(ii) ellos *no* quieren [que tú traigas *nada*]
     'they don't want that you bring-SUBJ nothing'

(iii) *ellos *no* dijeron [que tú trajiste *nada*]
'they didn't say that you brought-IND nothing'

This, of course, does not entail that the definition of a binding Domain is parameterized, any more than the transparency of infinitival clauses requires a parametric definition. It would simply mean that subjunctives and infinitives do not manifest the same AGR properties as indicatives.

8. Similar comments may apply to "logophoric" pronouns, which are sometimes seen as a phenomenon of embedded clauses (Sells 1987). However, they may also occur in matrix Domains, and they are understood to reflect what somebody said fairly directly, as in the following Latin example:

(i) Marcus dixit me felicem esse
Marcus said, me happy to-be
'Marcus$_i$ said that he$_i$ was happy'

Baker (1989) raises an interesting problem: How can a degree-0 learner determine whether relative clauses have resumptive pronouns? He points to English constructions like (ii), where the object of *invite* may be empty or may be a resumptive pronoun, whereas other languages allow only the pronoun in analogous forms.

(ii) John$_i$ is too tired to invite e$_i$/him$_i$ to our house for dinner

I have no solution yet to this problem, but (ii) may be structurally ambiguous: only the form with the pronoun may occur in "topic" position:

(iii) a. *to invite to your house for dinner, John is too tired
b. ?to invite him to your house for dinner, John is too tired

Cinque (1990) motivates a structural distinction for Italian analogues to (ii) with the empty element and the overt pronoun. His analysis makes the overt pronoun obligatory in a structure which has no appropriate predication relation. If such an analysis can be sustained, the learning problem becomes more tractable: the child needs evidence to postulate an extra (prepositional) node. In that event, the embedded clause must have an overt pronoun.

Chapter 3

1. In these languages complementizers are not freely deletable, whereas in English they may be deleted when lexically governed (see Aoun et al. 1987). If an embedded Comp is necessarily occupied by an overt complementizer, one understands why verbs do not move to Comp in embedded clauses: there is no appropriate position to which an inflected verb may move. This explanation is lost, however, if Comp is taken to project to CP, as in Chomsky 1986 and much recent work. In that case Comp is empty in the structure underlying Dutch *ik weet* $_{CP}$[*wat* $_{IP}$[*Jan leest*]] 'I know what John is reading', where *wat* is the Specifier of the embedded CP, and there is no apparent reason why the verb *leest* should not move leftward to yield the ungrammatical *ik weet wat leest Jan. (See Lightfoot 1990 for discussion.) Peter Coopmans (personal communication) reports that some dialects of Afrikaans have forms like *ik weet wat leest Jan*, so one should be wary of attempts to disbar such sentences by general principles of Universal Grammar.

2. It is misleading to postulate a "topicalization" operation moving the phrase to the front, as one often reads, and that is why I have used quotation marks around the term. Expletives like Dutch *er* and German *es* trigger verb movement but can not be "topics" in any usual sense of the term. For example, they are typically unstressed, whereas topicalized pronouns require stress. Genuinely topicalized pronouns also attract the finite verb: **HEM Jan vond in Utrecht* 'HIM Jan found in Utrecht', but *HEM vond Jan in Utrecht*. Consequently, topicalization is not the distinguishing property of verb-second structures.

3. Emonds defines specifiers as typically consisting of closed-class items, suggesting that children build phrase structure partly on the basis of identifying closed-class items (Lebeaux 1988 has developed this approach further). This guarantees that specifiers of VP must immediately precede the V'. Here I am concerned with specifiers of verbs rather than Spec of VP.

4. Clahsen and Smolka go further and make stronger claims. They take "move V" to operate from the earliest stage, initially affecting verbs and verbal complexes of all types, affecting only simple verbs at stage 2, and affecting finite simple verbs obligatorily at stage 3. De Haan (1987) observed that one Dutch child used only finite forms in first or second position at 26 months and that nonfinite forms occurred only sentence-finally. Since the child seemed to make no other use of a finiteness feature, de Haan suggests that "move V" is not operative and that the early grammars generate verbs expressing modal and temporal notions in first or second position and other verbs finally. This entails a complex and somewhat mysterious development whereby an early category of auxiliary is eliminated in favor of a more general verbal category. Whatever else may be involved, this is another instance of very young children's having at least a large class of verbs base-generated in sentence-final position, long before they show any capacity to produce embedded clauses.

Clahsen and Muysken (1986) show that the acquisitional sequence reported by Clahsen and Smolka (1986) conforms to findings in other longitudinal studies of the acquisition of German, and that this sequence differs substantially from the sequences followed by adult learners, who typically have considerable difficulty in acquiring verb-final order.

5. Reddick (1982) argues that the Early West Saxon dialect of Old English (manifested by Alfred's versions of the *Cura Pastoralis* and of Orosius' *Historiarum* and by the Parker manuscript of the Chronicle up to 891) was underlyingly verb-object. However, his argument is complex, and it depends on sets of assumptions about specific rules proposed elsewhere, which he criticizes. Pintzuk (1988) reanalyzes Reddick's data in favor of an object-verb treatment.

6. I have no account for why the verb had to move to the empty Comp, if that was indeed the case. One might try to derive the phenomenon by showing that an empty Comp in the relevant contexts would not be head-governed. This would still not account for why a subject occurs to the left of a fronted verb. It is difficult to think of interesting accounts when the data base is so thin and problematic.

7. Presumably the verb moves first to some inflectional position and then to the initial Y^0. It has often been assumed that the basic clausal structure was $_s$[NP VP INFL] while English had object-verb order (van Kemenade 1987), but

Willem Koopman (1985) argues for an underlying $_S$[NP INFL $_{VP}$[NP V]], also claiming that the VP was V-final but that otherwise the complement elements were unordered at D-structure. In fact, there are reasons to treat Old English diglossically, allowing variation between INFL-medial and INFL-final structures; INFL-final order was initially predominant, but eventually gave way to INFL-medial order by Middle English. This change was presumably linked to the replacement of object-verb order by verb-object. The position of INFL is important for interpreting sentences where an inflected verb seems to be neither in an initial Y^0 position nor in its base-generated position, and thus for interpreting some features of the statistical surveys discussed here. Since my goal here is not to settle all important questions about the structure of Old and Middle English grammars, I can make my argument about the nature of the child's triggering experience while staying open on the changing position of inflectional elements.

Santorini (1990) studies the change from verb-final to verb-medial in Yiddish, which occurred slowly, whereas the extension of verb-second to embedded clauses took place suddenly along with the operation of "topicalization."

8. This graph differs from a similar one offered by Hiltunen (1983, p. 111). I have corrected some errors in his figures for early Middle English; more important, I compare embedded clauses with main clauses, excluding conjunct clauses, which, as noted, sometimes lack the initial Y^0 position and show the properties of embedded clauses.

Chapter 4

1. A similar conclusion has been reached independently by Olga Fischer (1988a, 1988b), although on the basis of quite different analyses and without any assumptions about degree-0 learnability. She provides extensive discussion of traditional treatments of these constructions, which I shall rely on at some points.

2. See Russom 1980 for discussion. Russom argues that already in Old English the *to* infinitive was the productive form in most constructions and that the plain form was largely restricted to certain lexically defined contexts. If so, the standard handbooks are incorrect in depicting the *to* form as taking over from or replacing the plain form from late Old English onward.

3. So French contrasts **vous croyez Jean être malade* and *qui croyez-vous être malade*. It is standard to attribute the ungrammaticality of the first example to the fact that French has no exceptional procedure whereby *Jean* may receive case; therefore there is a violation of the case filter (which requires every lexical NP to have case; see Chomsky 1981). The second example is well formed, however, since case theory need not be directly involved; the variable corresponding to *qui* must be visible at LF, and it will be visible if it is either case-marked or (perhaps by a marked option) in an obligatory position (Hornstein and Lightfoot 1987). Since all clauses have subjects by the Extended Projection Principle (Chomsky 1981), the subject position of *être* is visible at LF. The same analysis could be adopted for Old English if (8b) were grammatical.

4. A "small clause" structure along the lines of *persuade* $_{SC}$*[NP [PRO to VP]]* may be more plausible. Hornstein and Franks (1988) and Hornstein and Weinberg

(1986) postulate such a structure on the grounds that the putative direct object of *persuade* shows certain subject-like properties with respect to superiority phenomena and other operations.

5. Obvious candidates would be object extraposition and stepwise clitic movement to Comp. Extraposition, which van Kemenade assumes for independent reasons, would yield a structure like (i) for her sentence (82a). Similarly for her other examples.

(i) þæt hie mid nanum þinge e$_i$ ne mehton [gesemede weorþan]$_i$
    that they with no thing   not could   reconciled become
    'that they could not be reconciled with anything'

She treats *him* in (ii) as a clitic attached to the complementizer *þæt*. Since she assumes that clitics generally move only within their clause, she claims that the clause boundary is eliminated with such infinitives; however, she does not consider the possibility that the clitic moves first to its local Comp and then to the higher Comp, like a *wh* word.

(ii) ... ofdrædd þæt him Godes yrre on becuman sceolde
     afraid that him God's anger on come   would
     'afraid that God's anger would descend on him'

Any adequate motivation for verb-raising in Old English would have to consider such alternatives, and would have to deal with the problem that if such a process did exist, then it was different from any of the processes found in modern grammars, being something of an amalgam of all of them: sometimes the infinitive adjoins to the right of the higher verb, as in Dutch, sometimes to the left, as in German, and sometimes a head is raised, as in Dutch and German, and sometimes part of a projection, as in West Flemish and Züritüütsch. Pintzuk (1988) discusses more shortcomings of the verb-raising analysis for Old English.

6. That paper takes phonological structure to be an abstract level of representation intervening between S-structure and phonetic form. Crucially, it follows "stylistic" reordering rules and precedes the elimination of syntactic structure. Its precise definition will depend on further investigation, but it can hardly be in doubt that such structures are available. In this regard it is precisely analogous to "LF," which also is an abstract level of representation containing the structures relevant for the assignment of scope relations and the like. See Chomsky 1988, note 10.

7. As is often noted, English shows an adjacency effect, which prevents a verb from governing an NP when separated from it:

(i) *Kim criticized vehemently Tim
    *who$_i$ did Kim expect last week in New York [e$_i$ to win]?

This requirement is subject to some variability which is not yet well understood. So the sentences of (ii) are markedly more acceptable than those of (i).

(ii) Kim seemed last week in New York to have made a complete recovery
     Kim was expected by almost everybody to accept the offer

It may be that there is no independent adjacency condition and that the ungrammaticality of (i) reflects the absence in English of an operation moving a verb to INFL (see section 6.2). In that case the difference between (16b) and (ii) would be keyed to different constituent structures.

8. Thus, if binding Domains are defined partially in terms of governors (as is argued in Chomsky 1981, and not just in terms of accessible SUBJECTS, as is assumed in chapter 2), the coalesced *to* will make the binding Domain for an infinitival subject the next clause up. So in *Jim expected himself to win, himself* is governed by *expect-to* and therefore has the matrix clause as its binding Domain. If binding Domains are defined as in chapter 2, in terms only of accessible SUB-JECTS, then the result is the same: the accessible SUBJECT for *himself* is in the higher clause, which therefore constitutes the binding Domain.

9. This is similar to the ambiguity of *the crowd is too angry to vote on this proposal*, where the understood subject of *vote* may be governed by *angry* (hence anaphoric in interpretation) or not (hence with an arbitrary reading). The corresponding question, however, *what is the crowd too angry to vote on?*, is unambiguous, and the lower subject is necessarily anaphoric. The S-structure must be (i), where the intermediate trace in the lower Comp is head-governed by *angry*; this, in turn, seems to entail that the empty subject be governed, hence anaphoric in interpretation. (See Aoun et al. 1987 for discussion.) It is important to note that a perception verb assigns case to an NP that it governs; this explains why an empty NP in this context may not be anaphoric. Case-marked empty NPs are defined as variables, and therefore a governed (anaphoric) PRO occurs only in non-case-marked positions, as in (i):

(i) what$_i$ is the crowd too $_{A'}$[angry $_{S'}$[e$_i$ $_S$[e to vote on e$_i$]]]

10. The material in this section was stimulated by an observation made by Maria Angela Botelho Pereira in a traffic jam in Rio de Janeiro, and the analysis was developed in collaboration with Lucia Lobato. The paradigm (26) is intriguing in that the infinitives do not have an overt morphological agreement marker where the personal pronoun also has distinct nominative and oblique forms, except in the little-used second-person singular.

11. By *tough* movement constructions, I mean infinitival complements to adjectives which involve movement of a *wh* object NP to Comp. For Portuguese, these include (i), where the infinitive must be uninflected, but not the passive ((ii)) or the middle ((iii)), where there is no object-to-Comp movement and the infinitive may be inflected.

(i)   esses relógios são difíceis de consertar
(ii) esses relógios são difíceis de ser*em* consertados
(iii) esses relógios são difíceis de se consertar*em*

Chapter 5

1. This chapter adapts and elaborates some sections of Lightfoot 1981a. Although the general line of argument is preserved, there are significant differences in the analyses offered, particularly with regard to the assignment of oblique case and its effects and with regard to the requirement that traces be head-governed.

2. Defining projection types in this way would allow transitive and intransitive verbs and adjectives. For any particular verb or adjective, the strict subcategoriza-

tion frame specifies whether it is transitive. In English, transitive verbs are common and transitive adjectives are rare; a system of markedness conventions might express such discrepancies and derive further predictions. Here I exploit the fact that transitive adjectives exist, and so I avoid Wasow's complications.

3. Also relevant to this claim were some issues relating to stative and dynamic interpretations and the fact that early passives marked the agent NP with a wide range of prepositions, whereas in Modern English *by* is fairly standard.

4. I accept Jack's (1978) correction of my earlier claim about the history of these expressions. However, it does not follow from the occurrence of objective genitives that there must have been a movement process in the core grammar of Old English.

5. It is sometimes claimed that such a view of lexical rules receives support from facts about language processing (see, e.g., Bresnan 1978 and Wasow 1978). These claims strike me as implausible.

6. Hornstein and Weinberg note that sentential PPs may not be stranded (*which concert did you sleep during?*, *what did you come because of?*), and that stranded prepositions form a unit with the preceding verb, not tolerating extraneous material:

(i) Jim spoke yesterday to Kim
    *who did Jim speak yesterday to?
    who did Jim speak to yesterday?

I shall assume this analysis, but there are tighter restrictions on preposition stranding with passives, as is well known. This might be due to ill-understood constraints on the form of predicates, as Hornstein and Weinberg suggested.

7. On this account, *Saskia* could also move to the subject of a passive verb: *Saskia was seen $_{NP}$[a $_{N'}$[portrait e$_i$]]. The ungrammaticality of this is due to the fact that *portrait* fails to receive case.

8. O'Neil (1982) discusses the demise of case inflections in terms of a general tendency for grammars to be simplified if left to themselves, and he notes the striking fact that Old English verbs governing a genitive or dative complement occur only with an impersonal passive (with the complement retaining its non-nominative inflection); with other passive verbs the complement assumes nominative case. The correlation is partially obscured by the fact that in Middle English many verbs taking a dative object may also take an accusative, as has often been noted. Given the accusative option, one would expect these verbs to occur with a personal passive in addition to the impersonal forms. See pp. 679–686 of Lieber 1979 for several examples and a good discussion.

9. Thus, *give* is subcategorized to occur with either ___ NP (PP), as in *give $5 (to John)*, where the postverbal NP denotes the item given, or ___ NP NP (*give John the book*), where the postverbal NP denotes the recipient. Only the immediately postverbal NP can become the subject of a passive: *$5 was given (to John)*, *John was given $5*. So in *John was given*, *John* cannot be interpreted as a recipient. The movement analysis leads to good results in this regard, and there is no need to invoke a lexical/movement distinction, *pace* Wasow (1977, p. 34).

Some dialects allow both *I gave it him* and *it was given him*. Here *give* is subcategorized to occur also in an initial frame ____ NP NP, where the postverbal NP denotes the item given (and is usually a pronoun) and the second NP the recipient. Again, only the immediately postverbal NP can become the subject of a passive. Notice that the verb is inside a participle but nonetheless assigns inherent case to the second object: *the book* must be case-marked in *John$_i$ was given e$_i$ the book*. The case is presumably assigned at D-structure and thus inherent: it is carried along with movement, and the trace may be a variable: *what$_j$ was John$_i$ given e$_i$ e$_j$*.

10. These elements all appear to take complement NPs, and can be modified by *very*; *near* has the comparative and superlative forms characteristic of adjectives. They are sometimes treated as prepositions, but they would be idiosyncratic in disallowing pied-piping (**I don't know worth what he bought a house/near whom he lives*).

11. In Dutch, a dative case has been lost fairly recently, and changes seem to be taking place in permissible passive forms. Den Besten (1980) offers some discussion. He shares the view, adopted here, that a trace left by movement into Comp must bear case, but he also assumes that a trace left by movement into another NP position may bear case, and he invokes an S-structure filter. He argues that Dutch and German distinguish verbal and adjectival passive, but on the theory adopted here several of the complications he notes fall away.

Chapter 6

1. Similar claims keying the loss of impersonal verbs to the loss of oblique cases have been made by Fischer and van der Leek (1983, 1987), Roberts (1985b), Allen (1986), and Brody (1989), although in somewhat different ways. The analyses of Roberts, Allen, and Brody all share the view that Old English had only inherent cases, and that structurally assigned cases emerged only in Middle English. I shall show later that this formulation cannot be right.

2. This is not to say, of course, that psych-verbs have a D-structure like (3) in all languages. Such a structure might be preempted for various reasons. For example, Ottósson (1990) argues that this D-structure is not available for psych-verbs in Icelandic because the "Specifier" position (the position of the experiencer in 3) is preempted for subjects.

3. A central claim of Fischer and van der Leek (1983) was that the new structure and meaning of *like* described in Lightfoot 1979 was not a novelty but rather a continuation of one of the patterns manifested in Old English. However, though many verbs showed experiencer NPs in the nominative case, Old English *lician* was not one of them. Allen (1986) and Denison (1990) show that there are no attested examples of *lician* with a nominative experiencer before the thirteenth century except in "slavish translations" of Latin. Therefore, the lexical entry is precisely as given in (5b).

4. Fischer and van der Leek (1983) made the important contribution of widening the perspective and seeking to couch *like*'s changes in terms of the impersonal verbs in general and the cases assigned to thematic roles. This makes word-order properties less central than in Lightfoot 1979 and 1981b, but not irrelevant: if the primary

data did not include a substantial number of experiencer-*like*-theme sequences, it would be hard to see what would have triggered a lexical entry with an externalized experiencer NP. Neither the earlier account (based on word-order change) nor the account offered here (keying the change to the new morphological case system) depends on the existence of a substantial number of ambiguous structures. Allen (1986) pointed out that most of the attested examples of *lician* are disambiguated structurally by at least one pronoun of unambiguous case, but the fascination of this change has always been due to the fact that it took place despite much apparent evidence for the earlier analysis, thus involving widespread obsolescence.

5. Lightfoot 1979 appeared to offer an explanation by virtue of a "Transparency Principle"—a rather imprecise, intuitive idea about limits on a child's ability to attain complex grammars, not unlike the "least effort principle" of Chomsky 1988. Many of the reanalyses discussed seemed to result from the complexity of the derivations in some way, and I wrote of a Transparency Principle which would, if formulated, disbar such complexity. The "principle" was never formulated, nor was it intended as an independent principle of Universal Grammar; see p. 358ff. of Lightfoot 1981c for discussion.

6. These changes affect the shape of what used to be thought of as the syntactic component, and one does not need to appeal to semantic or pragmatic factors to formulate the changes. This, of course, is not to say that there were no semantic consequences. For example, once *can, shall*, etc. were classified as instances of INFL, they could no longer occur with direct objects; they therefore ceased to occur with the kinds of meanings that they had in association with direct objects. This is part of what is explained by formulating the change in this fashion, and is thus an automatic consequence. It does not mean that the change must be formulated in semantic terms or that there was a semantic change requiring explanation (cf. Allan 1988; Plank 1984). I shall discuss the causes of these changes later, considering whether they were induced by prior meaning changes affecting the premodal verbs.

7. Since Allan does not say what he means by a distinct class of word-order changes, it is hard to know quite where the limits lie. If he adopts a schema like (7) of chapter 1, constraining phrasal categories to consist of a specifier and X′ in some order, then he can account for variation in word order. In that event, his theory amounts to a claim that category membership is invariant, and thus that there is some universal means of defining what category a word belongs to, independent of its accidental properties in a particular language. So words are assigned to categories on some notional or "semantic" basis. The fundamental difficulties with such approaches have been pointed out many times, and nobody has succeeded in illustrating such a model beyond a few very simple examples.

8. Plank (1984) poured sophomoric vitriol over the analysis of Lightfoot 1974, 1979 and then argued for an analysis in terms of gradually changing lexical features and a change in structures. He concluded that the emergence of the premodals as a distinct category "culminated, in the sense of approaching provisional completion, in the sixteenth and early seventeenth century in the standard language" (p. 348). If one ignores the obfuscation entailed in the notion "approaching provisional completion," identifying the "culmination" of the change in the sixteenth century echoes almost exactly the work that offended Plank so much. He argued

that the change took place quite gradually, but his argument was based largely on examining "fifteen or so further changes," some of which turn out on inspection to be unrelated to a categorial change and some of which not to be changes at all.

9. The most common preterite-present verbs survived as auxiliary verbs: *sculan*, which occurs 2240 times in Tatlock and Kennedy's Concordance to Chaucer (1927); *magan*, with 400 attestations; *cunnan*, with 600; *motan*, with 555; *willan*, with 1525. By comparison, *munan*, *dugan*, and *genugan* were not attested, *þurfan* had 14 occurrences, *unnan* one, *durran* 260, *agan* 277, and *witan* 530. I am indebted to Norma Belt for these figures.

10. And perhaps, as a result, subject for the first time to the phrase-structure schema that defines the way in which lexical categories project to a phrasal category. This would entail a structure $_{IP}[Spec_{I'}[I XP]]$, where Spec would typically be the subject NP and the XP complement would typically be VP. IP would be equivalent to what I have taken elsewhere to be "S". Chomsky (1986) uses such a structure, but I have not examined whether there was evidence in Early Modern English for such a structural innovation.

Roberts (1985a), assuming that languages with rich morphology lack AGR, argued that as verbal morphology became poorer AGR emerged as a distinct component of INFL. As a result, INFL would always be filled at D-structure (by either a modal, *do*, or AGR), and this would block V-to-INFL movement. Like Lightfoot 1974 and 1979, this ignored the lag between the reclassification of the premodals and the loss of V-to-INFL. Furthermore, the correlation is inaccurate: Duffield (1988) shows that Swedish and Danish, whose verb morphology is about as poor as that of English, nonetheless have the V-to-INFL operation.

11. This is consistent with a plausible view of the historical changes, if the notion 'weak' can be linked with the morphological distinctiveness that makes the modals categorially different from true verbs. However, it is less plausible to define 'weak' in terms of theta theory, which was essentially the view of Roberts, who argued (1985a, p. 35) that the premodals came to "appear in INFL, *because of* their lack of thematic-roles" [my emphasis—DWL]. Then one wants to know why the premodals lost their ability to assign thematic roles, entailing the structural change. Warner (1983) refuted the view (Lightfoot 1974, 1979) that the loss of direct objects to the premodals was an accidental *precondition* to the structural change, arguing instead that this was a *consequence* of the structural change (see above in the main text).

It should also be noted that the notion of "weak" inflection here is different from the weak inflection that precludes null subjects: English lost its null subjects long before losing the V-to-INFL operation.

Chapter 7

1. The existence of such forms is one reason why a person's grammar does not define all the expressions of his or her language, and why there may not be a mechanical device that can generate all these expressions. These forms are presumably learned, that is, shaped in direct response to experience, sometimes in adulthood.

Bibliography

Note: Particles are discounted in the alphabetization of names here; e.g., von Schon is alphabetized as Schon.

Adams, M. 1984. Multiple interrogation in Italian. *Linguistic Review* 4.1: 1–28.

Adams, M. 1987. From Old French to the theory of pro-drop. *Natural Language and Linguistic Theory* 5.1: 1–32.

Adamson, S., V. Law, N. Vincent, and S. Wright, eds. 1990. *Papers from the Fifth International Conference on English Historical Linguistics*. Benjamins.

Aitchison, J. 1979. The order of word order change. *Transactions of the Philological Society* 77: 43–65.

Akmajian, A. 1977. The complement structure of perception verbs in an autonomous syntax framework. In Culicover et al. 1977.

Allan, W. S. 1988. Lightfoot noch einmal. *Diachronica* 4: 123–157.

Allen, C. 1977. Topics in Diachronic Syntax. Doctoral dissertation, University of Massachusetts, Amherst.

Allen, C. 1986. Reconsidering the history of *like*. *Journal of Linguistics* 22.2: 375–409.

Anderson, J. M. 1986. A note on Old English impersonals. *Journal of Linguistics* 22.1: 167–177.

Anderson, J. M., and C. Jones, eds. 1974. *Historical Linguistics*. North-Holland.

Andrew, S. O. 1940. *Syntax and Style in Old English*. Cambridge University Press.

Aoun, J. 1986. *Generalized Binding*. Foris.

Aoun, J., N. Hornstein, D. W. Lightfoot, and A. S. Weinberg. 1987. Two types of locality. *Linguistic Inquiry* 18.4: 537–578.

Aoun, J., and D. W. Lightfoot. 1984. Government and contraction. *Linguistic Inquiry* 15.3: 465–473.

Bach, E. 1962. The order of elements in a transformational grammar of German. *Language* 38.1: 263–269.

Baker, C. L. 1978. *Introduction to Generative-Transformational Syntax*. Prentice-Hall.

Baker, C. L. 1979. Syntactic theory and the projection problem. *Linguistic Inquiry* 10.4: 533–581.

Baker, C. L. 1982. Review article on Wexler and Culicover 1980. *Language* 58: 413–421.

Baker, C. L. 1989. Some observations on degree of learnability. *Behavioral and Brain Sciences* 12.2: 334–335.

Barrett, C. R. 1953. Studies in the Word-Order of Aelfric's *Catholic Homilies* and *Lives of the Saints*. Occasional Papers III, Department of Anglo-Saxon, Cambridge University.

Battistella, E., and A. Lobeck 1988. The Role of the Category INFL in Word Order Typology and Syntactic Change. Manuscript, University of Alabama.

Bean, M. 1983. *The Development of Word Order Patterns in Old English*. Croom Helm.

Belletti, A., and L. Rizzi. 1988. Psych-verbs and theta-theory. *Natural Language and Linguistic Theory* 6.3: 291–352.

Bennis, H. 1983. A case of restructuring. In H. Bennis and W. U. S. van Lessen Kloeke, eds., *Linguistics in the Netherlands 1983* (Foris).

Berwick, R. C. 1985. *The Acquisition of Syntactic Knowledge*. MIT Press.

Besten, H. den 1980. A case filter for passives. In A. Belletti, L. Brandi, G. Nencioni, and L. Rizzi, eds., *Theory of Markedness in Generative Grammar* (Pisa: Scuola Normale Superiore).

Besten, H. den 1983. On the interaction of root transformations and lexical deletive rules. In W. Abraham, ed., *On the Formal Syntax of the Westgermania* (Benjamins).

Besten, H. den, and C. Moed-van Walraven 1986. The syntax of verbs in Yiddish. In Haider and Prinzhorn 1986.

Bickerton, D. 1984a. The language bioprogram hypothesis. *Behavioral and Brain Sciences* 7.2: 173–203.

Bickerton, D. 1984b. Learnability and the Structure of Parameters. Manuscript, University of Hawaii.

Bierwisch, M. 1963. *Grammatik des Deutschen verbs*. Berlin: Studia Grammatica 2.

Bock, H. 1931. Studien zum präpositionalen Infinitiv und Accusativ mit dem *to*-Infinitiv. *Anglia* 55: 114–249.

Bresnan, J. 1978. A realistic model of transformational grammar. In M. Halle, G. Miller, and J. Bresnan, eds., *Linguistic Theory and Psychological Reality* (MIT Press).

Brody, M. 1989. Old English Impersonals and the Theory of Grammar. *Working Papers in Linguistics* 1, University College London.

Burzio, L. 1986. *Italian Syntax: A Government-Binding Approach*. Reidel.

Callaway, M. 1913. *The Infinitive in Anglo-Saxon*. Carnegie Institution.

Canale, M. 1978. Word Order Change in Old English: Base Reanalysis in Generative Grammar. Doctoral dissertation, McGill University.

Changeux, J.-P. 1980. Genetic determinism and epigenesis of the neuronal network: Is there a biological compromise between Chomsky and Piaget? In M. Piattelli-Palmarini, ed., *Language and Learning* (Routledge and Kegan Paul).

Changeux J.-P. 1983. *L'homme neuronal*. Fayard.

Chomsky, N. 1965. *Aspects of the Theory of Syntax*. MIT Press.

Chomsky, N. 1973. Conditions on transformations. In S. Anderson and P. Kiparsky, eds., *A Festschrift for Morris Halle* (Holt, Rinehart and Winston).

Chomsky, N. 1981. *Lectures on Government and Binding*. Foris.

Chomsky, N. 1986. *Barriers*. MIT Press.

Chomsky, N. 1988. Some Notes on Economy of Derivation and Representation. Manuscript, Massachusetts Institute of Technology.

Cinque, G. 1990. On a difference between English and Italian 'Complement Object Deletion' constructions. In J. Mascaró and M. Nespor, eds., *Grammar in Progress: GLOW Essays for Henk van Riemsdijk* (Foris).

Clahsen, H., and P. Muysken. 1986. The availability of Universal Grammar to adult and child learners—A study of the acquisition of German word order. *Second Language Research*. 2.2.

Clahsen, H., and K.-D. Smolka 1986. Psycholinguistic evidence and the description of V2 in German. In Haider and Prinzhorn 1986.

Clark, R. 1989. Causality and parameter setting. *Behavioral and Brain Sciences* 12.2: 337–338.

Cole, P., G. Hermon, and L.-M. Sung 1990. Principles and parameters of long-distance reflexives. *Linguistic Inquiry* 21.1: 1–22.

Coopmans, P. 1984. Surface word order typology and Universal Grammar. *Language* 60.1: 55–69.

Culicover, P., A. Akmajian, and T. Wasow, eds. 1977. *Formal Syntax*. Academic Press.

Culicover, P. W., and W. K. Wilkins. 1984. *Locality in Linguistic Theory*. Academic Press.

Curtiss, S. 1977. *Genie: A Psycholinguistic Study of a Modern-Day "wild child"*. Academic Press.

Dahlstedt., A. 1901. *Rhythm and Word Order in Anglo-Saxon and Semi-Saxon, with Special Reference to Their Development in Modern English.* Malmstrom.

Denison, D. 1981. Aspects of the History of English Group-Verbs: With Particular Attention to the Syntax of the Ormulum. Doctoral dissertation, Oxford University.

Denison, D. 1985. Why Old English had no prepositional passive. *English Studies* 66.3: 189–204.

Denison, D. 1989. Auxiliary and impersonal in Old English. *Folia Linguistica Historica* 9.2.

Denison, D. 1990. The Old English impersonals revived. In Adamson et al. 1990.

Duffield, N. 1988. Modals, V2, etc. Manuscript, University of Southern California.

Edelman, G. M. 1987. *Neuronal Darwinism: The Theory of Neuronal Group Selection.* Basic Books.

Einenkel, E. 1916. *Historische Syntax. Geschichte der Englischen Sprache.* Volume 2. Strassburg: Karl J. Trübner.

Ellegård, A. 1953. *The auxiliary "do": The Establishment and Regulation of Its Use in English.* Almqvist & Wiksell.

Emonds, J. 1986. Parts of speech in generative grammar. *Linguistic Analysis* 16: 247–284.

Evers, A. 1975. The Transformational Cycle in Dutch and German. Doctoral dissertation, University of Utrecht.

Evers, A. 1982. Twee functionele principes voor de regel 'Verschuif het werkwoord'. *Glot* 5: 11–30.

Fischer, O. 1988a. The origin and spread of the accusative and infinitive construction in English. *Folia Linguistica Historica* 8: 143–217.

Fischer, O. 1988b. The rise of the passive infinitive in English. *Amsterdam Papers in English* 1.2: 54–107.

Fischer, O., and F. C. van der Leek. 1983. The demise of the Old English impersonal construction. *Journal of Linguistics* 19.2: 337–360.

Fischer, O., and F. C. van der Leek. 1987. A "case" for the Old English impersonal. In W. Koopman, F. van der Leek. O. Fischer, and R. Eaton, eds., *Explanation and Linguistic Change* (Benjamins).

Fourquet, J. 1938. *L'ordre des éléments de la phrase en germanique ancien: Etudes de syntaxe de position.* Paris: Les Belles Lettres.

Gardner, F. 1971. *An analysis of the Syntactic Patterns of Old English.* Mouton.

Gerritsen, M. 1980. An analysis of the rise of SOV patterns in Dutch. In Traugott et al. 1980.

Gerritsen, M. 1984. Divergent word order developments in Germanic languages: A description and a tentative explanation. In J. Fisiak, ed., *Historical Syntax* (Mouton).

Gleick, J. 1988. *Chaos: Making a New Science.* Heinemann.

Gorrell, J. H. 1895. Indirect discourse in Anglo-Saxon. *PMLA* 10.3: 342–485.

Greenberg, J. H. 1966. Some universals of grammar with particular reference to the order of meaningful elements. In J. H. Greenberg, ed., *Universals of Language* (MIT Press).

Grimshaw, J. 1986. Subjacency and the S/S′ parameter. *Linguistic Inquiry* 17.2: 364–369.

Grimshaw, J., and S. Pinker. 1989. Positive and negative evidence in language acquisition. *Behavioral and Brain Sciences* 12.2: 341–342.

Guy, G. R. 1981. Linguistic Variation in Brazilian Portuguese: Aspects of the Phonology, Syntax, and Language History. Doctoral dissertation, University of Pennsylvania.

Haan, G. de. 1987. A theory-bound approach to the acquisition of verb placement in Dutch. In G. de Haan and W. Zonneveld, eds., *Formal Parameters of Generative Grammar III.* (University of Utrecht).

Haan, G. de., and F. Weerman 1986. Finiteness and verb fronting in Frisian. In Haider and Prinzhorn 1986.

Haider, H. 1986. V-second in German. In Haider and Prinzhorn 1986.

Haider, H., and M. Prinzhorn, eds. 1986. *Verb-Second Phenomena in Germanic Languages.* Foris.

Harlow, S. 1981. Government and relativization in Celtic. In F. Heny, ed., *Binding and Filtering* (Croom Helm).

Harris, A. 1980. On the loss of a rule of syntax. In Traugott et al. 1980.

Hausmann, R. 1974. The development of periphrastic *do* in English. In Anderson and Jones 1974.

Hawkins, J. 1979. Implicational universals as predictors of word order change. *Language* 55: 618–648.

Hellan, L., and K. Koch Christensen, eds. 1986. *Topics in Scandinavian Syntax.* Reidel.

Higgins, R. 1973. The Pseudo-Cleft Construction in English. Doctoral dissertation, Massachusetts Institute of Technology.

Hiltunen, R. 1983. *The Decline of the Prefixes and the Beginnings of the English Phrasal Verb.* Turku: Turun yliopisto.

Hornstein, N., and S. Franks. 1988. Properly governed PRO and secondary predicates in Russian. To appear in R. Larson, S. Iatridou, U. Lahiri, and J. Higginbotham, eds., *Control and Grammar* (Kluwer).

Hornstein, N., and D. W. Lightfoot, eds. 1981. *Explanation in Linguistics: The Logical Problem of Language Acquisition.* Longman.

Hornstein, N., and D. W. Lightfoot. 1987. Predication and PRO. *Language* 63.1: 23–52.

Hornstein, N., and A. S. Weinberg. 1981. Case theory and preposition stranding. *Linguistic Inquiry* 12.1: 55–91.

Hornstein, N., and A. S. Weinberg. 1986. Superiority and generalized binding. In *Proceedings of North East Linguistics Society*. Graduate Student Linguistics Association, University of Massachusetts, Amherst.

Huang, J. 1982. Logical Relations in Chinese and the Theory of Grammar. Doctoral dissertation, Massachusetts Institute of Technology.

Hyams, N. 1983. The Pro-drop parameter in child grammars. In *Proceedings of the West Coast Conference on Formal Linguistics*.

Hyams, N., and S. Sigurjónsdóttir. 1990. The development of "long distance anaphora": A cross-linguistic comparison with special reference to Icelandic. *Language Acquisition* 1.1: 57–93.

Jack, G. 1978. *Rome's destruction* and the history of English. *Journal of Linguistics* 14.2: 311–312.

Jacobsson, B. 1951. *Inversion in English, with Special Reference to the Early Modern English Period*. Almqvist and Wiksell.

Jerne, N. K. 1967. Antibodies and learning: Selection versus instruction. In G. C. Quarton, T. Melnechuk, and F. O. Schmitt, eds., *The Neurosciences: A Study Program* (Rockefeller University Press).

Jerne, N. K. 1985. The generative grammar of the immune system. *Science* 229: 1057–1059.

Jespersen, O. 1922. *Language: Its Nature, Development and Origin*. Allen and Unwin.

Jones, C. 1988. *Grammatical Gender in English: 950 to 1250*. Croom Helm.

Joshi, A. K. 1989. A possible mathematical specification of "degree-0" or "degree-0 plus a little" learnability. *Behavioral and Brain Sciences* 12.2: 345–347.

Kageyama, T. 1975. Relational grammar and the history of subject raising. *Glossa* 9: 165–181.

Kayne, R. 1981a. ECP extensions. *Linguistic Inquiry* 12.1: 93–133.

Kayne, R. 1981b. On certain differences between French and English. *Linguistic Inquiry* 12.3: 349–371.

Kellner, L. 1892. *Historical Outlines of English Syntax*. Macmillan.

Kemenade, A. van. 1987. *Syntactic Case and Morphological Case in the History of English*. Foris.

Klavans, J. L. 1985. The independence of syntax and phonology in cliticization. *Language* 61.1: 95–120.

Klein, R. 1974. Word order: Dutch children and their mothers. *Publikaties van het Instituut voor Algemene Taalwetenschap* 9, Amsterdam.

Klima, E., and U. Bellugi. 1966. Syntactic regularities in the speech of children. In J. Lyons and R. Wales, eds., *Psycholinguistic Papers* (Edinburgh University Press).

Kohonen, V. 1978. *On the Development of English Word Order in Religious Prose around 1000 and 1200 A.D.: A Quantitative Study of Word Order in Context.* Abo Akademi Foundation.

Koopman, H. 1983. ECP effects in main clauses. *Linguistic Inquiry* 14.2: 346–350.

Koopman, H. 1984. *The Syntax of Verbs: From Verb Movement Rules in the Kru Languages to Universal Grammar.* Foris.

Koopman, H. 1986. The genesis of Haitian: Implications of a comparison of some features of the syntax of Haitian, French and West-African languages. In P. Muysken and N. Smith, eds., *Substrata versus Universals in Creole Languages* (Benjamins).

Koopman, W. 1985. The syntax of verb and particle combinations in Old English. In H. Bennis and F. Beukema, eds., *Linguistics in the Netherlands 1985* (Foris).

Koster, J. 1975. Dutch as an SOV language. *Linguistic Analysis* 1: 111–136.

Kouwenberg, S. 1989. SVO patterns in Ijo. Manuscript, University of Amsterdam.

Kroch, A. 1989a. Function and grammar in the history of English periphrastic *do*. In R. Fasold and D. Schiffrin, eds., *Language Change and Variation* (Benjamins).

Kroch, A. 1989b. Reflexes of grammar in patterns of language change. *Journal of Language Variation and Change* 1.3: 199–244.

Lakoff, R. 1968. *Abstract Syntax and Latin Complementation.* MIT Press.

Lasnik, H. 1981. Restricting the theory of transformations: A case study. In Hornstein and Lightfoot 1981.

Lasnik, H. 1989. The nature of triggering data. *Behavioral and Brain Sciences* 12.2: 349–350.

Lebeaux, D. 1988. Language Acquisition and the Form of the Grammar. Doctoral dissertation, University of Massachusetts, Amherst.

Lieber, R. 1979. The English passive: An argument for historical rule stability. *Linguistic Inquiry* 10.4: 667–688.

Lieber, R. 1982. A note on the history of the English auxiliary. *MIT Working Papers in Linguistics* 4: 81–99.

Lightfoot, D. W. 1974. The diachronic analysis of English modals. In Anderson and Jones 1974.

Lightfoot, D. W. 1979. *Principles of Diachronic Syntax.* Cambridge University Press.

Lightfoot, D. W. 1980. Sur la reconstruction d'une proto-syntaxe. *Langages* 60: 109–123. [English version in P. Ramat, ed., *Linguistic Reconstruction and Indo-*

European Syntax (Benjamins, 1980) and in I. Rauch and G. F. Carr, eds., *Language Change* (Indiana University Press, 1983).]

Lightfoot D. W. 1981a. A history of NP movement. In C. L. Baker and J. McCarthy, eds., *The Logical Problem of Language Acquisition* (MIT Press).

Lightfoot, D. W. 1981b. Explaining syntactic change. In Hornstein and Lightfoot 1981.

Lightfoot, D. W. 1981c. A reply to some critics. *Lingua* 55: 351–368.

Lightfoot, D. W. 1982. *The Language Lottery: Toward a Biology of Grammars.* MIT Press.

Lightfoot, D. W. 1986. Review of Culicover and Wilkins 1984. *Journal of Linguistics* 22.2: 480–485.

Lightfoot, D. W. 1987. Review of S. J. Keyser and W. O'Neil, *Rule Generalization and Optionality in Language Change. Language* 63.1: 151–155.

Lightfoot, D. W. 1988a. Syntactic change. In F. Newmeyer, ed., *Linguistics: The Cambridge Survey.* Cambridge University Press.

Lightfoot, D. W. 1988b. Creoles, triggers and universal grammar. In C. Duncan-Rose and T. Vennemann, eds., *Rhetorica, Pragmatica, Syntactica: A Festschrift for R. P. Stockwell.* Routledge.

Lightfoot, D. W. 1989. The child's trigger experience: Degree-0 learnability. *Behavioral and Brain Sciences* 12.2: 321–334.

Lightfoot, D. W. 1990. Old heads and new heads. In J. Mascaró and M. Nespor, eds., *Grammar in Progress: GLOW Essays for Henk van Riemsdijk* (Foris).

Lightfoot, D. W., and A. Weinberg. 1988. Review article on Chomsky 1986. *Language* 64.2: 366–383.

Macleish, A. 1969. *The Middle English Subject-Verb Cluster.* Mouton.

Matthei, E. 1981. Children's interpretation of sentences containing reciprocals. In S. L. Tavakolian, ed., *Language Acquisition and Linguistic Theory* (MIT Press).

Mazurkewich, I., and L. White 1984. The acquisition of the dative alternation: Unlearning overgeneralizations. *Cognition* 16.3: 261–283.

McNeill, D. 1966. Developmental linguistics. In F. Smith and G. A. Miller, eds., *The Genesis of Language: A Psycholinguistic Approach* (MIT Press).

Mehler, J. 1974. Connaître par desapprentissage. In E. Morin and M. Piattelli-Palmarini, eds., *L'unité de l'homme* (Editions du Seuil).

Mitchell, B. 1979. F. Th. Visser, *An historical syntax of the English language*: Some caveats concerning Old English. *English Studies* 60: 537–542.

Mitchell, B. 1985. *Old English Syntax.* Clarendon.

Morgan, J. L. 1986. *From Simple Input to Complex Grammars.* MIT Press.

Muysken, P. 1988. Are creoles a special type of language? In F. Newmeyer, ed., *Linguistics: The Cambridge Survey*, volume 2 (Cambridge University Press).

Naro, A. 1981. The social and structural dimensions of syntactic change. *Language* 57.1: 63–98.

Newport, E. C., H. Gleitman, and L. Gleitman. 1977. "Mother, I'd rather do it myself": Some effects and non-effects of maternal speech style. In Snow and Ferguson 1977.

O'Neil, W. 1982. Simplifying the grammar of English. In J. Anderson, ed., *Language Form and Language Variation: Papers Dedicated to Angus McIntosh* (Benjamins).

Ottósson, K. G. 1989. VP-Specifier subjects and the CP/IP distinction in Icelandic and mainland Scandinavian. *Working Papers in Scandinavian Syntax* 44: 89–100.

Ottósson, K. G. 1990. Psych-Verbs and Binding in Icelandic. Paper presented at Twelfth Scandinavian Conference on Linguistics, Reykjavik.

Piattelli-Palmarini, M. 1986. The rise of selective theories: A case study and some lessons from immunology. In W. Demopoulos and A. Marras, eds., *Language Learning and Concept Acquisition* (Ablex).

Pica, P. 1987. On the nature of the reflexivization cycle. *NELS* 17: 483–499.

Pinker, S. 1989. *Learnability and Cognition: The Acquisition of Argument Structure*. MIT Press.

Pintzuk, S. 1988. Verb Movement in Old English. Manuscript, University of Pennsylvania.

Pintzuk, S., and A. Kroch. 1985. Reconciling an exceptional feature of Old English clause structure. In J. T. Faarland, ed. *Germanic Linguistics: Papers from a Symposium at the University of Chicago* (Indiana University Linguistics Club).

Plank, F. 1984. The modals story retold. *Studies in Language* 8: 305–364.

Platzack, C. 1985. A survey of generative analyses of the verb-second phenomenon in Germanic. *Nordic Journal of Linguistics* 8.1: 49–73.

Platzack, C. 1986. COMP, INFL and Germanic word order. In Hellan and Koch Christensen 1986.

Pollock, J.-Y. 1989. Verb movement, UG and the structure of IP. *Linguistic Inquiry* 20.3: 365–424.

Quirk, R., and C. L. Wrenn. 1955. *An Old English Grammar*. Methuen.

Radford, A. 1988. Small children's small clauses. *Transactions of the Philological Society* 86: 1–43.

Randall, J. 1986. Retreat Routes. Paper presented to the Boston University Conference on Language Development.

Raposo, E. 1987. Case theory and Infl-to-Comp: The inflected infinitive in European Portuguese. *Linguistic Inquiry* 18.1: 85–110.

Reddick, R. 1982. On the underlying order of early West Saxon. *Journal of Linguistics* 18.1: 37–55.

Reszkiewicz, A. 1962. *Main Sentence Elements in "The book of Margery Kempe."* Warsaw: Komitet Neofilologiczny Polskiej Akademii Nauk.

Rizzi, L. 1982a. *Issues in Italian Syntax.* Foris.

Rizzi, L. 1982b. Comments on Chomsky's "On the representation of form and function". In J. Mehler, E. C. T. Walker, and M. Garrett, eds., *Perspectives on Mental Representation* (Lawrence Erlbaum).

Rizzi, L. 1989. On the format for parameters. *Behavioral and Brain Sciences* 12.2: 355–356.

Rizzi, L., and I. G. Roberts. 1989. Complex Inversion in French. Manuscript, University of Geneva.

Roberts, I. G. 1985a. Agreement parameters and the development of English modal auxiliaries. *Natural Language and Linguistic Theory* 3.1: 21–57.

Roberts, I. G. 1985b. Oblique case in the history of English. *University of Southern California Working Papers in Linguistics.*

Roeper, T. 1973. Connecting children's language and linguistic theory. In T. Moore, ed., *Cognitive Development and the Acquisition of Language* (Academic Press).

Roeper, T. 1979. Children's Syntax. Manuscript, University of Massachusetts, Amherst.

Ross, J. R. 1973. The penthouse principle and the order of constituents. In C. Corum, T. C. Smith-Stark, and A. Weiser, eds., *You Take the High Node and I'll Take the Low Node* (Chicago Linguistic Society).

Rouveret, A., and J.-R. Vergnaud. 1980. Specifying reference to the subject: French causatives and conditions on representations. *Linguistic Inquiry* 11.1: 97–202.

Russom, J. H. 1980. The plain infinitive in Old English. *Brown University Working Papers in Linguistics.*

Russom, J. H. 1982. An examination of the evidence for OE indirect passives. *Linguistic Inquiry* 13.4: 677–680.

Safir, K. 1981. Inflection-government and inversion. *Linguistic Review* 1.2: 417–467.

Sainsbury, R. 1971. The "feature positive effect" and simultaneous discrimination learning. *Journal of Experimental Child Psychology* 11: 347–356.

Sainsbury, R. 1973. Discrimination learning utilizing positive or negative cues. *Canadian Journal of Psychology* 27.1: 46–57.

Sankoff, G., and S. Laberge. 1973. On the acquisition of speakers by a native language. *Kivung* 6: 32–47.

Santorini, B. 1990. The History of the Verb-Second Constraint in Yiddish. Manuscript, University of Pennsylvania.

Schon, C. V. von 1977. The Origin of Phrasal Verbs in English. Doctoral dissertation, State University of New York, Stony Brook.

Sells, P. 1987. Aspects of logophoricity. *Linguistic Inquiry* 18.3: 445–479.

Shannon, A. 1964. *A Descriptive Syntax of the Parker Manuscript of the Anglo-Saxon Chronicle.* Mouton.

Sigurdsson, H. A. 1986. Moods and (long distance) reflexives in Icelandic. *Working Papers in Scandinavian Syntax* 25: 1–53.

Singler, J. 1984. Comments on Bickerton's "Creoles and UG: The unmarked case?" Paper presented at winter meeting of the Linguistic Society of America, Baltimore.

Singler, J. 1988. The homogeneity of the substrate as a factor in pidgin/creole genesis. *Language* 64.1: 27–51.

Smith, C. A. 1893. The order of words in Anglo-Saxon prose. *PMLA* 8: 210–244.

Smith, N. S. H., I. Robertson, and K. Williamson. 1987. The Ijo element in Berbice Dutch. *Language in Society* 16: 49–90.

Smith, N. V. 1981. Consistency, markedness and language change: On the notion 'consistent language'. *Journal of Linguistics* 17.1: 39–54.

Snow, C. 1977. Mothers' speech research: From input to interaction. In Snow and Ferguson 1977.

Snow, C., and C. A. Ferguson, eds. 1977. *Talking to Children: Language Input and Acquisition.* Cambridge University Press.

Sportiche, D. 1981. On bounding nodes in French. *Linguistic Review* 1: 219–246.

Sproat, R. 1985. Welsh syntax and VSO structure. *Natural Language and Linguistic Theory* 3.2: 173–216.

Stockwell, R. P. 1977. Motivations for exbraciation in Old English. In C. Li, ed., *Mechanisms of Syntactic Change* (University of Texas Press).

Stockwell, R. P., and D. Minkova. 1989. Subordination and word order change in the history of English. In D. Kastovsky, ed., *Kellner Memorial* (Mouton/de Gruyter).

Swieczkowski, W. 1962. *Word Order Patterning in Middle English.* Mouton.

Taraldsen, K. T. 1986. On verb second and the functional content of syntactic categories. In Haider and Prinzhorn 1986.

Tatlock, J., and A. Kennedy. 1927. *Concordance to the Complete Works of Geoffrey Chaucer.* Carnegie Institution.

Traugott, E. 1965. [Closs] Diachronic syntax and generative grammar. *Language* 41: 402–415.

Traugott, E. 1969. Toward a grammar of syntactic change. *Lingua* 23.1: 1–27.

Traugott, E. 1972. *The history of English Syntax.* Holt, Rinehart & Winston.

Traugott, E., R. Lebrum, and S. Shepherd, eds. 1980. *Papers from the Fourth International Conference on Historical Linguistics*. Benjamins.

Travis, L. 1987. Parameters of phrase structure. *McGill University Working Papers in Linguistics*.

Vennemann, T. 1974. Topics, subjects and word order: From SXV to SVX via TVX. In Anderson and Jones 1974.

Vennemann, T. 1975. An explanation of drift. In C. Li, ed., *Word Order and Word Order Change* (University of Texas Press).

Visser, F. T. 1963–1973. *An Historical Syntax of the English Language*. Leiden: Brill.

Warner, A. 1982. *Complementation in Middle English and the Methodology of Historical Syntax*. Pennsylvania State University Press.

Warner, A. 1983. Review article on Lightfoot 1979. *Journal of Linguistics* 19: 187–209.

Warner, A. 1990. Reworking the history of English auxiliaries. In Adamson et al. 1990.

Wasow, T. 1977. Transformations and the lexicon. In Culicover et al. 1977.

Wasow, T. 1978. Remarks on processing, constraints and the lexicon. In D. Waltz., ed., *Theoretical Issues in Natural Language processing 2*. Department of Computer Science, University of Illinois.

Weerman, F. 1989. *The V2 conspiracy: A Synchronic and Diachronic Analysis of Verbal Positions in Germanic Languages*. Foris.

Weinberg, A. S. 1990. Markedness vs. maturation: The case of Subject-auxiliary inversion. *Language Acquisition* 1.2: 165–194.

Wells, G. 1981. *Learning through Interaction: The Study of Language Development*. Cambridge University Press.

Wexler, K., and P. W. Culicover 1980. *Formal Principles of Language Acquisition*. MIT Press.

Wilcoxon, S. 1988. Binding in Mandarin Chinese: Another Look at *ziji*. Manuscript, University of Texas.

Zeitlin, J. 1908. *The Accusative with Infinitive and Some Kindred Constructions in English*. Columbia University Press.

Index